MAUPASSANT
THE NOVELIST

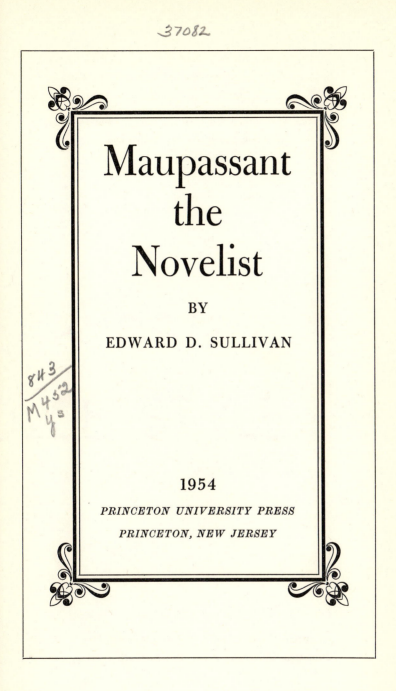

Maupassant the Novelist

BY

EDWARD D. SULLIVAN

1954

PRINCETON UNIVERSITY PRESS

PRINCETON, NEW JERSEY

Publication of this book has been aided by a grant from the
Princeton University Research Fund

Printed in the United States of America by
Princeton University Press, Princeton, New Jersey

TO MY WIFE

PREFACE

A GREAT many people have contributed in one way or another to the preparation of this study. I have profited much from the work of many earlier scholars in the field, especially from that of Edouard Maynial and René Dumesnil in France, and I owe a particular debt to the two outstanding Maupassant scholars in this country: Professor Artine Artinian, who generously gave me the benefit of his detailed knowledge of all things pertaining to Maupassant and who made available his admirable collection of Maupassantiana; and Francis Steegmuller, biographer of Maupassant, whose friendly encouragement, practical assistance, and example helped me over many rough places. I should like to express here also my gratitude to Professor André Morize, with whom I first studied the novels of Maupassant; to Professor Gilbert Chinard, who gave much constructive advice and who solved many problems in obtaining microfilms of unpublished material; to Professor Ira O. Wade for his sympathetic understanding and discernment; and to my other colleagues at Princeton, especially to Professor Maurice Coindreau, who encouraged me to publish my earlier brief studies on Maupassant.

I am greatly indebted to the Princeton University Research Fund for providing the necessary tools of research and a generous subsidy toward publication; and to the staff of the Princeton University Library for their efficient cooperation. *The French Review* has kindly given permission to reprint part of the chapter on *Notre Cœur* which first appeared in that publication in 1948.

In referring to Maupassant's novels and stories I have taken Conard as the standard edition, since it is more generally available than that of the Librairie de France. References to Maupassant's correspondence are to the fifteenth volume of the Librairie de France edition, which is more complete than Conard, and to Artine Artinian's *Correspondance inédite de Maupassant*, Paris, Wapler, 1951; together these two volumes provide a convenient collection of all the published letters. The following abbreviations are used:

Conard: *Œuvres complètes de Guy de Maupassant*, 29 vols., Paris, Louis Conard, 1908-1930. Since the volumes of this edition are not numbered, reference is made to the title of the volume, followed by (Conard) and the page; e.g. *Boule de Suif* (Conard), p. 19.

LF: *Œuvres complètes illustrées de Guy de Maupassant*, edited by René Dumesnil, 15 vols., Paris, Librairie de France, 1934-1938. Reference to this edition is given simply by the letters LF, followed by the number of the volume and the page, e.g. LF, xv, 231. The fifteenth volume, *Etudes, Chroniques et Correspondance*, was also issued separately by the Librairie Gründ in 1938.

E. D. S.

Princeton
November 1953

CONTENTS

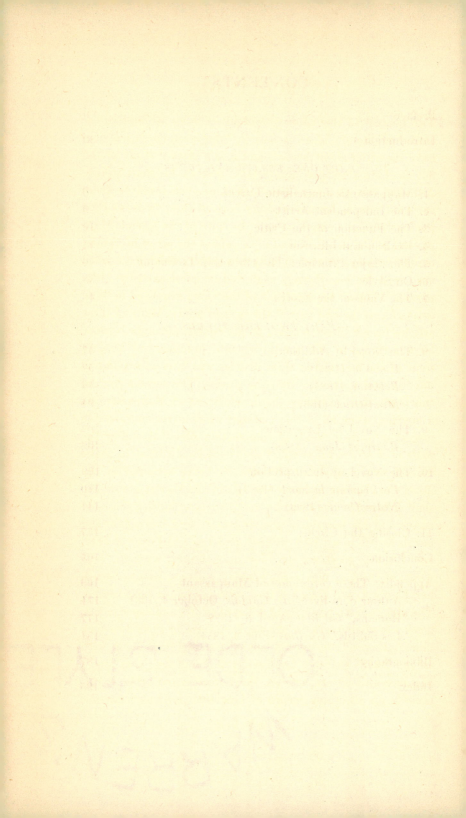

INTRODUCTION

THE purpose of this book is twofold: it is an attempt to examine the literary ideas of a writer who is supposed never to have theorized about his art, and it is a critical study of the novels of a man whose literary fame rests on his short stories. Although this may seem paradoxical, or even perverse, there are good reasons for undertaking both of these tasks and for joining them in a single volume. In spite of the legend, Maupassant did have a good deal to say about the art of literature, mainly in essays printed in daily newspapers which have, until very recently, been largely neglected or overlooked by Maupassant scholars. An exposition of the views expressed in these essays forms the first part of the present study. Many of these articles bear a direct relation to his novels, not only because he was trying to put the theory into practice, but because some of the material in these articles was later incorporated, directly and indirectly, into the novels. The second part of this book, then, examines the development of Maupassant as a novelist, using all of this material which gives considerable insight into his methods of composition. We shall follow the path of a successful *conteur* who consciously tried to make himself into a novelist, although he never acquired in the novel the absolute assurance he felt in the shorter genre. We shall follow his questionings and his uncertainties, his successes and his failures in the six novels and two unfinished novels he left to us. Two of these, *Bel-Ami* and *Pierre et Jean*, are, I think, great novels; they do not rank with the best works of the four nineteenth-century masters, Balzac, Stendhal, Flaubert, and Zola, but they certainly follow close behind. The other novels, products of different efforts and experiments, mark essential stages on the road, and are in their own way illuminating; all the novels, considered together, along with all the details that can be discovered about their creation in Maupassant's letters, articles, short stories, and other works, provide an absorbing record of how this particular novelist worked and allow us to estimate his achievements and understand his inadequacies.

Numerous anecdotes recall that Maupassant rebuffed eager questioners who sought to draw him into a discussion of books, tendencies or schools, and he himself wrote as early as 1877 that he never discussed literature or principles; he thought it perfectly useless since no one is ever converted.[1] It should be noted, however, that this remark is taken from a very long letter which is itself a profession of literary faith, "ma religion littéraire." The author of *Bel-Ami* had very little use for journalists and resented any intrusion into what he considered his private life. The best known incident, and one which contributed greatly to this particular Maupassant legend, was the interview by Jules Huret for his *Enquête sur l'évolution littéraire* in 1891, near the end of Maupassant's life. The novelist ended the questioning abruptly by saying that he never talked about his art, consequently Huret, with some malice, presented him as a man who had no interest in literary ideas.[2] Since then the notion has persisted that Maupassant was essentially unliterary and almost never wrote anything of a critical or theoretical nature. Many scholars and critics have believed that the preface to *Pierre et Jean* was his only effort in the literary essay.[3]

[1] Maupassant, letter (to Paul Alexis?) January 17, 1877; LF, xv, 223-226.

[2] Jules Huret, *Enquête sur l'évolution littéraire*, Paris, Charpentier, 1891, p. 187.

[3] Cf. Georges Pellissier, *Le Mouvement littéraire contemporain*, Paris, Plon-Nourrit, 1902, p. 13; reprinted in A. Lumbroso, *Souvenirs sur Maupassant*, Rome, Bocca frères, 1905, pp. 169-173. Lumbroso, a fervent admirer of Maupassant, defended his hero, though rather feebly, in a note: "Il y a aussi l'étude sur le roman au xixe siècle, dans la *Revue de l'Exposit. Univ. de 1889*, numéro de novembre." Croce, although he admired Maupassant as a great lyric poet in prose, remarked that he had no "transcendental ideal of art . . . nor did he ever direct a curious glance at the nature of art or engage in any kind of inquiry or criticism relating to it, having little taste for theorizing, discussions or polemics. . . . Exquisite in his sense for form, Maupassant was very slightly preoccupied with the technical side of composition, he was 'literary' only to a very small extent." (Benedetto Croce, *European Literature in the Nineteenth Century*, tr. by Douglas Ainslee, New York, Knopf, 1924, pp. 352-353.)

Although Maupassant may well have had an aversion to conversation on art and literature, this did not prevent him from writing during the course of his career a surprisingly large number of essays devoted to precisely these subjects. What has preserved the legend that he was the most unliterary of writers is the fact that few students of Maupassant's work have ever examined these essays, which, for the most part, have never been reprinted. Conard did not include them, stating rather grandly that he was publishing the works of the great novelist, not those of the journalist.[4] The most recent edition of Maupassant's works, published from 1934 to 1938 by the Librairie de France, reprinted forty-two of the essays, mostly in the last volume called *Etudes, Chroniques et Correspondance*, and unfortunately gave the impression that there were no more, especially since the elaborate bibliography listed only those essays which the Librairie de France edition had included. The preface to *Pierre et Jean*, which has been scorned as superficial by some and praised by others as highly intelligent and constructive, is not an isolated phenomenon in the work of Maupassant, but rather a summary of some of the main points of his artistic credo (much of it derived from Flaubert, of course) which he had elaborated from the beginning of his career in articles which appeared chiefly in the *Gaulois* and the *Gil Blas*. There are 227 essays or *chroniques* by Maupassant known to me, of which 185 have never been reprinted. They were written during the entire course of his literary life, the earliest in 1876 and the last in 1891.[5]

[4] *Boule de Suif* (Conard), p. vii.

[5] A check-list of Maupassant's newspaper articles was published by the author in collaboration with Francis Steegmuller as "Supplément à la bibliographie de Guy de Maupassant" in the *Revue d'Histoire littéraire de la France* (October-December, 1949, pp. 370-375). Very few writers on Maupassant have been aware of the extent of this material. Two German scholars first called attention to these essays, although their efforts seem to have been completely ignored in France. In 1907 Paul Mahn wrote a rather sketchy article on "Maupassant als Journalist" in *Das literarische Echo* (x, 77-85, 149-157), which he used in his biography, *Guy de Maupassant, sein Leben und seine Werke*, Berlin, Fleischel, 1908. Fritz Neubert, the only one to deal extensively with this body of Maupas-

INTRODUCTION

In these articles, Maupassant expressed himself freely on the theory of the novel and on literature in general, but what is most striking is that he almost never ventured into a technical discussion of the short story. One might reasonably expect the celebrated *conteur*, at least once or twice in the years when he was writing so many literary essays, to give us some idea of his conception of the genre in which he excelled. Yet he rarely discusses his own short stories, and then only to defend the choice of subject matter, as in his replies to the criticism by Albert Wolff and Francisque Sarcey of *Mademoiselle Fifi.*[6] Even when he devotes an article to the

sant's work, wrote two short monographs, *Die literarische Kritik Guy de Maupassants* and *Die kritischen Essays Guy de Maupassants (mit Ausschluss der literarischen Kritik).* The first appeared as *Supplementheft VIII der Zeitschrift für französische Sprache und Litteratur* in 1914; the second as *Supplementheft IX* of the same publication in 1919. Neubert was chiefly bent on showing that Maupassant's literary ideas derived from Flaubert and he quotes at length from the latter's correspondence; he tries to demonstrate also, particularly in his second monograph, that Maupassant's philosophical viewpoint was strongly influenced by Schopenhauer. Distressed that the Conard edition did not include Maupassant's essays, Neubert summed up his findings in a short article, "Maupassant als Essayist und Kritiker," in the *Germanisch-Romanische Monatsschrift* in 1920 (VIII, 165-178). Neubert's studies are interesting and I am indebted to him for first putting me on the track of this neglected body of writings, but he missed a great many articles, and references to many others are marred by errors in date, title, or the name of the newspaper in which they first appeared. In 1925 Gérard de Lacaze-Duthiers wrote two articles based on a very small sample of Maupassant's critical writings, "L'Œuvre critique de Guy de Maupassant," *La Nouvelle Revue critique*, June 15, 1925, pp. 289-296; and "Guy de Maupassant, critique d'art," *Revue mondiale*, July 15, 1925, pp. 169-172. Another brief account in 1925 was "Guy de Maupassant, critique d'art," by R. Lécuyer in the *Gaulois* of July 16. A. Guérinot made very effective use of about fifteen of the *chroniques* in an informative article "Maupassant et les Goncourt," *Mercure de France*, December 15, 1928, pp. 567-591. Maupassant's biographers have had knowledge of only a handful of items from this very rich source, with the notable exception of Francis Steegmuller, who, in his excellent work, *Maupassant, A Lion in the Path*, New York, Random House, 1949, has used much biographical information derived from a knowledge of the complete body of the essays.

6 Maupassant, "Chronique," *Gaulois*, July 9, 1882, and "Les Bas-fonds," *Gaulois*, July 28, 1882; LF, XV, 69-75. "Chronique" is the original title of the article which is usually referred to as "Réponse à Francisque Sarcey" and wrongly dated July 28 and July 20.

short stories of a writer like Turgenev[7] he speaks mainly of
qualities of realism or fantasy, never of structure, never of
anything which distinguishes the short story from the novel.
The reason for this is not hard to find. The short story was
his natural medium; after *Boule de Suif* he wrote a steady
stream of stories, seemingly without effort, producing them,
it was remarked, as naturally as an apple tree brings forth
apples. Whatever his native gifts in this genre, it should be
remembered that they were supplemented by the intensive
training and criticism he had received from Flaubert during
a long period of apprenticeship, with the result that he pos-
sessed his technique so completely that he could practice his
craft with ease but was incapable of theorizing about it. His
short stories were written without benefit of a preliminary
theoretical discussion; his novels, on the other hand, represent
a conscious search for a technique, which is reflected in the
emphasis he puts on novelistic theory in his essays. Each of
the six novels of Maupassant is a stage on the road toward
the secret of the novel, a road he followed hesitatingly, groping
his way, never very sure of himself, and at least once falling
flat on his face. From Flaubert he had learned the practice of
the short story and the theory of the novel. He set out to
follow those theories, adapting them to his own temperament,
experimenting, modifying them considerably as time went on,
but never wholly abandoning them. Our interest in this study
of his novels comes not only from the merits of the novels
themselves, but also from the opportunity that is offered us to
follow the creative process of a "natural" short story writer
as he tried to make himself into a novelist.

7 Maupassant wrote four articles on Turgenev: "L'Inventeur du mot
nihilisme," *Gaulois*, November 21, 1880, reprinted in LF, xv, 35-39; "Ivan
Tourgueneff," *Gaulois*, September 5, 1883, reprinted in LF, xv, 89-92;
"Ivan Tourgueneff," *Gil Blas*, September 6, 1883, signed Maufrigneuse,
a revision of the *Gaulois* article of 1880; and "Le Fantastique," *Gaulois*,
October 7, 1883, never reprinted.

PART ONE

ESSAYS AND IDEAS

1

MAUPASSANT'S
JOURNALISTIC CAREER

WORKING under the ever-watchful eye of Flaubert the master, Maupassant served a long literary apprenticeship, testing his skill at poetry, drama, and the short story. His eagerness to write at the same time articles for newspapers and magazines is explained by his need to supplement the very meager income he received as a government clerk, and we find his first article, a sketch of Gustave Flaubert, appearing in *La République des lettres* in 1876.[1] Flaubert, anxious to help his protégé, urged Raoul-Duval, then launching a new review, *La Nation*, to give Maupassant a trial as book-reviewer.[2] He provided his young disciple with a letter of introduction and some practical advice as well, namely, to save the editor's time and energy by proposing certain specific literary subjects he would like to treat. Flaubert suggested a few possibilities, most of them rather ambitious, such as the history of modern criticism, the question of art for art's sake, a study of George Sand or one of Alexandre Dumas. He hoped for a sensational début and even considered the idea of developing some involved literary hoax.[3]

As a result of his interview with Raoul-Duval, Maupassant learned that *La Nation* still lacked a "chroniqueur littéraire," and he was given the assignment of writing one or two book-reviews, after the publication of which Raoul-Duval would ask the directors to name Maupassant as regular literary critic. Delighted, Maupassant rushed off to buy the correspondence of Balzac which had just been published by Lévy. After completing his review he learned to his chagrin that literary ar-

[1] Maupassant, "Gustave Flaubert," *La République des lettres,* October 22, 1876; LF, xv, 3-7.

[2] Flaubert, *Correspondance*, Paris, Conard, 1930, viii, 354.

[3] *ibid.*, p. 355.

3

ticles signed Filon were appearing in *La Nation* and that Filon was to be retained as permanent literary critic while Maupassant would replace "un chroniqueur léger qu'on trouve trop bête."[4] The article on Balzac was published November 22, 1876, and the young critic immediately set about doing another. He was careful to write a humble letter to Raoul-Duval, thanking him for accepting the Balzac article and submitting the second one. He took great care not to encroach on the territory of Filon, saying of the article he was enclosing that he had tried to make it look more like a general literary study than a review of a recent book.[5]

Maupassant had proposed to Raoul-Duval the subjects suggested by Flaubert, but the editor had found them too long and serious and preferred something more amusing. "Pour lui plaire," wrote Maupassant to Flaubert, "je lui ai donné mon article sur Balzac, qui est de la critique à l'usage des dames et des messieurs du monde, mais où il n'est pas question de littérature."[6] Raoul-Duval found this charming, but the second article on "L'Invasion de la Bizarrerie" was rejected. In it Maupassant, using as a point of departure *Les Morts bizarres* of Jean Richepin, attacked lack of originality. Raoul-Duval's objection was that this would give Richepin more publicity than he deserved.

Maupassant's next step was to buy a reprint of Sainte-Beuve's *Tableau historique et critique de la poésie française et du théâtre français au xvie siècle* and write a review of it which was published January 17, 1877.[7] Further efforts met with no success, however. At Raoul-Duval's suggestion he turned to drama criticism and wrote an account of *L'Ami Fritz*, only to discover that the editor himself found the play stupid and was recommending that his friends not bother to see it. Meanwhile the young man was spending more money

4 Maupassant, letter to Flaubert, November 17, 1876; LF, xv, 217-218.
5 Maupassant, letter to Raoul-Duval, November 28, 1876; LF, xv, 219.
6 Maupassant, letter to Flaubert, January 8, 1877; LF, xv, 221.
7 "Les Poètes français du xvie siècle," *La Nation*, January 17, 1877; LF, xv, 12-17.

than he could afford, especially since he was obliged to buy the books he intended to review. He was getting little return and there was no sign of his being named to any regular position on the paper. He grew rather bitter about his lack of success and wrote to Flaubert that he was sure no paper would let him write really literary articles where he could say what he thought. *La Nation*, he assured the master, was an impossibly stupid publication, utterly conventional, and hostile to any new idea or unfamiliar form.[8] Maupassant decided to write one more article for *La Nation* and if no permanent assignment resulted, he would drop the whole affair, which is precisely what did happen.

His first brief contact with the journalistic world left him a little bitter and very wary; he wanted to dictate his own terms, an insistence on the part of an unknown which was not relished by the editors with whom he dealt. He outlined his position in 1878 in a letter to his mother, informing her that he had been offered a chance to do some literary articles and that Zola was urging him to accept. He was embarrassed by a good many scruples, however, most of which he conquered eventually. He was unwilling, he wrote, to be a regular contributor to the *Gaulois*, preferring to develop interesting subjects as they occurred; he insisted that he would publish only articles he felt worthy of his signature, and that he would put his name on no page that had cost him less than two hours of work.[9] Nothing came of this particular overture, and the young disciple continued to work with Flaubert, publishing an odd poem, an occasional story, and working on his dramas. He suffered periods of great discouragement, feeling unable to produce anything of merit, as in August 1878 when he wrote to Flaubert that he had tried to write some *chroniques* for the *Gaulois* in order to make a little money, but was unable to compose a line and sat staring, almost weeping, at the blank sheet before him.[10] In any case no more articles were published

8 Maupassant, letter to Flaubert, January 8, 1877; LF, xv, 222.
9 Maupassant, letter to his mother, April 3 [1878]; LF, xv, 236.
10 Maupassant, letter to Flaubert, August 21, 1878; LF, xv, 243.

until 1880 when he submitted to the *Gaulois* a somewhat fantastical account of how the *Soirées de Médan* had been composed.[11] With the enormous success of *Boule de Suif* the columns of the *Gaulois* were opened to him, and there began to appear in rapid succession short stories and articles from the facile pen of a young writer who had found himself.

From that time on he encountered little difficulty in getting his articles into print. He became a regular and frequent contributor to the *Gaulois*, signing his articles with his own name, and in October 1881, the *Gil Blas* began to publish his articles under the pseudonym of Maufrigneuse. The use of the pseudonym had one great advantage in that it enabled him to take material from an old *Gaulois* article and use it in the *Gil Blas* and vice versa, sometimes simply reproducing an entire article that he had previously published elsewhere. None of his contemporaries seems to have remarked this little game of self-plagiarism, though the identity of Maufrigneuse could hardly have been a secret. In any case the pen-name, which had been consistently used for the *Gil Blas* stories and articles, was publicly revealed in May 1884 to be that of Guy de Maupassant and after 1885 it was dropped completely.

The decade of the 1880's was a period of intense literary activity for Maupassant. Short stories, novels, travel sketches came from his pen in a steady stream, and the statistics of his production have been a constant source of amazement. If we now add to this the formidable array of his newspaper articles and essays, our astonishment must increase despite the fact that he contrived to publish at least twice practically every page he ever wrote. His travel books were composed of sketches he had sent to the *Gaulois* and other papers,[12] and he constantly cribbed material from one article for use in another or even in the novels themselves. Maupassant's articles—over

11 "Les Soirées de Médan; comment ce livre a été fait," *Gaulois*, April 17, 1880; LF, xv, 20-23.

12 *Sur l'eau*, published in 1888, is made up almost entirely of essays and sketches which had appeared much earlier; see my article *"Sur l'eau*: a Maupassant Scrap-book," *Romanic Review*, October 1949, pp. 173-179.

two hundred in number—treat an extraordinarily wide variety of subjects: they include travel sketches, which, according to his valet François, he composed without effort;[13] political articles, in which he berates politicians of all parties and condemns politics in general; some pure pot-boilers on odd items of news which aroused his interest or his scorn, or which furnished an excuse for a tirade on a favorite idea; and, what interests us most here, a very large number of essays and studies devoted to books, writers, literature, and the technique and theory of fictional art.

Toward the end of his career, as the state of his health worsened, his activity inevitably became less intense and he was forced to give up a good deal of the journalistic writing which provided so necessary a part of his income. In 1888 he wrote to Léon Hennique, who wanted him to do an article, that he had been forbidden by his doctor to do any writing at all, and that he had given up the *Gaulois* completely, had interrupted his work for *Figaro*, was obliged to dictate the articles he had promised to the *Gil Blas*, and would be unable to keep other engagements that he had made.[14] Nevertheless, he kept turning out articles almost to the very end, and as late as October 1891 he proposed to the publisher Paul Ollendorf a book of criticism and portraits in four parts on Flaubert, Bouilhet, Turgenev, and Zola, composed chiefly of previously published articles.[15] According to François, he planned to write, after finishing the novels and stories on which he was working, a general analysis of his own works and a study of the great authors who had most profoundly influenced him.[16]

Such was, in brief, the journalistic career of Maupassant. His newspaper work was never more than a side-line, carried on somehow in the midst of the rest of his writing. Yet this aspect of his career cannot be considered as unimportant, for it

[13] François Tassart, *Souvenirs sur Guy de Maupassant*, Paris, Plon, 1911, p. 118.
[14] Maupassant, letter to Léon Hennique, April 1, 1891; LF, xv, 399.
[15] Maupassant, letter to Ollendorf, October 28, 1891; LF, xv, 409.
[16] François Tassart, *op. cit.*, p. 262.

not only furnished him the background for his novel *Bel-Ami*, but also gave him a chance, or rather forced him, to set forth his ideas on life, literature, and society in a direct and un-equivocal manner. We can see these ideas in his literary works, woven into the substructure or put into the mouths of his characters, and a study of his *chroniques* will bring out more clearly various aspects of his technique and art. The fact that many articles served as preliminary sketches for scenes in some of the novels, or were incorporated in them with but slight modification, provides material for a study of their composition. In short, while some of the *chroniques* are mere pot-boilers, many are thoughtful and well-developed essays on the art of fiction which are of great interest in them-selves. Maupassant was not a great literary critic, but this large and long-neglected body of material deserves to be studied, particularly because of the intimate relation it bears to the rest of Maupassant's literary work.

2

THE INDEPENDENT ARTIST

IT WOULD BE rash to study Maupassant's numerous essays in the hope of reconstructing a doctrine or of making a systematic classification of his literary ideas. There are, naturally enough, contradictions and conflicts, since each article represents to some degree the preoccupations of the moment when it was written. Yet certain beliefs and tendencies stand out by virtue of constant repetition in varying form throughout his life and these evidently were fundamental notions to which he held fast. Many of these principles were equally fundamental to Flaubert, as will be perfectly apparent to anyone who has read the correspondence of Maupassant's master, but we are here not so much concerned with the source of Maupassant's ideas as with his literary credo and the effect of that credo on his work.

Despite the fact that he was a disciple—in a very literal sense—of Flaubert, and scored his first literary success under the auspices of Zola with *Boule de Suif* in *Les Soirées de Médan*, he was unwilling to be identified with any school or any doctrine. Flaubert was constantly urging him and his contemporaries not to imitate others but to develop their own originality, and Maupassant, even as a very young man, proclaimed his desire to remain independent and free to criticize. In 1876 when Catulle Mendès tried to persuade him to become a free-mason, Maupassant flatly refused, declaring that he was unwilling to join any group professing a doctrine or principles by which he would be bound, whether it was a political party, a religion, a sect, or a school. He added that his attitude gave him the right to defend his friends regardless of their affiliations.[1] Although he has been duly classified and catalogued among the Naturalists, he took many occasions to affirm his own individualistic approach, and protested as early as 1877

---

[1] Maupassant, letter to Catulle Mendès, 1876; LF, xv, 220-221.

that he no more believed in naturalism or realism than he did in romanticism—meaningless words which simply indicate an opposition of temperaments.[2] Similarly, when he wrote his first article for the *Gaulois* as publicity for *Les Soirées de Médan* he took pains to make it clear from the start that the group did in no way represent a school, and that he personally was unwilling to limit himself to a single dogma.[3] A few years later, when asked to write a preface for *Fille de fille* of Jules Guérin, Maupassant observed that a preface was usually a sermon in favor of some literary religion, but, he added, neither he nor the author had any religion of any kind. He expressed his impatience at vain attempts at classification, for he sees only one fundamental question: does a man have talent or not? Debates on literary classifications are incomprehensible to him: "Ces discussions oiseuses sont la consolation des Pions."[4]

This freedom which Maupassant, like Flaubert, demands for the artist naturally goes much further than mere freedom from arbitrary classification in a literary school. For him, art does not concern itself with morality; laws on pornography are stupid and dangerous, for the artist is indifferent to questions of morality when he composes his work: "Il marche, les yeux éblouis d'une vision, possédé par ce qu'on appelait jadis l'inspiration, sans s'inquiéter si elle est chaste ou impure. Il produit son œuvre conçue selon ses facultés, il élabore presque inconsciemment; il est une force, une machine productrice."[5] Yet the artist finds himself constantly attacked for violating the current code of morality, which is absurd, says Maupassant, for by present standards the works of the greatest French writer, François Rabelais, would have to be banned as pornographic. The same legislators who strive to throttle the artist by their laws on pornography demand also "un art démocratique, un art honnête," but, "l'art, messieurs, ne vous en

[2] LF, xv, 224. [3] LF, xv, 20.

[4] Maupassant, preface to *Fille de fille, roman parisien* by Jules Guérin, Bruxelles, Kistemaeckers, 1883. LF, xv, 93.

[5] Maupassant, "Discours académique," *Gil Blas*, July 18, 1882.

déplaise, n'a rien à faire avec tous ces mots. Il est et restera malgré vous aristocrate, sans se soucier le moins du monde de vos croyances."[6] The notion of "un art populaire" is absurd; any truly lofty work can be addressed only to the happy few capable of appreciating it.

The artist, according to Maupassant, must not only combat the restrictions imposed by the state, but he must also refuse any help and protection offered by the state; ". . . le patronage de l'État est et sera toujours funeste à l'art; . . . il n'enfantera jamais que trafics, agiotages commerciaux et le reste." It is obvious that painters are already hamstrung by the official competition; all of them have but a single goal: "quelque médaille décernée cérémonieusement par les chefs de bureau de la peinture." It is absurd to allow some incompetent official to judge matters he knows nothing about, therefore "Pas de protection, pas de patronage, pas de subvention!" No genius has ever been discovered by an academic competition; if a young man has talent he will make his own way, and concludes Maupassant: "Il n'y a pas de génies incompris. Il n'y a que des imbéciles prétentieux."[7] The Academy announced a poetry competition in 1883 and sought "une formule qui, sans arrière-pensée, embrassât à la fois, dans un idéal poétique, l'art et la morale, la religion et le patriotisme." When the subject, "Sursum corda," was announced, Maupassant all but exploded: "On ne comprendra donc jamais qu'il serait aussi stupide de vouloir imposer un sujet à un vrai poète que de forcer un chapelier à fabriquer des couteaux."[8] Painters have become the slaves of their Salon, musicians are prisoners of their Conservatoire, and all are officially classified; writers alone are free, says Maupassant, to speak to the intelligent public, and free they must remain.

[6] *ibid.*
[7] "Art et Artifice," *Gaulois*, April 4, 1881.
[8] "Sursum corda," *Gaulois*, December 3, 1883.

3

THE FUNCTION OF THE CRITIC

MAUPASSANT had very definite views on the function of the critic, but, as happens even to better critics, there is a curious contradiction between his theory and his practice. Unwilling to be catalogued as a member of a school and proclaiming absolute liberty for the writer, he demanded the same freedom for the critic. In fact, the critic should be free from any preconceived notions or any dogma, and be ready to welcome any new talent, any original work of art. This he expressed in the preface to *Pierre et Jean*,[1] adding that the writer should be judged not by any arbitrary standard but from his own point of view, and the critic's concern is to decide how well the artist succeeded in what he set out to do. Too many critics, says Maupassant, are merely readers—readers who require that a book appeal to their own peculiar temperament and mentality, and judge it on the basis of how well it satisfies their particular kind of imagination.[2] Elsewhere, Maupassant describes the eighteenth-century public who really understood the art of reading a book; this aristocratic, intelligent society was a refined and discerning judge: "Il cherchait les dessous, les dedans des mots, pénétrait les raisons secrètes de l'auteur, lisait lentement, sans rien passer, cherchait, après avoir compris la phrase, s'il ne restait plus rien à pénétrer. Car les esprits, lentement préparés aux sensations littéraires, subissaient l'influence secrète de cette puissance mystérieuse qui met une âme dans les œuvres."[3] This last is a rather fair summary of Maupassant's ideas on the function of a critic.

[1] *Pierre et Jean* (Conard), p. vi.   [2] *ibid.*, pp. viii-ix.

[3] Maupassant, "Etude sur Gustave Flaubert" *Revue bleue,* January 19 and 26, 1884; used as preface to *Lettres de Gustave Flaubert à G. Sand,* Paris, Charpentier, 1884, and as introduction to *Bouvard et Pécuchet,* volume VIII of *Œuvres complètes de Gustave Flaubert,* Paris, Quantin, 1885; LF, xv, 128. This essay, an excellent example of the way Maupassant reused his articles, is made up of material taken unchanged

Whenever he discusses principles of literary criticism, Maupassant proclaims the necessity of a completely open mind, although his own critical writing is marked by definite preferences and prejudices. Even in the letter of 1877 in which he outlines his literary faith certain affinities are apparent. At one point he writes: "Je ne crois pas que le naturel, le réel, la vie soient une condition *sine qua non* d'une œuvre littéraire. Des mots que tout cela," but a few lines later he qualifies this, saying, ". . . si je tiens à ce que la vision d'un écrivain soit toujours juste, c'est parce que je crois cela nécessaire pour que son interprétation soit originale et vraiment belle."[4] He shows clearly in his article on *Les Soirées de Médan* his antipathy for the romantics and more especially for the sentimental idealists like Feuillet: "Littérairement, ce qui nous parait haïssable, ce sont les vieilles orgues de Barbarie larmoyantes, dont Jean-Jacques Rousseau a inventé le mécanisme et dont une suite de romanciers, arrêtés, je l'espère, à M. Feuillet, s'est obstinée à tourner la manivelle, répétant invariablement les mêmes airs langoureux et faux."[5]

He gives a clear indication of his own preferences in his review of *A vau-l'eau* of Huysmans in 1882, for he was profoundly moved by this "histoire d'un employé à la recherche d'un bifteck," by Folantin, "cet Ulysse des gargotes," whose Odyssey is frightening in its truth. Though many are repelled by the narration of this hideous truth and prefer to be amused by someone like Cherbuliez, Maupassant sets forth his own views, saying: "Pour être ému, il faut que je trouve, dans un livre, de l'humanité saignante: il faut que les personnages soient mes voisins, mes égaux, passent par les joies et les souffrances que je connais, aient tous un peu de moi, me fassent établir, à mesure que je lis, une sorte de comparaison

---

or only slightly rewritten from the following: "Souvenirs d'un an: un après-midi chez Gustave Flaubert," *Gaulois*, August 23, 1880; "Gustave Flaubert d'après ses lettres," *Gaulois*, September 6, 1880; "Bouvard et Pécuchet," *Gaulois* (supplément), April 6, 1881; "Les Audacieux," *Gil Blas*, November 27, 1883; "La Finesse," *Gil Blas*, December 25, 1883.

[4] LF, xv, 224.   [5] "Les Soirées de Médan . . . ," LF, xv, 21.

constante, fassent frissonner mon cœur à des souvenirs intimes, et éveillent à chaque ligne des échos de ma vie de chaque jour. Et voilà pourquoi *l'Education sentimentale* me bouleverse, et pourquoi le roquefort avarié de M. Folantin fait courir en ma bouche des frémissements sinistres de remémorance."[6] He seeks above all a recognizable reality, and finds dull and insipid tales of impossible adventures, such as *Monte-Cristo* or *Les Trois Mousquétaires* which he was never able to finish, overcome by boredom at the accumulation of improbable and fantastic events.[7]

Henri Fouquier, who wrote under the pseudonym of Nestor in the *Gil Blas*, took exception to these remarks on Huysmans and Dumas; Maupassant in replying summed up a number of ideas which appear later in the preface to *Pierre et Jean*. Although he repeats his contention that literary principles are useless, he nevertheless sees some value in a discussion of these ideas; literary criticism should bring out the basic differences between writers of opposing temperaments and admit the right of each to create in his own fashion: "Et d'abord, en principe, je déclare à mon aimable confrère que je crois tous les principes littéraires inutiles. L'œuvre seule vaut quelque chose, quelle que soit la méthode du romancier. Un homme de talent ou de génie met en préceptes ses qualités et même ses défauts; et voilà comment se fondent toutes les écoles. Mais, comme c'est en vertu des règles établies ou acceptées par les écrivains d'un tempérament différent qu'on attaque les livres d'un rival, les discussions ont cela d'excellent qu'elles peuvent servir à expliquer les œuvres et à faire comprendre la légitimité des revendications artistiques, le droit de chaque littérateur de comprendre l'art à sa façon, du moment qu'il est doué d'assez de talent pour imposer sa manière de voir."[8] To Nestor's charge that Maupassant simply did not enjoy amusing or imaginative novels, the latter replied that he placed imagination on the same level as observation, but that a third gift was necessary: "Ce don, c'est l'art

---

[6] "En lisant," *Gaulois*, March 9, 1882.   [7] *ibid.*
[8] "Question littéraire," *Gaulois*, March 18, 1882.

littéraire. Je veux dire cette qualité singulière de l'esprit qui met en une œuvre je ne sais quoi d'éternel, cette couleur inoubliable, changeante avec les artistes, mais toujours reconnaissable."[9]

Maupassant's reply to Sarcey's criticism[10] of *Mademoiselle Fifi* sums up his conception of the task of the critic: "S'il me prend fantaisie de critiquer ou de contester le talent d'un homme, je ne puis le faire qu'en me plaçant à son point de vue, en pénétrant ses intentions secrètes. Je n'ai pas le droit de reprocher à M. Feuillet de ne jamais analyser des ouvriers, ou à M. Zola de ne point choisir des personnages vertueux."[11] This lofty statement rings just a little false when compared to the many violent attacks Maupassant made against Octave Feuillet, who was, in fact, his favorite whipping-boy. The sentence that follows gives us the real clue to Maupassant's critical position: "Il ne s'ensuit pas qu'il ne nous soit point permis de garder des préférences pour un certain ordre d'idées ou de sujets." There is an apparent contradiction between Maupassant's theories on the rôle of the critic and his own practice in critical writing. When his own literary works are subjected to critical scrutiny he is quick to demand absolute tolerance and a completely open mind on the part of the critic; but, when he himself assumes the rôle of critic he judges almost always from the point of view of his own aesthetic and his own tastes and preferences as a creative writer. The fact is that Maupassant never really considered himself a literary critic; in his many articles, even those signed Maufrigneuse, he is writing from the point of view of Guy de Maupassant the short story writer and novelist. As such, he does not hesitate to formulate rules which should bind literary critics, but it never occurs to him that these same rules should be binding on him when he reviews the work of others. Consequently, he finds nothing strange in his demanding that the professional critics judge a writer like Feuillet in terms of Feuillet's own

[9] *ibid.*

[10] Francisque Sarcey, "La Loi sur les écrits pornographiques," *Le XIXe Siècle*, July 4, 1882.

[11] "Chronique," *Gaulois*, July 9, 1882; LF, xv, 69-70.

intentions, while he, Maupassant, is at liberty to attack Feuillet's methods and aims because he finds them antipathetic to his own. When he speaks with admiration of *A vau-l'eau*, because he perceives in it a true presentation of something close to him, he is simply expressing a personal preference. But when Nestor replies that he is not at all interested in M. Folantin with whom he has absolutely nothing in common, Maupassant is indignant and declares that if the novel must treat only those subjects which fall within the experience of the reader, then it is the end of the novel as a genre. Nestor is a critic, and by the very nature of his profession should give the widest possible acceptance to all subjects and all methods, especially those that are least familiar. Maupassant is speaking as a professional writer who naturally tends to view literature in terms of his own artistic creed. That is why Maupassant's essays have a peculiar value, not because he is a great literary critic—he is not—but because everything he wrote is a reflection of his own creative process, of his own aesthetic.

Maupassant has very little hope that any absolute evaluation of a work of art can be made either by the critic or by the artist. Writing of the Salon of 1885, he declares the critics incompetent to pass judgment because they lack technical knowledge, while the artists are prejudiced, impressed only with their own method.[12] The situation is precisely the same in literature: "Si quelqu'un, par exemple, voulait avoir une opinion autorisée sur la valeur réelle d'une œuvre, à qui pourrait-il s'adresser parmi les écrivains connus ou diplômés. . . . En qui donc pouvons-nous avoir confiance pour apprécier un homme ou une œuvre? Hélas en personne. Nous avons le droit tout au plus de constater les choses grossièrement haïssables et fausses, les fautes de français et les fautes d'orthographe! Seul, le temps prononce une sentence infaillible et définitive."[13] In his critical writings Maupassant in no way pretends to render a definitive judgment of a work or a writer; his position is that of a fellow artist, not that of a critic.

[12] "Les Juges," *Gil Blas*, July 7, 1885.   [13] *ibid.*

4

REALISM AND IDEALISM

In one respect at least Maupassant admitted the existence of a common bond uniting the collaborators of the *Soirées de Médan*; all were reacting against the "esprit romantique" for the simple reason that "les générations littéraires se suivent et ne se ressemblent pas."[1] Men of his generation were brought up on the works of the romantic school and, in their youth, were full of admiration and enthusiasm for Hugo and Lamartine; yet when they came to write in their turn, they felt the need of creating something else, of finding new forms or of rediscovering still older methods.[2] But Maupassant's rejection of romanticism is based on something more fundamental than a mere desire for a change: he deplores the philosophical result and, even more, the idealism of the romantics, by which he means their deliberate attempt to give a false presentation of observable reality, depicting life not as it is, but as they would like to see it, deforming the truth by "idealizing" it.

The philosophical result of romanticism, which he finds so shocking, is the fact that Hugo has in part destroyed the work of Voltaire and Diderot. Romantic sentimentality has caused the disappearance of the old good sense and wisdom of Montaigne and Rabelais. The idea of pardon has been substituted for that of justice; emotion and sentimentality have replaced reason, and it is this romantic morality which causes the courts to free individuals whose crimes are inexcusable but whose situation arouses pity. He prefers Schopenhauer and Herbert Spencer to the masters of the romantic school because they offer a sounder view of life than the author of *Les Misérables*, adding that this criticism he makes of Hugo has nothing whatever to do with purely literary values.[3] Maupassant, following

[1] "Les Soirées de Médan . . . ," LF, xv, 20.
[2] Maupassant, "Romanciers contemporains: M. Emile Zola," *Revue bleue*, March 10, 1883; LF, xv, 30.
[3] "Les Soirées de Médan . . . ," LF, xv, 20-21. Maupassant seems to have

the lead of the Goncourts, frequently expressed a definite nostalgia for the eighteenth century, "ce dix-huitième siècle qui est et qui restera le grand siècle de la France, le siècle de l'art par excellence, de la grâce et de la beauté. . . ."[4] Whenever he needed a vantage point from which to attack the nullity of his own period, he invariably used the eighteenth century as the model of wit, art, good manners, and personal honesty. Above all, he found there the perfect antidote for the sentimental idealism of his own times which he so thoroughly abhorred. One has only to read *Manon Lescaut* or Godard d'Aucourt's *Thémidore* after George Sand's *Le Marquis de Villemer*, ". . . et soudain tout l'échafaudage compliqué de la sentimentalité moderne s'écroule, tous les raffinements d'idéalisme disparaissent, et la bonne logique ancienne se redresse devant nous."[5]

When he deals specifically with literature, however, he sets forth clearly certain ideas which are basic to him and which define sharply his own limitations, or at least the limitations he imposed on himself. He professes to see in the arguments over realism and idealism a meaningless quibble on words, but he leaves no doubt as to his own position, for he holds it to be an inflexible philosophical law that our imagination is limited to the impressions received through the sense organs; to him, this means that any "ideal conception," any paradise

---

been deeply vexed by the sentimentality which often influenced the courts' decisions and wrote feelingly on the subject in "Le Préjugé du déshonneur," *Gaulois*, May 26, 1881, which was used again in substantially the same form in "L'Amour à trois," *Gil Blas*, March 4, 1884; the latter article was also used as a preface to Paul Ginisty's book *L'Amour à trois* the same year, reprinted in LF, xv, 144-147. See also: "Pétition d'un viveur malgré lui," *Gil Blas*, January 12, 1882; "Chronique," *Gaulois*, April 14, 1884; and "Le Sentiment et la Justice," *Figaro*, December 8, 1884.

[4] "Bibelots," *Gaulois*, March 22, 1883.

[5] "A propos du divorce," *Gaulois*, June 27, 1882. See also "Maison d'artiste," *Gaulois*, March 12, 1881; "L'Esprit en France," *Gaulois*, June 19, 1881; "La Politesse," *Gaulois*, October 11, 1881; "Les Femmes," *Gil Blas*, October 29, 1881; "La Finesse," *Gil Blas*, December 25, 1883; "Etude sur Gustave Flaubert," *Revue bleue*, January 19 and 26, 1884 (LF, xv, 128); "Contemporains," *Gil Blas*, November 4, 1884.

invented by any religion is absurd, and the artist must limit himself to his direct experience of life, attempting to understand it and interpret it in a communicable form. Anyone who presents life as more beautiful than it is, who tries to imagine it as different from the reality he sees, is either a charlatan or an imbecile, a "romancier pour les dames."[6]

The realist, according to Maupassant, seeks to reveal in an artistic manner what he apprehends through his senses, recognizing that his sense organs may be deceptive, but avoiding any willful, deliberate alteration of the results of his observations. Zola, who calls himself a naturalist and who violently attacked the romantics on whom he was nourished, nevertheless used, as they did, the same techniques of enlargement, but applied them in a different manner. Maupassant ascribes to Zola a view which is exactly his own: for Zola, the work of art is the product of truth, and the deliberate distortion of what one sees can only produce a work that is false; the writer cannot give reign to his imagination, he must observe and describe scrupulously what he has seen.[7] Although these statements sound unduly rigid, they are immediately qualified, for the temperament of the writer and the particular way in which his senses operate must be taken into account. He will be faithful to his own vision of the world, refusing to adulterate in any way the impressions he receives, yet recognizing that the truth as he sees it is never the absolute truth. Zola defined his naturalism as "la nature vue à travers un tempérament," which Maupassant accepts as the clearest and most perfect definition of literature in general. The absolute truth, "la vérité sèche," does not exist, for no one is a perfect mirror, says Maupassant; but even if we know that we cannot attain absolute truth, we must, as artists, be meticulously exact in reporting the world as we see it and at least not give false testimony about our own impressions.[8]

[6] "Les Soirées de Médan . . . ," LF, xv, 21.
[7] "Romanciers contemporains: M. Emile Zola," LF, xv, 81.
[8] ibid., p. 82.

Maupassant's most fully developed discussion of realism and idealism is to be found in "Autour d'un livre,"[9] a review of *Un Mâle*, a novel by Camille Lemonnier. This novel, a rather violent tale of passion and death, is valuable, according to Maupassant, for the creation of an "atmosphère champêtre et sauvage." When it had first appeared as a feuilleton it had been attacked as naturalistic or realistic, as appealing to the baser passions. Maupassant defends it on that ground, but criticizes it as being more of an epic poem than a novel. The peasants are heroes glorified by the author and seen through the magnifying glass of a poet and not with the cold, accurate eye of a novelist. It is therefore idealistic rather than realistic, as he defines those terms: for the true artist, the idealists are dreamers whose special function is to present life as transformed by the rose-colored glasses of poetry; the realists, on the other hand, are men whose goal is to render life as it is in all its brutal truth. Both are logical, although to Maupassant's mind no real novelist should set out deliberately to be an idealist or a realist—rather he should be both, that is, uniquely concerned with a sincere presentation of his own vision of life, without regard for schools or literary fashions. Since we have no other guide except life as it appears to us, it would be folly to represent it as better than nature made it. Anyone who would thus try to change or correct the world as it has been created is guilty of pride and arrogance.

Although Maupassant defines an idealist as a kind of inaccurate dreamer he is aware that the public understands by idealistic literature something improbable, sympathetic, and consoling. The reader wants nothing more than to be moved, and if his sympathies are aroused by the book, the author is termed an idealist. Such readers cannot stomach a really great writer, says Maupassant, and in a forceful paragraph defines what he means by a great writer: one who is sincere but without illusions, whose domain is far above sentimental nonsense and false poetry, who takes hold of the reader and drags him

[9] "Autour d'un livre," *Gaulois*, October 4, 1881, reprinted in appendix.

out of his illusory tranquillity and makes him face life as it is; he exposes the unwilling reader to the misery and egoism of the human existence, its lack of lasting pleasure and the ever-present shadow of death which awaits us all, but which we prefer to ignore; he shows us to ourselves, unadorned and un-embellished, and most of us refuse to accept the image as our own. To escape the dreariness of their lives most readers hope to find in fiction comforting or exciting illusions. Those who are in their own lives dishonest and wicked demand purity in fiction to cleanse their soul by the spectacle of an ideal world, of a conventional existence. There are writers of talent who dispense this literary palliative in varying doses: some provide "la littérature mélasse à l'usage des petites bour-geoises"; and still others, "la littérature tord-boyaux (par-don!) à l'usage des portières."

This debate over idealism and realism is dismissed by Mau-passant as having no real connection with art and literature. It is in fact nothing more than a quarrel between hypocrisy and the sincerity of the mirror, or the reader's exasperation at the temperament of a particular writer. We are hypocrites to the marrow, we think only of saving appearances, and demand a hypocritical literature.[10] He does not hesitate, in a review of *Bouvard et Pécuchet*, to call Flaubert an idealist, but he is quick to add his own definition of the term, which is not that of the general public: "Ici il est curieux de remarquer la tendance constante de Gustave Flaubert vers un idéal de plus en plus abstrait et élevé. Par idéal je n'entends point ce rococo romantique qui séduit les imaginations bourgeoises. Car l'idéal, pour la plupart des hommes, n'est autre chose que *l'invrai-semblable*. Pour les autres, c'est tout simplement le domaine de l'idée. Gustave Flaubert, quoi qu'en aient dit les inconsci-

[10] Cf. "Chronique," *Gaulois*, July 9, 1882: "Le romancier se trouve donc placé dans cette alternative: faire le monde tel qu'il le voit, lever les voiles de grâce et d'honnêteté, constater ce qui est sous ce qui paraît, montrer l'humanité toujours semblable sous ses élégances d'emprunt, ou bien se résoudre à créer un monde gracieux et conventionnel comme l'ont fait George Sand, Jules Sandeau et M. Octave Feuillet." **LF,** xv, 70.

ents, a toujours été le plus acharné des idéalistes; mais, comme il avait aussi l'amour ardent de la vérité, sans laquelle l'art n'existe pas, tous ceux qui confondent, comme je viens de l'indiquer, l'idéal avec l'invraisemblable ont fait de lui un matérialiste forcené."[11]

The so-called idealists, represented in Maupassant's mind chiefly by George Sand, Jules Sandeau, and Octave Feuillet, devote themselves exclusively to the reader's happiness and willingly sacrifice truth, probability, and psychological accuracy to achieve this end. On the other hand, those who ardently seek the truth, like Flaubert and the Goncourt brothers, drive ahead indifferent to the effect of their findings on the reader. "Ils sont les esclaves respectueux de la Vérité, des passions et des tempéraments humains. La loi de la vie est leur seule loi. Ils ne cherchent pas à produire un effet qui pourra émouvoir ou attendrir; mais ils cherchent à découvrir le mobile secret et certain des actes, à soulever le voile de la réalité, à prendre sur le fait la mystérieuse nature. Peu leur importe de plaire au lecteur, de conquérir ses sympathies ou d'exciter sa colère par des moyens artificiels, peu leur importe d'indigner, d'irriter, de bouleverser, de dégoûter, d'ennuyer ou de séduire. Ils ne se préoccupent seulement de la sincérité de leur œuvre. Ils ne sont point les serviteurs du succès, mais les serviteurs de leur conscience d'artistes."[12] If they were seeking merely popular success, he adds, Flaubert would never have written *L'Education sentimentale*, nor would the Goncourt brothers have published *Germinie Lacerteux*. It is interesting to note that, in this same article, Maupassant does not include Balzac in the camp of those who "regardent, observent, notent, étudient l'Etre en toutes ses manifestations." He holds rather to the view expressed by Baudelaire that Balzac was above all a "visionnaire," and specifically excludes him, saying, "Je ne parle pas du grand Balzac, dont la manière, toute d'intuition, était encore fort différente."

11 "Bouvard et Pécuchet," *Gaulois* (supplément), April 6, 1881.
12 "La Jeune Fille," *Gaulois*, April 27, 1884.

Maupassant's realism, then, is based on accuracy of observation, a sincere and artistic effort to present the results of this study, and an awareness that the final result will not be an absolute truth but a partial and relative one. This relative truth, however, can be valuable, but only if it is an accurate and unadulterated representation of the writer's vision; all else is false. But, if nature is seen, it is seen through a temperament, and the ultimate value of a work of art derives from the originality and greatness of the temperament which interprets and arranges the raw material.[13] All his life the disciple of Flaubert proclaimed the doctrine of accurate observation. "Voir; tout est là, et voir juste. J'entends par voir juste voir avec ses propres yeux et non avec ceux des maîtres."[14] Like the painter in "La Vie d'un paysagiste"[15] he can say: "Vrai je ne vis plus que par les yeux. . . . Mais il faut voir, ou plutôt il faut découvrir. L'œil, le plus admirable des organes humains, est indéfiniment perfectionnable; et il arrive, quand on pousse, avec intelligence, son éducation, à une admirable acuité." But observation without reflection is sterile: insight must accompany sight, enabling the artist to see meaning and significance in objects which are commonplace and unevocative to others. The simple and direct sensation that a given object produces on our senses is not to be confused with the far more complex and illuminating experience which is provided by the artistic representation of that same object; the most repugnant sight can therefore become a thing of beauty when transformed by the brush of the painter or the pen of a writer.[16]

Maupassant insists that the realist must be an artist and that art is essentially a selective process. In the preface to *Pierre et Jean* he wrote that the realist, if he is an artist, does not try to give merely a banal photograph of life, but a more complete, more striking, more penetrating vision than reality

---

[13] LF, xv, 224.
[14] Maupassant, letter to Maurice Vicaire, July 17, 1885; LF, xv, 334-335.
[15] "La Vie d'un paysagiste," *Gil Blas*, September 28, 1886; LF, xv, 167.
[16] "Au Salon," *Le XIXe Siècle*, April 30, 1886; LF, xv, 162-163.

itself seems to offer. Similarly in his first essay on Flaubert in 1876, when he compares his master to Balzac, he holds that the author of the *Comédie humaine*, though a powerful genius, lacks the artistic faculty. Balzac is like a man who has far more material than he needs to build a house but uses it all because he is unable to make a choice; he creates nevertheless an immense work, but one less beautiful and less durable than if he had been more of an architect and less of a mason, more artistic and less personal.[17] Flaubert, on the other hand, carefully chooses what is essential, and unhesitatingly rejects the rest, so that from the finished work no piece can be taken away without destroying the harmony of the whole.

The novelist cannot simply set himself to copying life because in so doing he would cease to function as an artist, and it is equally true that many events which actually occur would sound utterly improbable in a novel.[18] In creating a character the writer draws on observations of the many people he has encountered in life; a fictional person will be composed of characteristics and mannerisms found in not one but many living models. Whenever a new book by Goncourt, Zola, or Daudet appears, people try to lift the masks of the characters and discover the identity of the model. Was la Faustin a portrait of Rachel or of Sarah Bernhardt? The question is an idle one to Maupassant; the answer is neither and both: "un personnage formé de toutes." All of human life belongs to the novelist and he may take his material where he finds it; but Maupassant holds that the conscientious artist will make certain that the mask cannot be lifted: "L'artiste a le droit de tout voir, de tout noter, de se servir de tout. Mais les masques qu'il met sur ses personnages, il faut qu'on ne les puisse lever."[19] It is on this same principle that he defended himself

[17] "Gustave Flaubert," *La République des Lettres*, October 22, 1876; LF, xv, 6.
[18] "Les Bas-fonds," *Gaulois*, July 28, 1882; LF, xv, 73-75; "Un Drame vrai," *Gaulois*, August 6, 1882.
[19] "Les Masques," *Gil Blas*, June 5, 1883.

against the criticisms levelled at *Bel-Ami* two years later.[20]

But the process of making an artistic selection from what reality offers is not in itself sufficient. A great work must have infused in it another quality: it must suggest something universal and fundamental, have a symbolic value. In an essay on the Venus of Syracuse he sets forth an article of his artistic credo which goes beyond the simple-minded "realism" with which he is often identified. "Une œuvre d'art n'est supérieure que si elle est en même temps un symbole et l'expression exacte d'une réalité."[21]

It is perfectly clear that Maupassant finds little of value in the "idealistic" novel, in spite of his thesis that all literary theories are equally admissible and that an author should be judged within the framework of his own intentions, ideas which he sets forth in the preface to *Pierre et Jean* and wherever he is writing not as a critic himself but as a guide to critics. His own preferences and prejudices stand out sharply in the articles in which he discusses the works of his contemporaries. Even in his celebrated preface he disposes rather quickly of the idealistic novel, saying that its chief interest lies in the development of the plot so that at the end of the book there remains no desire on the part of the reader to know what will happen further to the characters, who are, as a matter of fact, people without a future. Curiously enough it is this same criticism, that the characters have no future, that everything of interest happened to them in the past, which Jean-Paul Sartre levels at Maupassant, whom he takes as a typical realist. We shall have occasion to refer again to Sartre's strictures, but first let us examine what Maupassant holds to be the major principle of his novelistic technique.

[20] "Aux critiques de *Bel-Ami*—Une Réponse," *Gil Blas,* June 7, 1885; LF, xv, 154-157.

[21] "Sur une Vénus," *Gil Blas,* January 12, 1886; repeated in *La Vie errante* (Conard), p. 122.

5

THE MAJOR PRINCIPLE: THE OBJECTIVE TECHNIQUE

THE core of Maupassant's novelistic creed is to be found in a single principle from which practically all of his ideas on technique derive: it is the belief, which he clung to even when he himself tried to write psychological novels, that the only valid novelistic technique is that which attempts to reveal the inner man by his acts, without recourse to direct analysis. It was a principle set forth explicitly by Flaubert and acknowledged by Maupassant to be a dogma of the master which he made his own. In the preface to *Pierre et Jean*, he tries to suggest that his attitude is that of liberal, open-minded acceptance of all theories, but it is nevertheless clear that his preference is for the objective method. In his earlier articles, however, he is often far less mild-mannered and holds that the psychological novel is absurd and pretentious, for we are subject to the limitations of our sense organs, and morally isolated by our inability ever to penetrate the mind of another. The novelist is not an omniscient God from whom his characters have no secrets; to Maupassant, the novelist is not above or within his characters; he is on their level, their equal, seeing them as a man sees other men, guessing at their inner nature from the evidence of their outward actions. The task of the novelist is to be a more perspicacious observer than the layman and to present his findings in an artistic manner.

His discussion in the preface to *Pierre et Jean* of the different techniques required by the psychological and by the objective approaches is simply the echo of ideas expressed earlier in his career in a number of articles written when he was attempting to put into practice the Flaubertian theories he had readily adopted. His most succinct expression of the basic principle of the objective novel appears in his article on Flaubert in 1884; he was apparently rather well pleased with it himself, for he lifted the paragraph verbatim and used it in another article a few months later. Flaubert's method, he wrote, was based not so much on observation as on penetration: "Au lieu d'étaler la psychologie des personnages en des dissertations explicatives, il la faisait simplement apparaître par leurs actes. Les dedans étaient ainsi dévoilés par les dehors, sans aucune argumentation psychologique."[1]

Behind this literary technique was a concept of life which Maupassant believed to be based on an inflexible philosophic law: "Nous ne pouvons rien imaginer en dehors de ce qui tombe sous nos sens."[2] Yet every phenomenon observed by our senses is part of a rigorous series of causes and effects and is capable of rational explanation. In 1881, at least, this celebrated pessimist expressed a somewhat naïve belief that the progress of science would one day lead surely to complete certainty of knowledge: "Les savants chercheront sans fin l'inconnu. Et pourtant le grand pas est fait. On marche dans le certain, vers le certain; on sait que tout effet a une cause logique, et que, si cette cause nous échappe, c'est uniquement parce que notre esprit, notre pénétration, nos organes et nos instruments sont trop faibles."[3] Whatever the future may hold in store, each man lives in solitary confinement, relying on his imperfect senses for his knowledge of the world and of other men.

Maupassant quickly abandoned this belief that science would one day arrive at absolute knowledge. As time went on, he stressed again and again man's solitude, his inability to understand his fellow men or be understood by them. "Soli-

---

[1] "Etude sur Gustave Flaubert," *Revue bleue*, January 19 and 26, 1884; LF, xv, 110. Repeated in "Les Subtils," *Gil Blas*, June 3, 1884, which is reprinted in the appendix.

[2] "Les Soirées de Médan . . . ," LF, xv, 21.

[3] "Au Muséum d'histoire naturelle," *Gaulois*, March 23, 1881. In "Adieu mystères," *Gaulois*, November 8, 1881, he wrote: "Plus de mystères; tout l'inexpliqué devient explicable un jour; le surnaturel baisse comme un lac qu'un canal épuise; la science, à tout moment, recule les limites du merveilleux."

tude"[4] is the despairing cry of a man who is tortured by his inability to know what goes on in the minds of his friends. "Quel mystère que la pensée inconnue d'un être, la pensée cachée et libre, que nous ne pouvons ni connaître, ni conduire, ni dominer, ni vaincre!" Occasionally he expresses an ironically bitter pleasure in his solitude, suggesting that it is perhaps just as well that one cannot look directly into the inmost recesses of another's mind. He develops the theme of La Rochefoucauld (but without mentioning him) that "Il n'y aurait pas d'honnête homme pour un œil sondant le fond des consciences."[5] His optimistic view of the progress of science was but a momentary enthusiasm. In 1884, the tone of many of his newspaper essays is as pessimistic as anything he wrote later, and in "Les Subtils"[6] he looks with scorn on the futile efforts of those who desire certainty. Since the beginning of the world, the most penetrating minds have grasped but fragments of the hidden secrets of man and the universe, and he quotes Flaubert's remark in *Bouvard et Pécuchet* that science, which is based on the meager data of the partially known, may be inapplicable to the vast undiscoverable region of the still unknown.

Apart from the vast realm which will ever remain part of the unknown, there is the domain of observable phenomena, accessible to man; but most of us, through familiarity or inertia, fail to use the faculties at our disposal and remain needlessly blind. "Mais l'homme a les yeux fermés pour l'homme. Il ne sait pas regarder ce qu'il voit dès l'enfance, juger d'un coup d'œil ce qui passe devant son regard en établissant toujours le mieux et le pire, contempler enfin notre vie comme ferait un singe grimpé dans un arbre et qui estimerait l'homme une caricature de sa race."[7] The novelist, who, by Maupassant's definition, has clearer vision than the rest of us, is able

[4] "Solitude," *Gaulois*, March 31, 1884; *Monsieur Parent* (Conard), pp. 261-270; LF, IV, 305-311.

[5] "Le Fond du cœur," *Gil Blas*, October 14, 1884.

[6] "Les Subtils," *Gil Blas*, June 3, 1884.

[7] "A propos de rien," *Gil Blas*, March 30, 1886.

to reveal things to us by his greater powers of observation and deduction; but even he can examine directly no other mind but his own, and consequently the psychological novel in its attempt to explore directly the minds of its characters is absurd and pretentious. Those who try to penetrate the mysterious mechanism of motives and the secrets of causes are doomed to failure and lose themselves in the inextricable labyrinth of psychological and physiological phenomena.[8]

Maupassant's marked aversion for the psychological novel was expressed in a number of articles before he summed up his views in the preface to *Pierre et Jean*, which, interestingly enough, is essentially a psychological novel. The most important of these articles, titled simply "Romans," was written as a review of Jean Richepin's *Quatre petits romans*, which serves as a peg on which to hang a discussion of the art of the novel and particularly of the function of psychology in the novel. Richepin, in his preface which had just been printed in the *Gil Blas* of April 12, 1882, had extolled the virtues of the psychological novel in general and of his own works, *Sœur Doctrouvé* and *Monsieur Destrémeaux*, in particular, and had attacked excessive description, saying: ". . . le roman psychologique est le plus beau, le plus difficile, le plus magistral de tous les genres de romans. . . . Quoi de plus curieux, en effet, de plus intéressant, de plus délicat, de plus subtil, de plus fort, que de fouiller les coins obscurs d'une conscience et de montrer à nu les mille et une péripéties du drame intime qui se joue dans le cœur d'un être humain? Voilà une description autrement ardue à faire, autrement troublante à lire, que les descriptions à la mode, où l'on ne peint que l'extérieur des personnages et le milieu qui les entoure. La belle malice, de m'inventorier un appartement avec une minutie d'huissier!"[9]

Maupassant, while agreeing with him on some points,[10] was disturbed by this last phrase which summed up the chief ob-

---

[8] "Les Subtils," *Gil Blas*, June 3, 1884.

[9] Jean Richepin, "Ma Préface," *Gil Blas*, April 12, 1882.

[10] Maupassant, "Romans," *Gil Blas*, April 26, 1882, reprinted in appendix.

jections to the so-called realistic or naturalistic schools, that is, the "Ecoles de la vraisemblance." Admitting that there have been abuses, and granting that psychology is of fundamental importance in a novel, Maupassant sees an absolutely necessary link between description and psychology; to eliminate description would remove the essential life-giving setting, flatten the characters and deprive them of their individual traits, and, in a word, exclude all artistry, leaving only the labor of the psychologist. The creation of atmosphere is indispensable if the book is to have any life, and to illustrate the point Maupassant chooses Dickens as an example, describing the care with which he makes familiar to the reader the scene of the action and the tics and habits of his characters.

Maupassant divides novels into two categories: those that are clear and those that are vague, the latter being novels which are heavy and confused because they depend almost entirely on psychological explanations. For him, the works of Stendhal, remarkable though they are, are typically "vague," for it is only after reflection that their hidden qualities become apparent; they lack the artistry that produces an immediate well-ordered clarity.

Reiterating his fundamental premise that the outward gesture will reveal the inner nature, Maupassant goes on to declare that observable facts are simply the translation of thoughts and sensations. To explain the inner workings of the mind by rigorous logic is too easy; the artist will show the character in action in a milieu which has become familiar to the reader, leaving to the latter the task of deducing from the evidence given the psychological basis of the character. The novelist never has the right to qualify or determine a character by an explanation of his motives; he must be seen in action, not talked about. The reader, amply provided with facts and actions, must be allowed to draw his own conclusions.[11] This basic premise of Maupassant's novelistic creed recurs again and again in one form or another whenever he launches

[11] *ibid.*

into a discussion of literature; for example in a letter, he put it thus: "Pour moi, la psychologie dans le roman ou la nouvelle se résume à ceci: mettre en scène l'homme secret par sa vie."[12]

He has a fondness for dividing novels into categories, but he constantly returns to the fundamental division between the "objective" novelists and "psychological" novelists. In the article on "Les Subtils"[13] he neatly labels the former "metteurs-en-scène" and the latter "métaphysiciens." But among those who go beyond physical appearances to delve into the workings of the mind he finds additional distinctions to be made. On the one hand are those who, probing into the human soul, attempt to simplify, to find the typical and the characteristic; on the other hand are those who search out the vaguest, most fugitive sensations of the mind, neglecting no nuance, preferring complexity to simplification. These last are "les subtils," whose great merit is that they constantly demand superior intelligence and close attention on the part of the reader if he is to follow them in their meandering exploration of the human brain. Flaubert is of course the arch-type of the objective novelist, while the Goncourts are specifically "subtils." The rest of the essay is devoted to an analysis of two young writers who represent two different types of "subtils": Catulle Mendès and Paul Bourget.

The chief criticism that has been levelled at the objective technique is that, while the system is adequate to treat the simple and primitive minds of the people in Maupassant's short stories, it can only break down when dealing with more complicated, more self-conscious, more introspective minds; or, as Henry James put it: "M. de Maupassant has simply skipped the whole reflective part of his men and women— that reflective part which governs conduct and produces character."[14] Maupassant recognized that certain subjects presented almost insuperable difficulties to the writer who worked

12 LF, xv, 422.
13 "Les Subtils," *Gil Blas*, June 3, 1884.
14 Henry James, "Guy de Maupassant," *Fortnightly Review*, March 1, 1888, p. 385; *Partial Portraits*, London, Macmillan, 1888, p. 285.

from observation. One such subject is the young girl: we seldom see her, says Maupassant, she lives outside of the social circles we frequent, it is difficult to know her thoughts and feelings and to interpret accurately her actions and words. His comments on this subject were inspired by the publication of Edmond de Goncourt's *Chérie* and Zola's *La Joie de vivre*, both of which dealt with a young girl. Maupassant considered this a very original undertaking, for, although *Paul et Virginie* disclosed to us the heart of a young girl, it is a poem rather than a work of observation; Octave Feuillet had portrayed a *jeune fille* in *Julia de Trécœur*, but, like George Sand and Jules Sandeau, was less concerned with exact truth or psychological accuracy, than with diverting the reader and playing on his emotions. The task of Zola and Goncourt was very different and more demanding, and Maupassant has nothing but praise for these two books: Goncourt, in a "tableau d'une âme de fillette" gives us a definitive analysis with all the subtlety of his style; Zola's book is profoundly human, marked by a bitter irony, one of his greatest novels. Maupassant, in 1884, was impressed particularly by the difficulty of observing a creature so well-hidden, so undeveloped as a young girl. "C'est encore là," he writes in this same article, "ce qui, sans doute, a retenu jusqu'ici les romanciers précis devant cette difficile tentative. Ecrire la vie d'une jeune fille jusqu'au mariage, c'est raconter l'histoire d'un être jusqu'au jour où il existe réellement. C'est vouloir préciser ce qui est indécis, rendre clair ce qui est obscur, entreprendre une œuvre de déblaiement pour l'interrompre quand elle va devenir aisée. Que reste-t-il de la jeune fille dans la femme cinq ans après? Si peu qu'on ne la reconnaît plus."[15] Henry James in *The Awkward Age* deals with the same problem and gives a perfect illustration of Maupassant's last remark in Aggie, who becomes so completely transformed immediately after her marriage, that she is apparently an entirely different person.

By training and temperament Maupassant was decidedly

[15] "La Jeune Fille," *Gaulois*, April 27, 1884.

more at home in the objective technique, and even in the preface to *Pierre et Jean*, where he gives at least the illusion of open-minded acceptance of all forms and methods, it is clear where his preferences lie. What disturbs him most about the strictly psychological approach is that the novelist can only substitute himself for each of his characters, transfer his own sensibility to them, since he cannot imagine perceptions other than those he himself has experienced. In other words, the psychological novel is necessarily autobiographical, and we may expect to find in the two novels which are frankly psychological studies, *Fort comme la mort* and *Notre Cœur*, some of the substance of Maupassant's own life and preoccupations. *Pierre et Jean* is a psychological novel, but in this case the objective method has been used and adapted to the particular problem of analysis presented by the subject.

Gide has expressed the same notion, but, naturally enough, has made a very different use of it. In the *Journal des Faux-Monnayeurs*, he writes: "Un caractère arrive à se peindre admirablement en peignant autrui, en parlant d'autrui—en raison de ce principe que chaque être ne comprend vraiment en autrui que les sentiments qu'il est lui-même capable de fournir."[16] The consequence of this for Gide, instead of leading him to renounce any efforts to delve into the mind of his characters, inclines him to search and analyze all the more thoroughly, for his goal is to find himself, the real authentic self, and his scrutiny of others springs only from his desire for self-revelation. Hence each work of Gide is a chapter in a long autobiography. Maupassant, on the other hand, tried to separate himself from his characters, to observe them from the outside, and, when relating their point of view or their reactions, to subordinate his personality to theirs. Contrasting the *chroniqueur* and the novelist, he defines the qualities and function of the writer of fiction: "Le romancier . . . doit, tout en donnant à son œuvre la marque de son originalité propre, se faire

---

[16] André Gide, *Journal des Faux-Monnayeurs, Œuvres complètes*, 15 vols., Paris, NRF, 1932-1939, XIII, 38.

autant de tempéraments qu'il met en scène de personnes; il doit apprécier avec leurs jugements divers, voir la vie avec leurs yeux, donner le reflet des faits et des choses dans tous ces esprits contraires, différamment organisés suivant leur tempérament physique et les milieux où ils se sont développés."[17]

The key to Maupassant's technique lies in the belief, so often expressed, that the imagination is strictly limited by the senses, which logically forces him to adopt the objective method. The task he sets himself is the artistic interpretation of man and of life; but he treats only observable phenomena, that part of man and that part of life which can be perceived through the senses. Now if there are hidden recesses in men's minds which contain psychological peculiarities no trace of which appears on the surface, which give no hint even to the most acute observer, then Maupassant concludes that no such hidden places exist *because* they are not visible on the surface. His whole view of life from which derives his conception of the novel limits his scope, cuts him off from a domain into which he attempted to penetrate only toward the last years of his life. Certain passages of his writings reveal that he at least glimpsed the complex workings of the memory and the subconscious, which were to furnish such a rich vein for later writers to exploit. But other novelists before him had penetrated their characters more deeply; Stendhal, for example, offers us in effective fashion the contrast between Julien Sorel's external appearance and the psychological ferment within. What would a witness have noted as he watched Julien hold Mme de Rênal's hand? The whole drama of the scene is precisely in the fact that little of it appears on the surface. Stendhal takes his position within his character and works from the inside outward. Maupassant is almost always outside his character, and remains there. He can infer what is going on within from what he sees from without. He is an observer, but a privileged one, possessing more of his character's history

[17] "Messieurs de la chronique," *Gil Blas*, November 11, 1884.

than we ever could of the background of any of our contemporaries. Yet even when he exposes directly the workings of his character's mind, as in *Pierre et Jean*, he keeps his external station, noting only those elements which would have been manifest to a person of some acuity. He has thus limited the range of the novelist; he is never omniscient, though he may think he is, because he stands off, refusing to enter, satisfying himself by saying: If there is anything behind this, signs of it will appear, signs which I can appreciate with the senses, and can then interpret.

Yet for all his self-imposed limitations he shows an awareness of the mysteries of memory and the subconscious with which he nevertheless feels incapable of dealing. His preoccupation with hallucinations and terror in many of his short stories is well-known. There is a suggestion in *Fort comme la mort* and elsewhere of the evocative power of odors and perfumes which can unexpectedly conjure up a whole section of the past.[18] Less well known are a number of very curious passages in his newspaper articles. In 1881 he wrote: "Dans notre mémoire, ce magasin d'antiquités des sensations et des idées, nous retrouvons parfois, tout à coup, un vieux souvenir oublié, qui nous fait revivre en une seconde toute une période lointaine de notre existence."[19] Again a few years later he develops the theme more fully: "Singulier mystère que le souvenir! On va devant soi, par les rues, sous le premier soleil de mai, et tout à coup, comme si des portes depuis longtemps fermées s'ouvraient dans la mémoire, des choses oubliées vous reviennent. Elles passent, suivies par d'autres, vous font revivre des heures passées, des heures lointaines.

"Pourquoi ces retours brusques vers l'autrefois? Qui sait? Une odeur qui flotte, une sensation si légère qu'on ne l'a point notée, mais qu'un de nos organes reconnaît, un frisson, un même effet de soleil qui frappe l'œil, un bruit peut-être, un

18 Cf. Edouard Maynial, *La Vie et l'Œuvre de Guy de Maupassant*, Paris, Mercure de France, 1906, pp. 230-231.
19 "Au Muséum d'histoire naturelle," *Gaulois*, March 23, 1881.

rien qui nous effleura en une circonstance ancienne et qu'on retrouve, suffit à nous faire revoir tout à coup un pays, des gens, des événements disparus de notre pensée."[20]

All this sounds very Proustian, of course, but Maupassant never made any serious attempt to explore any further or to incorporate any of these ideas in his fiction. He was satisfied to have found a neat introductory paragraph to an article and stopped there. From the same premises Proust went on and pursued time until he recaptured it and fixed it in a masterpiece. Maupassant dreads the very thought of such a pursuit, such a delving into the recesses of the mind, lest we expose all sorts of secret vices and villainy; and he is relieved that such an inquisition is impossible: "Oh! quelle chance d'être fermés comme nous sommes à toute investigation du voisin, d'être toujours mentalement sur la terre, toujours séparés de tous dans le mystère de notre pensée. . . .

"S'il fallait, non pas avouer mais seulement reconnaître en silence toutes les hontes secrètes de notre pensée, tous les désirs coupables qui nous effleurent, tous les éveils infâmes de nos passions, de nos instincts, de notre sensualité, de notre envie, de notre cupidité, nous demeurerions effarés devant notre gredinerie."[21]

Yet Maupassant is aware that the subconscious has become a field of exploration for the novelist. Psychology, he writes, was once the domain of philosophers who published their studies in weighty serious books; today it is the novelist who attempts to penetrate and explain the obscure workings of the will, the mystery of the subconscious and the instincts. He quotes from the first page of a story, *L'Irréparable*, by Paul Bourget: "Par dessous l'existence intellectuelle et sentimentale dont nous avons conscience, et dont nous endossons la responsabilité probablement illusoire, tout un domaine s'étend, obscur et changeant, qui est celui de notre vie inconsciente." It is this domain, says Maupassant, that is being developed now

[20] "Malades et Médecins," *Gaulois*, May 11, 1884.
[21] "Le Fond du cœur," *Gil Blas*, October 14, 1884.

by many novelists using many different methods.[22] Maupassant himself held aloof, aware that the field which others were working was rich, yet forced by his own doctrine to remain on the other side of the fence in his own territory, where the results of his labor were by no means insignificant.

[22] "Les Subtils," *Gil Blas*, June 3, 1884.

ON STYLE

MAUPASSANT'S remarks on style at the end of the preface to *Pierre et Jean* are essentially a plea for simplicity and an attack on over-complicated manipulation of syntax and a self-conscious choice of words, a criticism which Edmond de Goncourt, with ample justification, took as a personal affront. Maupassant has elsewhere set down a number of observations on style, faithfully following the doctrine of Flaubert and applying those principles to the work of his own contemporaries. His attitude toward the Goncourts seems vacillating and inconsistent, at times full of praise for their work, at others condemning the style identified with them. The simplest explanation is probably that he admired the results achieved by the Goncourts, even though their manner was so different from his own, but he abhorred those who imitated the subtleties and complexity of their style.[1]

For him, as for Flaubert, the fundamental basis of style is a complete and perfect harmony between the idea and the expression. In an article called "Styliana" he ascribes to a "great writer," that is to say Flaubert, the definition of style which he adopts as his own: "J'entendais dernièrement un homme de lettres de vraie race définir le style à peu près ainsi: 'Une chose qui blesse le public, qui indigne le plus souvent les critiques, et qui révolte l'Académie.' Il ajoutait 'Le style, c'est la vérité, la variété, l'abondance de l'image; le choix infaillible de l'épithète unique et caractéristique; la justesse absolue du mot pour signifier la chose; la concordance rythmique de la phrase avec l'idée.'

"Il disait encore: 'La phrase doit être souple comme un clown, cabrioler en avant, en arrière, en l'air, de toutes les façons; ne jamais faire deux culbutes pareilles, étonner sans

---

[1] Cf. A. Guérinot, "Maupassant et les Goncourts," *Mercure de France*, December 15, 1928, pp. 567-591.

cesse par la variété de ses poses et la multiplicité de ses allures.'

"Il disait aussi: 'L'idée est l'âme du mot; le mot, le corps de l'idée; la phrase forme l'harmonie de cette âme et de ce corps.' "[2]

The essence is not in the fact but in the manner of presenting it, "une accordance absolue de l'expression avec l'idée," as Maupassant says in his study of Flaubert in 1884.[3] Therefore Musset was not an artist in the same sense that Baudelaire, Hugo, and Leconte de Lisle were. Words have a soul, he insists, and most readers, even most writers, are satisfied with the simple meaning. Many are totally insensitive to this quality, but it cannot be taught: "Autant parler musique à des gens qui n'ont point d'oreille." Style to Flaubert was not a mannerism, but rather "une manière unique, absolue, d'exprimer une chose dans toute sa couleur et son intensité." The form to him was the work itself: "Il ne comprenait point que le fond pût exister sans la forme, ni la forme sans le fond." Hence his immense labor to discover the *mot juste* for what he wanted to express.[4] In one of his earliest articles, written in 1876, while Flaubert was still alive, Maupassant set forth clearly the belief that style is not a personal peculiarity but an absolute perfection to be attained by unremitting labor: "Flaubert n'a point son style, il a le style; c'est-à-dire que les expressions et la composition qu'il emploie pour formuler une pensée quelconque sont toujours celles qui conviennent *absolument à cette pensée*, son tempérament se manifestant par la justesse et non par la singularité du mot."[5]

Much as he stressed the importance of style, Maupassant held that it was only one aspect of literary art. Great books have been written, which though they lack the quality of style, nevertheless have a force and life which are immediately recognizable. "En dehors de l'art, pas de salut. L'art est-ce le

[2] "Styliana," *Gaulois*, November 29, 1881.
[3] LF, xv, 128.   [4] *ibid.*, pp. 129-130.
[5] "Gustave Flaubert," *La République des Lettres*, October 22, 1876; LF, xv, 5.

style? dira-t-on. Non assurément, bien que le style en soit une large partie. Balzac écrivait mal; Stendhal n'écrivait pas; Shakespeare traduit nous donne des soulèvements d'admiration."[6] One can even be a great writer without being, in Maupassant's sense, an artist: "Pour être un artiste, il ne suffit pas à un écrivain de penser avec puissance, de penser même avec génie, et d'exprimer sa pensée clairement et fortement.

"Cela suffit pour être un grand homme.

"L'artiste cherche à mettre dans son œuvre autre chose que la pensée; il veut y mettre cette chose mystérieuse et inexplicable qui est l'Art littéraire. Qu'est-ce que cela qu'ignorent tant de romanciers? Comment l'expliquer au juste?

"L'artiste ne cherche pas seulement à bien dire ce qu'il veut, mais il veut donner à certains lecteurs une sensation et une émotion particulières, une jouissance d'art, au moyen d'un accord secret et superbe de l'idée avec les mots." Merely changing the position of a word may be enough to produce immediately, "un effet saisissant de beauté, de vie. . . ." In short this is the function of the artist: "Il met la délicate musique de l'expression sur la chanson de la pensée."[7]

The choice of each individual word and its position are of the utmost importance. When Maupassant made his brilliant début with *Boule de Suif* Flaubert had not seen the manuscript, but read the story for the first time when it had already been set up in page-proofs. Maupassant invited his criticism, adding that, since the volume was already in proof and the number of lines could not be altered, only individual words could be changed: "Mais l'épithète est une chose grave qui peut toujours être modifiée."[8]

Although it is possible for a great intellect to bring forth a masterpiece which still lacks the quality of style, there are certain subjects, particularly those dealing with mediocre people in a routine existence, which require all the resources

6 "Question littéraire," *Gaulois*, March 18, 1882.
7 "La Femme de lettres," *Figaro*, July 3, 1884.
8 Maupassant, letter to Flaubert [March 1880]; LF, xv, 285.

of literary art and style to give interest and significance to the banal material. Reviewing *La Ferme du Choquard* in the *Gil Blas* in 1883, Maupassant develops this point treating Victor Cherbuliez none too gently: "C'est un roman du genre champêtre. Il faut dans ces œuvres d'une apparente simplicité, une science profonde du style, un art infini des nuances, une habileté hors ligne pour émouvoir avec des personnages inférieurs avec des faits d'une apparente banalité.

"Les qualités de M. Cherbuliez sont tout autres. Un homme d'une extrême originalité peut seul, par le fait même de sa nature, donner de la couleur et de l'intérêt aux choses médiocres de la vie. Un homme d'un tempérament moyen, qui plaît plutôt par des effets, rendra insipides, en les faisant passer par son cerveau, les sujets déjà ternes par eux-mêmes." Most of his criticism is for the style of the novel: "D'où vient l'invincible somnolence qui vous prend en lisant ce gros roman? Elle vient de la pâleur du style, de l'uniforme banalité de la phrase, du français-suisse enfin."[9]

Absolute perfection of style is achieved not by brilliant flashes of inspiration but by dogged, persistent labor. Consequently Maupassant is scornful of the romantics in general, because he felt that they simply did not work hard enough at their task. In a moment of discouragement and loneliness in 1881, he wrote to his mother: "Je sens cet immense égarement de tous les êtres, le poids du vide. Et au milieu de cette débandade de tout, mon cerveau fonctionne lucide, exact, m'éblouissant avec le Rien éternel." His brain is lucid enough to catch himself up and criticize what he has just written: "Cela a l'air d'une phrase du père Hugo: mais il me faudrait beaucoup de temps pour rendre mon idée claire dans un langage précis. Ce qui me prouve une fois de plus que l'emphase romantique tient à l'absence de travail."[10]

There is a further distinction to be made. Working diligently on one's style is not enough; however great the labor

[9] "M. Victor Cherbuliez," *Gil Blas*, May 1, 1883.
[10] Maupassant, letter to his mother [January 1881]; LF xv, 293.

involved, it will be in vain if one seeks merely a particular elegance and distinction of phrase: the only valid effort is an impersonal search for the absolute. Maupassant draws this distinction sharply in his review of *Païenne* by Juliette Lamber (Mme Adam): "Elle soigne son style. Soigner son style ne veut pas dire travailler son style. La nuance est délicate à saisir. On soigne son style quand on a un certain idéal de phrase élégante, sonore, mais monotone et un peu cérémonieuse. On travaille son style quand on pioche sa phrase, sans parti-pris de lui donner une certaine forme convenue dont on désire ne pas sortir."[11]

He distinguishes among contemporary writers two groups who stand at opposite poles: those who labor over their style too little, and those who complicate it excessively. The latter group is easily identified with the followers of the Goncourts. His description of the two camps is not lacking in malice: "Il est parmi les prosateurs deux groupes qui passent leur temps à s'entre-mépriser: ceux qui travaillent presque trop leur phrase, et ceux qui ne la travaillent pas assez. Les premiers n'arrivent jamais à l'Académie; les seconds, à moins d'être vides comme l'Odéon un jour de première, y parviennent presque toujours. Leur prose coule, coule, incolore, insipide, sans mordre l'esprit, sans secouer la pensée, sans troubler les nerfs. On appelle cela être correct.

"Mais celle des autres est compliquée, machinée, criblée d'intentions, hérissée de procédés, semée de nuances. Tout y est voulu, médité, préparé. Chaque adjectif a des lointains et chaque verbe un son qui doit s'accorder avec l'idée qu'il exprime. En une page, jamais deux fois la même allure de phrase ne doit se reproduire, jamais deux mots pareils, jamais deux consonnances ne doivent se rencontrer à cent lignes de distance; et il doit exister dans le retour des lettres initiales des mots, une certaine symétrie mystérieuse qui concourt à l'harmonie de l'ensemble."[12]

[11] "Bataille de livres," *Gaulois*, October 28, 1883.
[12] "Profils d'écrivains," *Gil Blas*, June 1, 1882.

In a later article he develops his criticisms of the practitioners of the complicated style, but makes it perfectly clear that he has a very great respect for the Goncourt brothers, although their less talented disciples indulge in strange excesses in their efforts to imitate the masters. François Poictevin, author of *Ludine*, is one of these, and Maupassant finds him interesting for his defects as well as his virtues. He is afflicted by a strange and almost incurable disease: "la maladie du mot." A subtle and delicate observer, he thinks that a special vocabulary is required to express these almost imperceptible nuances that he feels. He therefore invents words and twists language so that one needs a key to read him, for he complicates the thought as well as the expression. Maupassant sounds just a little exasperated when he utters the plea which will be reechoed in the preface to *Pierre et Jean* some years later: "Et, vraiment je me demande s'il n'est pas possible de dire les choses les plus délicates, de saisir les impressions les plus fuyantes et de les fixer clairement avec les mots que nous employons ordinairement."[13] He goes on however to make clear the distinction between the masters and the disciple: "Ce livre est curieux surtout parce qu'il est le type nouveau de cette littérature maladive, mais singulièrement pénétrante, subtile, chercheuse qui nous vient de ces deux maîtres modernes, Edmond et Jules de Goncourt. Le disciple n'a pas la sûreté du patron, sa dextérité à jouer avec la langue, à la disloquer à sa guise, à lui faire dire ce qu'il veut. Il est souvent confus, il peine, il s'efforce, il souffre, mais il nous rappelle en certaines pages ces chefs-d'œuvre *Manette Salomon* et *Germinie Lacerteux*."[14]

The art, the style of the Goncourts can be understood only by the few. M. Poictevin can never hope to appeal to a large public. Even the purer, simpler style which Maupassant practices cannot, he knows, be fully appreciated by the average reader. To him, art is essentially aristocratic, but of all the arts paint-

13 "Bataille de livres," *Gaulois*, October 28, 1883.
14 *ibid.*

ing and literature are most deceptive because, while they seem readily accessible there are few people really competent to judge painting or prose.[15]

When Jules Vallès reproached Maupassant for not writing for the proletariat, the latter set forth his conception of art as necessarily aristocratic in an article in the *Gaulois*, "A propos du peuple." Vallès dreams only of revolution and barricades, wrote Maupassant, and while he respects this literary ideal, he claims the right to retain his own. No artist, sculptor, or musician addresses himself to the people. "L'art, quel qu'il soit ne s'adresse qu'à l'aristocratie intellectuelle d'un pays . . . le romancier pourrait être utile au peuple si le peuple savait le comprendre et l'interpréter. . . . Mais, si le peuple était capable de lire les romanciers, les vrais romanciers, il y pourrait trouver le plus utile des enseignements, la science de la vie. Tout l'effort littéraire aujourd'hui tend à pénétrer la nature humaine et à l'exprimer telle qu'elle est, à l'expliquer dans les limites de la stricte vérité."[16] Underlining the chief difficulty of the proletarian novel, Maupassant adds that unfortunately the working classes for whom Vallès writes do not read his novels in any case.

Zola writes for the general reading public, and, addressing himself to such a wide audience, is less concerned with niceties of style. His great worth, according to Maupassant, lies in his massive power; he is a great poet in prose, not because of his particular mode of expression, but because his imagination is so abundant that it perpetually breaks through the limits of his style. Yet this style is admirably suited to his needs. "Il a eu l'audace du mot propre, du mot cru," which aroused violent opposition; but that is only one element: "Son style, large, plein d'images, n'est pas sobre et précis comme celui de Flaubert, ni ciselé et raffiné comme celui de Théophile Gautier, ni subtilement brisé, trouveur, compliqué, délicatement séduisant, comme celui de Goncourt; il est surabondant et

[15] "Au Salon," *Le XIXᵉ Siècle*, April 30, 1886; LF, xv, 161.
[16] "A propos du peuple," *Gaulois*, November 19, 1883.

impétueux comme un fleuve débordé qui roule de tout."[17]
With great natural gifts as a writer, Zola did not seek to perfect his instrument, and says Maupassant, he even seemed to
be insensitive to certain vibrations and harmonies of language
to which more refined and delicate spirits have responded.
But Zola, writing for the general public, has no need of these
subtleties: "il écrit clairement, d'un beau style sonore. Cela
suffit. . . ."[18]

[17] "Romanciers contemporains: M. Emile Zola," *Revue bleue,* March
10, 1883; LF, xv, 83.
[18] *ibid.,* p. 84.

THE VALUE OF THE ESSAYS

MAUPASSANT'S stature as critic and theorist has been, until now, judged almost entirely on the basis of one document, the preface to *Pierre et Jean*, an essay which has inspired extraordinarily diverse opinions as to its worth. Pol Neveux, however, who wrote the introduction for the Conard *Œuvres complètes*, had undoubtedly seen a good many of Maupassant's *chroniques*, and shared Conard's view that they should not be republished, for he flatly declared that Maupassant had no critical ability whatsoever, and that the clarity and precision of thought and language, so evident in his fiction, are utterly lacking in his essays.[1] He specifically included the famous preface in his condemnation. His violent denial of any critical ability in the author whose stories he so much admired can be explained in part at least by the fact that, in going through the newspaper files, he must have turned up a number of Maupassant's purest pot-boilers and been discouraged from going any further. Neveux, strangely enough, was eloquent in his praise of *Sur l'eau*, which he considered one of the author's greatest masterpieces, though it turns out that this volume was put together from over twenty of the same much-decried *chroniques*.

It is quite true that many, too many in fact, of these articles were written for the moment and intended to be forgotten. In this study I have tried to weed out the space-fillers inspired by *fait-divers* and concentrate on a number of thoughtful essays which have remained buried in newspaper files but which deserve, I believe, a re-examination. If many of his essays were written with the sole view of filling up two columns in the *Gaulois* or the *Gil Blas*, others were born of a sincere desire to clarify his position, to defend his art, or to

---

[1] *Boule de Suif* (Conard), p. lxv.

attack tendencies he believed to be dangerous or absurd. It is these last that form the basis of this study and from which I have felt justified in quoting rather fully. I cannot share the opinion of Pol Neveux that Maupassant's critical writings reveal nothing but a lack of precision and the feeblest argumentation. When he deals with any subject that touches on his art and his own literary convictions, he writes with vigor in a clear and precise prose charged with feeling. He is not, to be sure, a great and original critic, he is not at all an aesthetician; he is simply a writer, an artist, who, by force of circumstances, has at hand a medium which permits him to give expression to his most cherished beliefs. What a great writer has to say about his own art may not necessarily have a general application, but it should not be overlooked as a way of arriving at a clearer understanding of the aim of that particular artist.

The essay on "Le Roman," used as an introduction to *Pierre et Jean*, is, as I have shown, a summary of many ideas more fully developed in his earlier articles. When it appeared, the essay was attacked by critics such as Anatole France, who complained that Maupassant was limiting unduly the task of the critic.[2] Since that day, however, this brief introduction, even though it was believed to be a rare example of Maupassant's venturing into criticism, has survived and has even achieved some fame as a lucid, well-reasoned exposition of the task of the critic and the organization of the novel. Henri Peyre mentions several writers who "have proposed a constructive program for critics, which the latter have heeded only too little. Three at least should have forced critics to re-examine the very foundations of their art."[3] The three are Maupassant, in this preface, Zola in an essay on "La Critique

---

[2] Anatole France, "M. Guy de Maupassant critique et romancier," *Le Temps*, January 15, 1888; reprinted in *La Vie littéraire*, Paris, Calmann-Lévy, 1890, II, 28-35.

[3] Henri Peyre, *Writers and their Critics, a Study of Misunderstanding*, Ithaca, Cornell University Press, 1944, p. 287n.

contemporaine,"[4] and Flaubert in his *Correspondance*. Joseph Warren Beach, more clearly than anyone else, saw the strict relation established in the preface to *Pierre et Jean* between the literary ideas and their actual elaboration in novelistic technique, when he wrote: "Among the theorists of realism, the one who has probably given the best account of how the realistic ideal affects the organization of matter in a novel is Guy de Maupassant, in his famous preface to *Pierre et Jean* (1887). He is really grounding his apology for the realists in fundamental principles of art in general. Seldom or never, in a discussion of the novel, had any English critic employed terms which so brought this bourgeois form of art into relation to other forms of art."[5]

Maupassant's outline of a program for critics is, of course, no radical innovation; he has simply discovered for himself and expressed in his own terms what many others had proclaimed before him. As Spingarn wrote, "Carlyle in his essay on Goethe, almost uses Goethe's own words, when he says that the critic's first and foremost duty is to make plain to himself 'what the poet's aim really and truly was, how the task he had to do stood before his eye, and how far, with such materials as were afforded him, he has fulfilled it.' This has been the central problem, the guiding star of all modern criticism. From Coleridge to Pater, from Sainte-Beuve to Lemaître, this is what critics have been striving for, even when they have not succeeded; yes, even when they have been deceiving themselves into thinking that they were striving for something else."[6] The same plea has been echoed more recently by François Mauriac, who writes frequently in the daily press, but who, like Maupassant, remains more a novelist than a critic, especially when he writes: "Qu'on nous juge

[4] Emile Zola, *Documents littéraires*, Paris, Bernouard, 1928, pp. 254-286.

[5] Joseph Warren Beach, *The Twentieth Century Novel, Studies in Technique*, New York and London, Century, 1932, p. 122.

[6] J. E. Spingarn, *The New Criticism*, New York, Columbia University Press, 1911, pp. 16-17.

et, si c'est nécessaire, qu'on nous condamne, mais que ce soit selon notre loi."[7]

The keystone of the whole structure of Maupassant's ideas about literature is, as we have seen, the objective method, which he consistently opposes to the method of psychological analysis. This writer, who so persistently protested his desire to remain unattached to any school, has become for many the typical representative of realism or naturalism, and oddly enough, his name is invoked to support utterly contradictory theories. For Percy Lubbock he serves as a convenient example of the "dramatic" technique, relating his story as if it were taking place before our eyes;[8] but, for Jean-Paul Sartre, Maupassant stands for all the nineteenth-century novelists whom Sartre sweepingly rejects on the grounds that they recount not living stories, but only events which happened in the past and have no effect upon the present: "Ainsi l'aventure est un bref désordre qui s'est annulé."[9]

The distinctions Maupassant established between the objective novel and the psychological novel are convenient and have a general validity. Gide made the same classification of the two kinds of novels, although with less absoluteness than Maupassant, and made a far better case for the psychological novel, where the author is not limited to a self-portrait, "mais ce qu'il peint, il aurait pu le devenir s'il n'était pas devenu tout lui-même."[10] An interesting discussion of the objective method may be found in Wellek and Warren's *Theory of Literature*,[11] where they define the technique broadly, rejecting Lubbock's conception of it as the only valid artistic method. Maupassant's own view was exceedingly rigid, and limited him severely when he attempted to enlarge his own novelistic

[7] François Mauriac, *Journal*, Paris, Grasset, 1937, II, 110.
[8] Percy Lubbock, *The Craft of Fiction*, New York, Scribners, 1921, pp. 112-114.
[9] Jean-Paul Sartre, *Situations II*, Paris, Gallimard, 1948, p. 181.
[10] André Gide, *Un Esprit non prévenu*, Paris, Kra, 1929, pp. 37-39.
[11] René Wellek and Austin Warren, *Theory of Literature*, New York, Harcourt, Brace, 1949, pp. 231-233.

technique. His is a stricter observance, even, than that of Henry James in *The Awkward Age*, cited by Lubbock as the perfect illustration of the objective novel, in which it is James's declared intention to let the story tell itself, to let the characters reveal themselves by their own actions and speech. But by Maupassant's standards, James plays the game with loaded dice; he has eliminated the probing, analyzing author, to be sure, but he has in fact replaced him by a hypothetical invisible spectator who haunts the book and is conjured up whenever deductions need to be drawn from a scene; such phrases as ". . . there would have been for an observer of his handsome controlled face . . . ," recur again and again. Furthermore his characters are not so much introspective as extraordinarily perceptive: they analyze one another constantly and at great length; they are very complicated people, but each is so astute that the others' complexity is delightfully apparent. The author has renounced his privilege of omniscience, but he more than makes up for it by conferring that gift on all his characters. Maupassant has his greatest success with the objective method in his short stories and in some of his early novels, notably in *Bel-Ami*, when he applied it to relatively simple people whose inner life is adequately projected by their actions. Once, in *Pierre et Jean*, he successfully extended the method and was able to join the dramatic sobriety of the objective technique to the need for "going behind" which was imposed by the very nature of his subject. Later, in *Fort comme la mort* and *Notre Cœur*, when he dealt with more complex human beings, people of some subtlety and sensitivity, he was at a loss; the strictly objective approach would not do, for, as James remarked, it could support only a very light weight, and he was unwilling and unable to cut loose completely from his own canons and adopt whole-heartedly the kind of Bourget psychologizing that was being urged on him. James's solution of using supremely analytical characters was no solution at all, at least not for Maupassant. Pérez Galdós in Spain solved the problem in his own way by noting and recording as a realist the romantic effusions of his characters, who literally pour forth their souls,[12] but again this was of no recourse to the Frenchman, who, among his own countrymen, could follow Bourget to some extent but not at all George Sand.

The critical writings of Maupassant are intimately bound up with his ventures in the novel, as we shall see when we examine his efforts in that genre. He refused to think of himself as a literary critic, even in his most effective articles, and wrote of his art and of his fellow-writers strictly from the point of view of a practitioner. He was able to spell out in detail the task of the critic without feeling for a moment that his remarks should apply to himself. Naturalism, as Zola lamented, lacked an official critic; there was no one to beat the drum for the new literature and prepare the public to receive it. Taine was the most likely candidate, but he had, in effect, declined the honor, so it was Zola himself who took up the burden early in the fight. He was seconded later by Maupassant, both of them novelists first of all and only doubling as critics.

It is to Maupassant's credit that he insisted vehemently in his articles in the press on the right of new artists to be heard, on the need for a perpetual renewal of any art and its techniques. His brief word of welcome to the symbolists in the preface to *Pierre et Jean* is but a reaffirmation of earlier and more eloquent statements on the necessity of breaking with old ideas and ever seeking new paths in art. A declared enemy of dogma and tradition in art, he saw revolt and renewal as eternal truths, and though he held firmly to his own ideas he had no desire to impose them on others. "La pensée marche, travaille, enfante," he wrote in 1881, "tout s'use, tout passe,

---

[12] Cf. Joachim Casalduero, *Vida y Obra de Galdós (1843-1920)*, Buenos Aires, Editorial Losada, 1943, p. 82: "No penetramos en el alma de los personajes, porque es un poco inútil. Tienen su alma tan a flor de piel, tan en los labios; expresa su exterior con tal exactitud lo que sienten y lo que piensan, que si ahondáramos en ellos no encontraríamos nada, tan totalmente en gestos, miradas, silencios y palabras se vierte su corazón."

tout change, tout se modifie. Les idées ne sont pas de nature plus immortelle que les hommes, les bêtes et les plantes."[13] He urged poets to take advantage of the immense broadening of the field of poetry brought about by Baudelaire; the traditional poetic subjects have been exhausted, but the proper subject of poetry is everywhere, potentially in everything: "C'est qu'il est difficile d'être poète aujourd'hui, après tant de maîtres. Il faut briser les chaînes de la tradition, casser les moules de l'imitation, répandre les fioles étiquetées d'elixirs poétiques, et oser, innover, trouver, créer! On a ramassé pour les sertir, toutes les pierres fines qui traînent au soleil; mais il en est d'autres assurément, plus cachées, plus difficiles à voir. Cherchez, poètes, ouvrez la terre: elles sont dedans; remuez les fanges si vous les croyez dessous; fouillez partout dans les profondeurs, car toutes les surfaces ont été retournées."[14] In sculpture he had a particular antipathy for the Venus de Milo, "type éternel et insipide du Beau, . . . quel audacieux brisera tes reins célèbres qui inspirent depuis si longtemps tous les gratteurs de marbre pâle, comme si l'Art ne devait pas se renouveler sans cesse, se transformer, mourir à chaque âge et renaître différent, changer toujours ses formes et ses moyens?"[15] His creed applied to all the arts and he welcomed the independent painters who held their exposition at the Tuileries in 1886: "Il faut ouvrir les yeux sur tous ceux qui tentent du nouveau, sur tous ceux qui cherchent à découvrir l'Inaperçu de la Nature, sur tous ceux qui travaillent sincèrement, en dehors des vieilles routines."[16] This man who, against his will, has been so narrowly identified with a particular school, had, after all, a rather wide horizon.

Our examination of Maupassant's literary essays, which were so scorned by Pol Neveux, leads us inevitably to a study of his novels. In fact, it is Neveux himself who most aptly

[13] Maupassant, "Adieu mystères," *Gaulois*, November 8, 1881.
[14] "Les Poètes grecs contemporains," *Gaulois*, June 23, 1881.
[15] "Notes d'un démolisseur," *Gil Blas*, May 17, 1882.
[16] "La Vie d'un paysagiste," *Gil Blas*, September 22, 1886; LF, xv, 166.

expressed the necessity for this joint consideration of essays and novels, when he wrote, still on Maupassant's inadequacy as a critic, that when he sets forth literary principles he simply derives them from his own methods of work, turning his particular individual techniques into generalized axioms.[17] Maupassant as a critic was surely not such a nullity as Neveux claims; but it is true that his articles are directly related to his novels, and sometimes the relation is a little too close for comfort, as we shall presently see in the process of examining those novels.

[17] *Boule de Suif* (Conard), p. lxvi.

PART TWO
THE NOVELS

THE NOVEL BY ADDITION

UNE VIE (1883)

DURING the period of his apprenticeship, that is, before 1880, the year of *Boule de Suif* and the death of Flaubert, Maupassant tried his hand at poetry, drama, stories, and essays, and, as early as 1877, began to make plans for writing a novel. In a letter to Flaubert dated December 10, 1877, he wrote: ". . . j'aurai achevé de refaire mon drame[1] (tout à fait remanié) vers le 15 janvier. Enfin, je vous le soumettrai peu de temps après votre retour. J'ai fait aussi le plan d'un roman que je commencerai aussitôt mon drame terminé."[2] A letter to his mother about the same time reports his progress and his difficulties: "Je travaille en ce moment beaucoup à mon Roman. Mais c'est rudement difficile; surtout pour la mise en place de chaque chose et les transitions. Enfin dans quatre ou cinq mois je serai bien avancé."[3] In March 1878 he had informed her that he had interrupted work on the novel to finish his poem *La Vénus rustique*.[4] The poem was finished in April, but the novel apparently progressed very slowly. That summer, Flaubert, to whom he had sent the plan of his novel, inquired: "Que devient la *Vénus rustique*? et le roman dont le plan m'avait enchanté?"[5]

Just what this early effort in the novel was, whether it was something he eventually abandoned or whether it was the beginning of *Une Vie* which was not published until 1883, we do not know. It is not likely that the work in question was the Voltairian tale, *Le Docteur Héraclius Gloss*, which Maupassant never published,[6] and which could no more prop-

---

[1] *La Trahison de la Comtesse de Rhune.*   [2] LF, xv, 234.

[3] Artine Artinian, ed., *Correspondance inédite de Guy de Maupassant*, Paris, Wapler, 1951, p. 36.

[4] LF, xv, 236-237.

[5] Flaubert, *Correspondance*, Paris, Conard, 1930, viii, 136.

[6] First published by Jean Ossola in the *Revue de Paris*, November 15 and December 1, 1920.

erly qualify as a novel than could the series of sketches which make up *Les Dimanches d'un bourgeois de Paris*. More probably the novel the plan of which delighted Flaubert was actually *Une Vie* or at least an early version of it. There exists an early manuscript of the novel which contains a number of lengthy episodes which were not included in the final version.[7]

Une Vie was a long time in the making. A curious reference in 1881, presumably to this, buried in an unimportant *chronique* Maupassant wrote for the *Gaulois* (where he used his own name, not a pseudonym) shows him struggling to compose: ". . . et sur ma grande table, le roman commencé s'arrêtait au milieu d'une page blanche inachevée la veille au soir."[8] What seemed to give him the most trouble was the problem of transition, as he mentioned in the letter to his mother quoted above; he labored over the arrangement of all the parts to make a unified whole, seeking a logical development that would carry through the novel. It was a problem he was unable to solve in his first novels, and he grumbled to Flaubert that Zola had simply avoided the difficulty. Reporting that Zola had read aloud two chapters of *Nana*, the young writer reveals his own preoccupations: "La division du livre ne me plaît pas. Au lieu de conduire son action directement du commencement à la fin, il la divise, comme le *Nabab*, en chapitres qui forment *de véritables actes* se passant au même lieu, ne renfermant qu'un fait; et, par conséquent, il évite ainsi toute espèce de transition, ce qui est plus facile."[9] The *conteur* was extremely sensitive to the difficulties of the longer genre, and working grimly at his task, could not overcome his annoyance when a celebrated novelist chose to ignore completely that aspect of the novel with which he was most concerned.

[7] Cf. Louis Barthou, "Maupassant inédit. Autour d'*Une Vie*," *Revue des deux mondes*, October 15, 1920, pp. 746-775.

[8] Maupassant, "Zut!" *Gaulois*, July 5, 1881.

[9] Maupassant, letter to Flaubert, December 2, 1878; LF, xv, 250-251.

Not only his own inclination but external pressures as well made it imperative that he write a sustained work, a novel. Particularly after his success with *Boule de Suif*, followed by *La Maison Tellier* and *Mademoiselle Fifi*, had established his reputation in the short story, the public and the critics waited expectantly for his first novel. The *conte*, then as now, was a lesser genre, and it was rarely that a collection of stories attracted the same attention or conferred as much prestige as a novel; "un conte est sans doute un chef-d'œuvre à moins de frais qu'un roman," said Jules Lemaître.[10] Maupassant, whom we now think of first as a writer of short stories, won during his lifetime far more critical attention for his novels than for his collections of tales, some of which were barely mentioned by the reviewers. Professor Artinian, who pointed this out, noted also that the six novels sold more copies up to 1891 than the twenty-one volumes of tales.[11] Maupassant was well aware at the very beginning of his career that he must produce some novels if he was to achieve the reputation he sought.

In writing *Une Vie*, the most natural method for him, although it was the chief source of all his trouble with "transitions," was a simple application of his short story technique, that is, the grouping of a number of short story incidents and sketches around a central figure until the proportions of a novel were attained. Instead of revealing a fragment of life, as in a *conte*, he wanted to lay bare a whole life, *Une Vie*, and thought he could accomplish this by mere accretion of details and incidents. The great defect is that, while within each episode or scene there is a rigorous selection of significant detail, he tends to include all possible episodes, some of which simply do not fit the pattern and tone of the novel.

The general outline of the story is simple enough. The life that is the subject of the book (*A Woman's Life* in the Eng-

---

[10] Jules Lemaître, *Les Contemporains*, 1ère série, Paris, Lecène et Oudin, 1887, p. 309.

[11] Artine Artinian, *Maupassant Criticism in France 1880-1940*, New York, King's Crown Press, 1941, p. 37 and p. 108n.

lish translation) is that of Jeanne Le Perthuis des Vauds, daughter of a family of the lesser Norman nobility, who, shortly after leaving the convent where she has been educated, marries a local squire, Julien de la Mare. Her life is a somber tale of unhappiness and frustration at every turn. Her husband's infidelity both with the maid Rosalie by whom he has a child, and with a neighbor, Mme de Fourville, is the first great blow, to which is added the shock of learning from letters found after her mother's death that she too had been unfaithful. After Julien is killed by Mme de Fourville's husband, Jeanne devotes herself completely to her son Paul, only to continue to meet with a series of misfortunes, for he runs off, gets into debt, lives with a girl by whom he has a child, looks to his mother only for financial help. Her fortune has dwindled until she is forced to sell the château and live with Rosalie, the maid her husband had seduced, who is now a well-to-do widow, shrewd and capable in the manner of the Norman peasant. The only spark left in Jeanne's existence is her interest in her grandson; she takes care of him after the death in childbirth of the girl Paul had married just before his son was born.

Jeanne is, of course, the central figure in the novel and the various events are assembled around her, but she plays no active role in any of the things that happen. She is passive and uncomprehending until the last moment; she has no influence on events, although all of them affect her. "L'humble vérité" is the epigraph Maupassant gave to his book, but the humble truth he chose to present was essentially undramatic—there is no conflict, only suffering. Jeanne is too negative to give any kind of unity to the work, and some admirers of Maupassant's first novel prefer to find the cohesive force in the unity of place, which is the region of Caux in Normandy.[12] This is not very convincing, for one could find the same unity

[12] Edouard Maynial, *La Vie et l'œuvre de Guy de Maupassant*, Paris, Mercure de France, 1906, p. 131; René Dumesnil, *Guy de Maupassant*, Paris, Armand Colin, 1933, p. 188.

of place in a number of collections of Maupassant's stories of Norman setting.

As a matter of fact *Une Vie* is not much more than a collection of short stories. It has been pointed out by Maynial that several incidents in the novel were based directly on previously published short stories.[13] He noted specifically four stories which were incorporated into *Une Vie*, all published in newspapers in 1881 but collected in a book for the first time in the posthumous *Le Père Milon*. The four stories are: "Par un soir de printemps,"[14] which furnished the extraneous episode of Tante Lison, an old maid who feels her loneliness when she sees Julien's solicitude for his fiancée Jeanne; "Le Saut du Berger,"[15] the story of the fanatical priest who beats a dog which was giving birth before a group of peasant children, and who pushes over a cliff a shepherd's hut with the lovers whose trysting place it was; "Vieux Objets,"[16] which tells how old objects evoke one's past life; and "La Veillée," which relates how the letters left by a woman after her death reveal her infidelity. In all these cases the borrowing is direct; Maupassant simply retouched the story to fit into the scheme of his novel, retaining many sentences and even paragraphs in their original form. The names of the characters remain unchanged or nearly so: Tante Lison in "Par un soir de printemps" keeps her identity in passing from the story to the novel, as does Jeanne, while the young man Jacques becomes Julien in *Une Vie*. "Le Saut du Berger" is closely reproduced in the novel, although in the longer work it is not

13 Edouard Maynial, "La Composition dans les premiers romans de G. de Maupassant," *Revue bleue*, October 31 and November 7, 1903, pp. 562-565, 604-608.

14 "Par un soir de printemps," *Gaulois*, May 7, 1881; *Œuvres posthumes I* (Conard), pp. 11-17; LF, I, 301-307. Cf. *Une Vie* (Conard), pp. 66-74.

15 "Le Saut du berger," *Gil Blas*, March 9, 1882; *Œuvres posthumes I* (Conard), pp. 31-36; LF, II, 67-71. Cf. *Une Vie* (Conard) pp. 260-285.

16 "Vieux Objets," *Gil Blas*, March 29, 1882; *Œuvres posthumes I* (Conard), pp. 37-41; LF, III, 33-37. Cf. *Une Vie* (Conard) pp. 330-332. Neither Conard nor LF gives the date of first publication of this story which can be found in the *Gil Blas* of the date given above.

the priest who sends the lovers to their death, but the jealous husband, who, presumably, was informed by the priest. The theme of "La Veillée," the finding of documents which are a posthumous revelation of some misdeed, was a favorite one of Maupassant which he treated in a number of stories[17] and even used to pad out some of his articles when he was particularly hard up.[18]

These four stories are not the only cases of Maupassant's borrowing from himself in *Une Vie*. "Histoire vraie," the story of a man who, having made his servant pregnant, tries to marry her off to a canny, hard-bargaining Norman peasant, is an early version of the same situation in *Une Vie*, where, however, the Baron handles the negotiations instead of Julien.[19] Two of Maupassant's *chroniques* which appeared before *Une Vie*, but which have never been reprinted, contain sections which were re-used in the novel. Maupassant's own experience is transferred to Jeanne and her husband on their honeymoon voyage in "Histoire corse" which contains a description of Corsica and the maquis and the story of Paolo Palabretti. Part of the account of Jeanne and Julien's trip to Corsica is taken from another article "Voyage de Noce," which was occasioned by a book of Juliette Lamber, *La Chanson des nouveaux époux*.[20] Along with these direct borrowings of material from stories and articles, there are numerous echoes in *Une Vie* of situations, themes, and characters which he had already sketched out in shorter works during the period when he was composing his novel. The story "Ma Femme"[21] de-

[17] Cf. "Le Lit" (1882), "Suicides" (1883), "La Confession" (1884), "Un Fou" (1885), "Nos Lettres" (1888).

[18] "Pétition d'un viveur malgré lui," *Gil Blas*, January 12, 1882; "Comment on cause," *Gil Blas*, November 29, 1887.

[19] Conard and LF give the date of first publication of "Histoire vraie" as *Gil Blas*, January 20, 1885. Actually it first appeared under the title "Mirza" in the *Gaulois* of June 18, 1882. Mirza, incidentally, is the name of the dog beaten by the Abbé Tolbiac in *Une Vie*.

[20] "Histoire corse," *Gil Blas*, December 1, 1881; "Voyage de noce," *Gaulois*, August 18, 1882.

[21] "Ma Femme," *Gil Blas*, December 5, 1882; *La Maison Tellier* (Conard), pp. 265-276; LF, II, 351-358.

rives from an incident included in the "vieux manuscrit," later published by Barthou, but not in the final version. "Le Pardon"[22] offers a sketch of a girl who closely resembles Jeanne, while "Une Veuve"[23] presents again the Tante Lison type. Appearing after publication of the novel was "Première Neige"[24] which relates a woman's flight in the snow, though for very different reasons from those of Jeanne.

What all this adds up to, obviously, is that during the period he was composing his first novel, Maupassant's pre-occupation with the subject was such that it is reflected in all other aspects of his literary production. Were these short stories and sketches written with the novel in mind, that is, as notes or studies for the novel, as publication of work in progress? Or were they simply observations set down at a given moment with no other intention save that of defining a character or exploring a favorite theme, which he later found he could incorporate into the novel? Maynial holds to this latter idea and suggests that Maupassant was able to re-use this material easily because the characters he deals with are so lacking in complexity, so average and ordinary that almost any event could be applied to them without creating a contradiction. According to this same critic Maupassant simply ignored the problem of composition and unity in *Une Vie* (and in *Bel-Ami*) and began to be seriously concerned with the question of the form of the novel as a whole only when he was writing *Pierre et Jean*, the preface to which reveals his awareness of the necessity of unity. Maynial, however, did not know that all the ideas in the celebrated preface had been expressed by Maupassant much earlier in his newspaper essays during the period he was composing his first novels. In 1881 his grasp of literary principles and theory was

22 "Le Pardon," *Gaulois*, October 16, 1882; *Clair de Lune* (Conard) pp. 89-99; LF, II, 257-263.
23 "Une Veuve," *Gaulois*, September 1, 1882; *Clair de Lune* (Conard) pp. 115-124; LF, II, 191-198.
24 "Première Neige," *Gaulois*, December 11, 1883; *Œuvres posthumes I* (Conard), pp. 191-201; LF, IV, 105-116. Cf. *Une Vie* (Conard) pp. 162-166.

as firm as in 1888; what he lacked was a practical method of applying the theory, and his whole novelistic career is, in a sense, a search for the method which would create the unity he knew was demanded. *Une Vie* is aptly described by Maynial as an album; its value lies in the individual excellence of each sketch, but the binding element is weak and ineffective.

Louis Barthou pointed out the same borrowings from short stories as Maynial had done, but, since he published at the same time the "vieux manuscrit," a discarded version of part of *Une Vie*, he was mainly impressed by the labor and effort Maupassant had put into his writing. Barthou was convinced that the independent stories were thoroughly integrated into the novel, and gave an impression of complete unity. He inclined to the view that the stories were composed independently of the novel and later adapted for insertion in the longer work: "Cet art habile et heureux d'accommoder, sinon des restes, du moins des essais, servit surtout à Maupassant dans *Une Vie*. Ce roman, qui donne avec tant de force l'impression de l'unité et dont la ligne générale est à la fois si simple et si droite, est en réalité, pour une grande partie, une tapisserie qui emprunte à des contes déjà parus des scènes importantes, cousues au sujet principal avec un art supérieur."[25] M. Barthou's enthusiasm for the subject at hand has carried him too far. There is indeed a great deal of art in *Une Vie* but it is the art of a *conteur*. Maupassant's skill is evident within each scene, but when the scene is put into the novel it doesn't quite fit, and all the revisions and additions he made were not sufficient to conceal the joint. By a curious process of reasoning, however, in this same article, Barthou reaches this same conclusion, admitting that in all Maupassant's novels there are parts which are dead, but what survives are those episodes which could have been short stories.

The question of whether Maupassant wrote the stories specifically for the novel or quite independently of it is not a

[25] Louis Barthou, "Maupassant inédit—autour d'*Une Vie*," *Revue des deux mondes*, October 15, 1920, pp. 746-775.

really important one. What does matter is that these fragments of the novel could be published independently as separate works, as short stories. The method of composition is
the same: the accumulation of short story material around a
character or a place. Certainly the novel he was struggling with
was uppermost in his mind during the early 1880's at least,
and since he made his living by his pen, he had to grind out
stories and articles to support himself, making use of anything at hand that could be adapted without too much effort.
So he furnished stories to the *Gaulois, Gil Blas,* and other
publications by giving them incidents from a version of the
novel he had decided to discard, sections from the manuscript
he was working on at the moment, or a variant of a theme
already elaborated. His articles were often written with the
least possible effort, and, under cover of his pseudonym, Maufrigneuse, in the *Gil Blas,* he was able to re-sell material already published in the *Gaulois.* The professional writer, who
lives solely on the return from his publications, is inclined to
sell in one way or another everything he sets on paper. Maupassant managed to sell everything at least twice, and some
pieces were used profitably three and four times.[26] Since he
appears to have kept close track of everything he published,
it is quite likely that at least some of the incidents in *Une Vie*
were written originally without any thought of the novel, but
later struck him as usable when he was looking for a way to
fill out a chapter.

The technique he adopted for *Une Vie* was naturally what
he called the objective method, that is, describing externals
from the point of view of a particularly keen observer in such
a way that the character, his thoughts, and his motives would
be made plain without any need for psychological analysis
by an omniscient author. This is in apparent harmony with

[26] "La Guerre" appeared first in the *Gaulois* (April 10, 1881) over his
own name and then in the *Gil Blas* (December 11, 1883) signed Maufrigneuse; it was put into *Sur l'eau* in 1888 and finally turned up as a
preface to a novel by V. M. Garchin, *La Guerre,* in 1889. *Sur l'eau,* it
has been shown, is composed almost entirely of previously published
articles pasted together.

the theories he so often expressed, but in *Une Vie* it still remains a short-story technique; he had not yet found the way to adapt the method to the novel. Our analysis of his literary essays has shown that these theories were not clarified in his mind for the first time when he wrote *Pierre et Jean*, but, as a matter of fact, were the basis of his whole self-conscious approach to the novel from the earliest days of his association with Flaubert, and it was perhaps his rigid and somewhat simple-minded efforts to adhere strictly to his doctrine which limited his range as a novelist. *Pierre et Jean*, as a novel, marks a liberation; not that he rejected the theories which had been his guide, but because he had at last found one way to adapt them to his own needs and was no longer following them slavishly. He is careful to point out in the preface to that novel, that his remarks do not apply to *Pierre et Jean*. The preface does not mark a new stage in his development but is a summation of the past; it is the novel itself which is indicative of a marked evolution of his technique.

Une Vie, adhering strictly as it does to the objective technique, is somewhat disappointing to the modern reader. It is absorbing, it impresses one for the most part by its reality, but yet it leaves one dissatisfied. There are scenes of extraordinary vividness, as at the very beginning when we follow Jeanne's journey in a carriage from the convent to her home, accompanied by her parents and the servant Rosalie. The journey is traced step by step; the positions of the people in the carriage, the pounding of the rain, the end of the storm, the countryside at night, every detail is noted. We follow them into the château, inspect Jeanne's room which looks out on the water, and see Jeanne at night unable to sleep, looking over the moon-bathed countryside, dreaming of love and the man, as yet unknown, who is to be her husband. All this is intensely visual description; it is as if we were invisible and bodyless observers, riding in the carriage accompanying the characters every step of the way. The only thing which seems not to be an immediate perception of the senses is Jeanne's dreaming about love. But this is not true psychological analysis: it derives not so much from a penetration of Jeanne's mind as from our awareness of her situation, her sudden freedom on emerging from the convent that we know unhesitatingly what her thoughts *must* be. She is not a person whose mind is revealed to us, but rather simply the product of a situation which determines her reactions. She is not enough of an individual to break through the cliché in which she is caught and think about anything that she likes; or rather, one feels that even if she did, the author, clever observer though he may be, would be totally unaware of it and would continue to ascribe to her those thoughts and dreams that a girl fresh from a convent school *ought* to have.

The novel leaves us dissatisfied not because the picture of life as Maupassant gives it is a pessimistic one, but rather because he has failed to convince us. Even the reader who is by nature more inclined to optimism than Maupassant is irked that the author has not succeeded in making him accept (if only temporarily) his own view. Most of all we feel cheated because *Une Vie* comes so close to being a truly great work. It has suggestions of *Madame Bovary* and *L'Education sentimentale*, in that it is a study of mediocrity; but Jeanne is in no way comparable to Emma as a person or as a creation, and she, to say nothing of Julien, has none of the desiccated vigor of that strange "fruit sec," Frédéric Moreau. The difficulty stems from the fact that the characters lack something, fail to give the impression of completely living people; they are best summed up as "primaires." The dominant theme of the so-called naturalistic novel, as Thibaudet remarked, was the "histoire d'une vie manquée."[27] Emma and Frédéric are failures in the sense that mediocre as they are, they contain within themselves the potentiality of something else. They both dream of a brilliant and spectacular life, and although each succumbs as the result of the same fatal error of accept-

[27] Albert Thibaudet, *Réflexions sur le roman*, Paris, Gallimard, 1938, pp. 136-137.

ing the dream as the fulfillment, we sense that given other circumstances they would be capable of greater things. They are human beings caught by a particular series of events, but the characters in *Une Vie* are nothing more than the sum of the events which surround them. Jeanne's life is not "manquée"; she was never capable of anything greater in the first place.

With her Maupassant seems to have followed strictly one of his most cherished beliefs, the idea that women have but two functions: love and maternity, so that, in spite of the admirable descriptions of her appearance, her actions and even her thoughts, she is constricted by the limited role the author assigned to women. It is her misfortune that, reduced to the two functions of love and maternity, she is deceived in both. She appears to be the central character in the novel but actually her position is marginal; never quite comprehending what is going on, she remains always a little apart; the effect of any event on her is seldom direct, but rather tangential. Tragic effect is greatest at the center of the catastrophe, at the point occupied by the figure with whom we have been directly concerned; the case of the innocent bystander may be pathetic, but not more. Jeanne is throughout an innocent bystander, terribly innocent and terribly alone. She is happiest with her father and mother, but the discovery of the love letters sent to her mother abruptly estranges her, separating her from even the memory of her mother. She is never united with Julien save for a brief period during their honeymoon in Corsica when she comes to know physical love. But once back home Julien soon ceases to be the ardent lover "comme un acteur qui a fini son rôle et reprend sa figure ordinaire,"[28] and all but ignores her. Her husband is a stranger to her, just as in a different way her son is. She is separated from Paul by the very affection she blindly lavishes on him, and as time goes on everything becomes to her more and more unreal and incomprehensible.

[28] *Une Vie* (Conard) p. 125.

Julien too is a "primaire"; he is sensual, he is stingy, he is crude; the only interesting thing about his character is the way in which it is presented. In introducing his personages Maupassant's usual method is to give us a physical description of them and a sketch of their personality the first time they appear. He outlines their character and then fills in the outline by showing their actions as the story develops. He does this with Jeanne, her mother and father, with the Abbé Picot and the Abbé Tolbiac, and, very briefly, with Rosalie. But when he brings in Julien he describes his appearance in detail but carefully refrains from any comment on his character. Here he applies the objective treatment with absolute rigor, leaving entirely to the reader the interpretation of the evidence presented by the author. Julien is to the reader at first just what he is to the baron and the baroness, a well-brought-up young man, polite, easy-mannered, rather colorless, and there is no hint of anything more unless you linger over the reference to his beard hiding "une mâchoire un peu trop forte." As we see more of him, some of his remarks begin to reveal the inner man; on the trip to Etretat when Jeanne describes lyrically her desire to travel in wild and romantic countries like Corsica, Maupassant notes: "Le vicomte, moins exalté, déclara:—Moi, l'Angleterre m'attire beaucoup; c'est une région fort instructive."[29] On the honeymoon we follow his laborious efforts to find out how much money is in the purse given Jeanne by her mother, his suggestion that he keep the money for her, and finally his doling out to her grudgingly a few francs at a time. Julien's character begins to take shape before the reader; no longer colorless and correct, he is strongly marked by his miserliness and his sensuality, coupled with a streak of indifference which is a kind of egotistic cruelty. His stinginess is revealed in a series of separate scenes, almost anecdotes, such as his beating the unfortunate Marius who had ruined his ridiculous livery; and when the genial but obtuse M. de Fourville kisses his wife in the presence of Julien

[29] *ibid.*, p. 53.

and Jeanne, Julien's expression reveals to the reader, if not to innocent Jeanne, that Mme de Fourville is his mistress. But this technique is far from subtle; Maupassant displays his clues too prominently, as if he were afraid some readers might miss his point. The method of gradually disclosing his character has a momentary interest but adds nothing to him; he can still be reduced to a few adjectives.

So with most of the other characters: the baron, Jeanne's father, is a stock type, the eighteenth-century Rousseauistic *gentilhomme*, indistinguishable from dozens of others like Edmée's father in George Sand's *Mauprat*. The mother, "petite mère," is a sluggish lump of flesh, who has read *Corinne* in her youth and who does little but muse over her box of souvenirs of the past. She wins attention only for a moment, and that posthumously, when her love letters are read by Jeanne.

Those who come off best among the minor characters are those who appear to come straight out of one of Maupassant's short stories. Désiré Lecoq, the peasant who for 20,000 francs was induced to marry Rosalie, who was already the mother of Julien's child, makes the most of the brief scene in which he appears, obstinately bargaining with the uncomfortable baron. As we have seen, he actually did come out of "Histoire vraie" first published as "Mirza" in 1882.

By far the most successful characterization in the whole book is that of Rosalie: not Rosalie the servant seduced by Julien, but Rosalie who returns to take care of her former mistress and who dominates the last chapters by her quietly human presence. She is now the well-to-do widow of Désiré Lecoq, her son (by Julien) is, as she says, "un bon gars qui travaille d'attaque," and who had recently been married. She has a fund of common sense, which with her native Norman shrewdness enables her to straighten out Jeanne's tangled financial affairs, since she is wise enough to seek professional advice. She takes over Jeanne completely, sells the château, installs her in a smaller house, which she runs with a benevolent despotism, for her mistress has sunk back into the same lethargic existence as "petite mère." Rosalie is a living person, not simply a stock peasant type; she is suggested rather than abstracted. Maupassant seems to give her scant attention, but with her his objective technique is at its best, because, unlike the case of Julien, we do not feel the presence of the author who is deliberately and self-consciously making his points.

Une Vie, Maupassant's first novel, is not without its virtues: some vivid scenes, some sharply-drawn characters, but they remain as pieces, as pages of an album, because they were never really integrated into the whole. He was still a short-story writer, trying to become a novelist. This somber tale of a woman's life which dwells on the pettiness and mediocrity of Jeanne's unhappy existence is pitched in a minor key. That is why the incidents he introduces which were or could have been short-stories fail to fit in harmoniously, for they are of necessity in a major key.

In spite of its many weaknesses the novel is impressive for its "documentary" value, as in a "documentary" film: you are made to feel that all this is real, if not a great expression of a fundamental truth. Maupassant describes vividly and economically both settings and characters. He paints his people from the outside; he stands off and observes them, but never really gets close to them. This is implicit in his method, but *Une Vie* falls short of being a great novel because the method is not used with any subtlety; it seems artificial and forced because the intentions of the author, and his technique, are too apparent. When Julien suddenly reveals himself by an action, we are impressed not so much by what we have learned about Julien but by the effort the author has made to get his point across. The characters in *Une Vie* have no life of their own. They are predetermined by the author, who, from behind the scenes, pulls the strings of his puppets. They are never in any danger of getting out of the author's control; they may be consistent, but they lack substance.

BEL-AMI (1885)

MAUPASSANT began work on his second novel in the summer of 1884,[1] just after he had completed *Yvette*, a long short story. *Bel-Ami* was finished by the end of February 1885[2] and was published on May 15.[3] With this novel he unquestionably satisfied his desire to prove that he was capable of producing a work of considerable length, for *Bel-Ami* is the longest of his novels, 441 pages in the original Havard edition. Apparently he was still sensitive, even after the success of *Une Vie*, to criticisms of his lack of *souffle*, and was especially gratified by the ample proportions of his new work, if we are to accept the testimony of his valet François, who quotes him as saying: "J'ai fini *Bel-Ami*, j'espère qu'il satisfera ceux qui me demandait toujours quelque chose de long; car il y a des pages et des pages, et serrées."[4]

Bel-Ami shows a great technical advance over *Une Vie*, and, of all his novels, best demonstrates his objective method. He adheres less rigidly to his theories, does not hesitate at times to go beyond the externals in the presentation of his characters, although his attitude remains scrupulously objective. In *Une Vie* scenes were elaborately prepared which immediately revealed a character through his actions, but the methods employed were so obvious that the reader could hardly be impressed. In *Bel-Ami*, by freeing himself just a little from the necessity of describing everything from an external vantage point, he handles his characterization smoothly without interrupting the flow for a set piece which is unduly cumbersome. Brunetière, comparing Bourget's *Cruelle Enigme* with Maupassant's novel, found that Bourget's work suffered from an excessive analysis of psychological motivation; he considered the directness of *Bel-Ami* far more effective, but added

---

[1] Maupassant, letter to his mother; LF, xv, 325.

[2] Maupassant, letter to Victor Havard; LF, xv, 327.

[3] It appeared in serial form in the *Gil Blas* from April 8 to May 30, 1885.

[4] François Tassart, *Souvenirs sur Guy de Maupassant*, Paris, Plon, 1911, pp. 30-31.

that such a method was possible only with characters who are not very complex or introspective. What Maupassant has done in *Bel-Ami* is to begin to extend his method of objective presentation to what goes on beneath the surface, to allow himself from time to time to view his character's mind at work, which saves him from the necessity of laboriously describing only speech and actions so that the inner man will be revealed. He does not analyze, he presents; his characters are not tortured introspectives in this novel, they are generally not very eager to delve into their own secret motives. Maupassant allows himself simply to lift the veil and reveal their thoughts, but makes no more comment than he does for their actions. The contrast with Bourget is clear: in *Bel-Ami* we find no psychological analysis by the author, but only a limited kind of psychological exposition.

In composing his second novel Maupassant followed essentially the same system he had used in the first, taking themes and incidents he had elaborated before, sometimes copying or revising passages previously published, and grouping all his material about a single character. We shall presently show in detail how he borrowed from himself in writing *Bel-Ami* and also how he used his borrowings more discreetly and skillfully than in *Une Vie*. But it should be noted at once that the superiority of *Bel-Ami* lies in the fact that he has created a character who has some substance, some life, so that the incidents grouped around him have something to adhere to. The joints in the structure are not nearly so noticeable as in the first novel. It is difficult to remember Jeanne as a person, the truth she represents is too humble or too negative, although this novel is mentioned more often than any other by periphrastic critics who like to refer to Maupassant as "l'auteur d'*Une Vie*." But Duroy, who is Bel-Ami, is not easily forgotten, and is evoked surprisingly often by critics today in any discussion of characters like Flaubert's Frédéric Moreau or Marivaux' Jacob of *Le Paysan parvenu*.

Bel-Ami is a novel of ascent; *Une Vie* recorded a descent. Jeanne sinks from mediocrity to nothingness; Duroy rises from mediocrity to material success. Not that he ceases himself to be mediocre; he is ambitious, but his ambition is not a Balzacian passion or the calculating singleness of purpose of Julien Sorel; it is tempered by laziness and sensuality. He does make the most of his opportunities and by his own standards and by the standards of his society he is a success; he has risen in the world.

Bel-Ami is the story of "a life," this time a man's life, and follows a simple chronological line, relating everything to the chief character, excluding all digressions and incidents which would remove him from the center of interest. Georges Duroy, former *sous-officier* with some years of service in Africa and now an ill-paid clerk for a railroad company, is first seen as he wanders about Paris, closely calculating his end-of-the-month finances, debating whether he should have a beer or two now and do without lunch the next day. His meager salary is hopelessly insufficient for his needs, and he is thinking of accepting a better-paid job, even though it is the menial post of groom at a riding club. At this critical point in his life, he meets an old regimental friend, Forestier, a journalist, who invites him to dinner the next day, and suggests he try his hand at journalism. He is taken on as Forestier's assistant, or leg-man, and, since the African question is currently the subject of much debate, is asked to write a series of feature articles on his African experiences. Utterly incapable of putting his recollections down in writing, he seeks help from Forestier's wife, who swiftly and professionally puts his article together for him. From this point on he rises steadily, then more and more rapidly, constantly making use of a number of women who find him irresistible. His most durable, but often interrupted liaison is with Mme de Marelle; this affair is for pleasure only, his other conquests being essentially business matters. After Forestier's death, he marries Madeleine Forestier, and begins to write political articles which

resemble strangely in style and tone those of his late friend.[5]
He then goes on to pay his court to Mme Walter, wife of the
owner of his paper, *La Vie française,* makes her his mistress,
but soon tires of her. Meanwhile, growing more and more
sure of himself, he decides that he can do without his wife's
influence and intelligence, in a search for bigger game. Watch-
ing her every movement, he catches her *en flagrant délit* with
a cabinet minister, Laroche-Mathieu. A divorce ensues and
likewise the resignation of the minister. His final coup is to
make himself attractive to Mme Walter's daughter, Suzanne,
and thereupon induce her to run away with him, thus forcing
Walter's consent to the marriage in order to quiet rumors.
Typically enough, Walter, an old hand at political plots and
business intrigues, is not unduly upset but rather admires his
new son-in-law for the skill with which the affair was carried
off. The book ends with Duroy coming out of the Madeleine
with his bride on his arm, but his thoughts are for Mme de
Marelle, with whom he will undoubtedly resume his liaison.

Woven into the main theme of Duroy's progress are many
scenes and incidents which form the substance of the book.
They do not, however, distract our attention or throw Duroy
out of focus, but rather provide a vivid background for his
activities. *Bel-Ami* gives an unflattering picture of the Pari-
sian newspaper world, not the world of *Le Temps* and *Le
Journal des débats,* but a sketch of a wretched little political
paper, created to serve special interests and which becomes
powerful as the schemes of its owners flourish. Included as
well are the details of political and financial deals, and a portrait of M. Walter, financier and manipulator of politicians.
There are well-developed scenes of Duroy at the Folies-Ber-
gère; the sharply etched, totally unsentimental account of
the visit of Duroy and Madeleine, after their marriage, to
Georges' parents in Normandy: a deftly satirical report of a

[5] It is perhaps no more than a slight coincidence that the hero of
Giraudoux' *Siegfried et le limousin,* who is recognized by his journal-
istic style long after he had disappeared during the war, is also named
Forestier.

fencing exhibition for a charitable purpose; and a portrayal of Duroy's struggles with his fear the night before a duel.

The fact that almost all the scenes and incidents in the book seem to fall naturally into place without giving the impression of being set pieces, interesting but extraneous, as was the case in *Une Vie*, is all the more surprising when we realize that Maupassant followed the same system in *Bel-Ami* as he had in his earlier effort. He inserted in *Bel-Ami* paragraphs, pages, and whole scenes which he had used elsewhere, sometimes reproducing them almost intact, more often rewriting them considerably to fit the new situation. The principle remained the same in both novels, taking material used elsewhere in stories and articles and embodying it in the longer work, but the results were different because the work of adaptation, the cementing of the joints, was far more skillfully done in *Bel-Ami*. Edouard Maynial classes *Bel-Ami* with *Une Vie*, calling them both "albums,"[6] groups of sketches and stories loosely bound together. Maynial was impressed by his discovery that parts of the stories "Mots d'amour," "Un Lâche," and "Promenade" were repeated textually in *Bel-Ami*; but one can find numerous other borrowings and many more remote echoes of earlier stories in this novel, and be impressed, not so much by the discovery, as by the skill with which the insertions were made. There are in *Bel-Ami* only two substantial textual borrowings of a whole incident. The first, taken from "Un Lâche," was used to describe Duroy's emotions on the eve of his duel. The novel follows the short story paragraph by paragraph, almost word for word, but Duroy, unlike his counterpart, does not commit suicide, but numbly goes through the motions of the duel in which neither party is hurt. Maupassant first published "Un Lâche" on January 27, 1884 in the *Gaulois*, some months before he set about writing *Bel-Ami*, but presumably he had been planning his new novel for some time and the story may well have

[6] Edouard Maynial, "La Composition dans les premiers romans de G. de Maupassant," *Revue bleue*, October 31 and November 7, 1903, pp. 562-565, 604-608.

been composed with the intention of including it in the novel. Indeed, one is tempted to consider this incident as a piece of autobiography, although there is no evidence to support the notion, other than the fact that Maupassant returned again and again to the subject of duels in his articles, attacking the custom with extraordinary bitterness. In 1881 in his *chronique* titled "Le Duel" he railed against the "niaiserie du point d'honneur," declared flatly that "Le duel est la sauvegarde des suspects. Les douteux, les véreux, les compromis essayent par là de se refaire une virginité d'occasion." A man fully preoccupied with his work or his art has no time to waste in *salles d'armes*. Why pick up a sword when the pen is a much more terrible weapon: "Vraiment, l'insulte entre journalistes est un moyen trop facile de se passer de talent."[7] Even in the preface he wrote for *Les Tireurs au pistolet* by the Baron de Vaux,[8] he expresses his scorn for duels, though he grants that pistol-shooting is a fascinating exercise, and whenever an occasion presented itself, he did not fail to continue his attacks.[9] In any case, whatever the source of the episode, whether autobiographical or not, whether it was composed for the novel or inserted as an afterthought, it fits the character of Duroy perfectly and has a logical place in the movement of the novel.

The second major borrowing is from the short story, "Le Legs," which appeared in the *Gil Blas* on September 23, 1884, when Maupassant was actively engaged in writing *Bel-Ami*. The text of the story is repeated in the novel almost word for word,[10] but is expanded to fit the situation, which concerns the debate over whether the legacy of Vaudrec should be accepted

[7] Maupassant, "Le Duel," *Gil Blas*, December 8, 1881.

[8] Baron de Vaux, *Les Tireurs au pistolet*, Paris, Havard, 1883. Maupassant's preface is taken mainly from his article, "Le Pistolet," *Gaulois*, December 15, 1882.

[9] Cf. "Notes d'un démolisseur," *Gil Blas*, May 17, 1882; "Contemporains," *Gil Blas*, November 4, 1884; "Le Sentiment et la Justice," *Figaro*, December 8, 1884; "Mépris et Respects," *Gil Blas*, March 10, 1885.

[10] Cf. *Bel-Ami* (Conard), pp. 459-472.

or not. This is clearly a case of a short story carved out of the manuscript of the novel he was working on. Maupassant never included it in any volume of short stories, and it remained hidden until Francis Steegmuller published his translation of it in his biography of Maupassant in 1949, pointing out the similarity to the episode in *Bel-Ami*.[11]

The other borrowings from himself, including some not mentioned by Maynial or Dumesnil, are interesting for what they can tell us of Maupassant's technique of composition. "Mots d'amour"[12] is in the form of a letter from a man to his mistress telling her with brutal frankness why he has dropped her. There is a close resemblance to Duroy's exasperation with Mme Walter after she has become his mistress; he cannot endure childish pet names and cajoling expressions from the lips of an older woman. The theme has been thoroughly reworked, however, in transferring it to the novel, and about all that remains of the original text is the conclusion that a mature woman should be a Dido and not try to be a Juliette. Another preliminary sketch of Duroy's relation with Mme Walter is suggested in the chronique "Vains conseils,"[13] again in the form of a letter, this time from a cynical older man to a young man who is trying to free himself from a liaison like Duroy's. The advice given, cynical and not particularly helpful, can be reduced to two rules: "Il ne faut jamais prendre une maîtresse qui ne peut plus vous être infidèle," and "Il faut se garder autant que possible des liaisons qu'on ne peut pas dénouer avec de l'argent."

The story "Promenade,"[14] mentioned by Maynial, contributes one paragraph with slight modifications to *Bel-Ami*, the scene where Georges and Madeleine Duroy, riding in a fiacre in the Bois de Boulogne, are filled with a sort of amorous

[11] Francis Steegmuller, *Maupassant, a Lion in the Path*, New York, Random House, 1949, pp. 376-382.
[12] "Mots d'amour," *Gil Blas*, February 2, 1882; *Mademoiselle Fifi* (Conard), pp. 183-190; LF, II, 47-53.
[13] "Vains conseils," *Gil Blas*, February 26, 1884.
[14] "Promenade," *Gil Blas*, May 27, 1884; *Yvette* (Conard), pp. 201-212; LF, V, 145-151.

tenderness, as if by contagion, at the spectacle of all the couples about them. In "Promenade" this Bois de Boulogne theme is treated in a totally different manner, for in it a lonely old man is moved by the same sight to commit suicide by hanging himself. The same paragraph served in both places since it was simply the description of a locale. The curious part is that Maupassant should have bothered to look up his story and copy out the paragraph instead of describing afresh a scene with which he was most familiar. Or was it perhaps some trick of conscious or subconscious memory which caused him to reproduce the same words when he again sought to describe the same incident? It is not likely, for he was not noted for a phenomenal memory, and too many other passages reveal the hand of the conscious artist reaching back into his files for a passage which had satisfied him particularly and then refurbishing it to fit its new surroundings.

The ride in the Bois de Boulogne is part of the development of a very important theme in *Bel-Ami*, the "jalousie posthume" of Duroy. Aware that people have noted the resemblance between his own articles and those of Forestier, whose widow he married, Duroy is annoyed by his colleagues who persist in calling him Forestier. At first he is indiscreetly curious about his predecessor's life with Madeleine, then obsessed by the idea that she must have been unfaithful to Forestier. Feeling certain she had deceived her first husband (though not with Duroy at least), he goes from jealousy almost to hatred, which in part inspires his efforts to bring about the divorce. This whole section of *Bel-Ami* is obviously adapted from a short story, "Le Vengeur";[15] many phrases recur and exactly the same line of development is followed. In the story, however, the wife admits she had deceived her first husband, whereupon her present husband, enraged because this liaison was with another and not with him, beats her unmercifully as if aveng-

[15] "Le Vengeur," *Gil Blas*, November 6, 1883; *Œuvres posthumes I* (Conard), pp. 175-181; LF, iv, 47-53. Cf. *Bel-Ami* (Conard), pp. 345-360. Conard and LF both note: "Voir *Bel-Ami*, IIe partie, fin du chapitre 2."

ing a friend. A comparison of the two texts shows clearly Maupassant's method and skill. "Le Vengeur" is brutal, concise, and direct; the style is typical of the short story, wasting no words, driving relentlessly on toward the conclusion. In *Bel-Ami* the transposition of this material is successfully effected for the story is modified, expanded, developed, and the whole tone is changed. The incidents in *Une Vie* cause the reader to stumble, or at least to change his pace; "Le Vengeur" as it appears finally in *Bel-Ami* is slowed down and softened to fit the tempo of the novel which is necessarily, as Ortega says, a sluggish genre.

The theme of posthumous or retrospective jealousy was apparently first suggested to Maupassant by the discussion of the legalizing of divorce. In 1882 he wrote an article for the *Gaulois* called "A propos du divorce"[16] in which he treated the subject from a single point of view—the second husband's jealousy of the first. In "Le Vengeur," written in November 1883, he attributed the same feelings to a man marrying a widow. Then, midway between "Le Vengeur" and *Bel-Ami*, in June 1884 after divorce had become legal, he discussed the effect on literature of the new law which created a new situation full of dramatic possibilities. Maupassant observed that marrying a divorcée was not the same as marrying a widow, but both in his story and in his novel he ignored the difference. A long section of this article reads like a kind of outline of both "Le Vengeur" and the section on Duroy's jealousy in *Bel-Ami*; it represents a transitional stage in the development of the idea, and since it has never been reprinted, is worth quoting in full:

"Certains maris seront obsédés par le souvenir du premier et ne cesseront de questionner leur femme, jour et nuit, sur ce qu'il faisait, sur ce qu'il disait, sur ce qu'il pensait, sur toute sa manière d'agir et de se comporter dans toutes les situations de la vie. Ils finiront même par l'appeler de son petit nom tout

---

[16] "A propos du divorce," *Gaulois*, June 27, 1882.

court: 'Qu'est-ce qu'Octave aurait fait à ma place, en cette circonstance?'

"Il y aura là, assurément, un gros élément de comique.

"Un grand nombre d'effets pourront être tirés de cette situation. Un mari, jaloux rétrospectivement, est torturé par la crainte que son prédécesseur n'ait été trompé par leur femme.

"L'Autre était bête, il le sait; ridicule, il le sait; brutal, il le sait; sournois, il le sait; certes, cela n'aurait pas été volé; cependant il a une peur horrible que cet accident n'ait eu lieu, et il emploie toutes ses ruses à le découvrir.

"Elle a, en parlant de l'autre, un petit ton méprisant et gai, tout à fait réjouissant, tout à fait favorable au successeur, mais aussi un peu inquiétant. Car enfin . . . si cela était arrivé . . . quelles garanties aurait-il, lui, le nouveau, pour la suite.

"Et puis, il veut bien épouser une femme qui a eu un mari, mais pas une femme qui a eu un amant!

"Alors, à force d'astuce, à force de la questionner, de se moquer lui-même du n° 1, de le blaguer, de répéter: 'Comme ce serait drôle, si tu l'avais trompé, comme ce serait drôle, c'est ça qui m'amuserait à savoir. En voilà un qui le méritait, hein, quelle brute?'

"Il finit par la faire avouer. Elle laisse comprendre. Elle sourit d'une telle façon qu'il devine.

"Alors, tout à coup, mordu au cœur, exaspéré, il commence à la traiter de gueuse, de fille, puis, vengeant l'autre, il la gifle, la bat, l'assomme et finit par l'abandonner, ne pouvant vivre avec cette idée qu'elle a trompé son prédécesseur."[17]

In the "Notice" to the Libraire de France edition of *Bel-Ami*[18] Dumesnil pointed out that Maupassant used in *Bel-Ami* some previously published short stories, but he mentions specifically only "Un Normand," "Le Horla," and "L'Homme-Fille." From "Un Normand"[19] comes the description of Rouen seen from Canteleu (Part II, chapter I), and a similar passage

---

[17] "Le Divorce et le Théâtre," *Figaro*, June 12, 1884.
[18] LF, xi, iii.
[19] "Un Normand," *Gil Blas*, October 10, 1882; *Contes de la Bécasse* (Conard), pp. 143-154; LF, ii, 249-256.

is to be found at the beginning of "Le Horla." A comparison of these texts will not convince one that Maupassant made any direct borrowing or even that he had the earlier passage in mind when he wrote *Bel-Ami*. He appears to have described again a scene he knew well from a vantage point he had often frequented. The same view is outlined again, in still a different form in "Le Garde,"[20] written during the period he was composing *Bel-Ami*. Dumesnil sees in "L'Homme-Fille"[21] a preliminary sketch of the character of Duroy but the connection is of the vaguest. There is no striking resemblance between Duroy and "l'homme-fille"; Duroy is the same general kind of opportunist, but lacks the feminine traits of the type Maupassant describes. The definition he gives could be applied to Duroy in some ways but it could fit any number of people as well, and Maupassant was deliberately generalizing: "Car nous sommes tous, en France, des hommes-filles, c'est-à-dire changeants, fantasques, innocemment perfides, sans suite dans les convictions ni dans la volonté, violents et faibles comme les femmes." The most one can say is, as Dumesnil remarks elsewhere, that the story is an "esquisse très vague du caractère de Bel-Ami."[22]

There are, however, a few other more definite borrowings and adaptations in *Bel-Ami* which have not been pointed out and which should be mentioned in any discussion of Maupassant's technique of composition. After dining at Walter's, Duroy takes a stroll with Norbert de Varenne, poet and writer for *La Vie française*, who delivers himself of a long and pessimistic speech on the subject of old age, solitude and death. The ideas he expresses are familiar to readers of Maupassant for they have been stated explicitly in many of his works and form a kind of substructure for almost everything he wrote. The framework and the entire substance of Norbert de Varenne's speech are to be found specifically in an article and

[20] "Le Garde," *Gaulois*, October 8, 1884; *Yvette* (Conard), pp. 233-247; LF, v, 297.

[21] "L'Homme-Fille," *Gil Blas*, March 13, 1883; *Toine* (Conard), pp. 49-56; LF, iii, 103-107.

[22] LF, xv, 497.

a story both of which appeared a week apart in the *Gaulois*
early in 1884. The story, "Solitude"[23] provides the setting of
two men, one young the other old, strolling after dinner; the
older man discourses on his loneliness, his feeling of being unable to communicate directly with other men. The article
"Causerie triste,"[24] which has never been reprinted, is an
essay on old age and death, occasioned by Maupassant's hor-
ror of crowds, particularly the crowds of Carnival time. ("Quel
plaisir éprouve-t-on à se réunir si c'est uniquement pour se
jeter des saletés à la face?") At twenty, he says, one can be
happy through sheer *joie de vivre*. "Mais plus tard, lorsqu'on
voit, lorsqu'on comprend, lorsqu'on sait! Lorsque les cheveux
blancs apparaissent et qu'on perd chaque jour, dès la trentaine,
un peu de sa vigueur, un peu de sa confiance, un peu de sa
santé, comment garder sa foi dans un bonheur possible? . . .
la mort, l'inévitable mort sans cesse nous talonne et nous dé-
grade." These two pieces in the *Gaulois* contain all the ideas
put into the mouth of the unhappy poet of the novel, but the
form of expression has been thoroughly revised, hardly any
phrases appearing exactly alike in both versions. But, curiously enough, in the middle of this section of *Bel-Ami* occurs
a paragraph which obviously comes directly with but slight
changes from a story, "La Tombe,"[25] written in July 1883. This
tale is in the form of a speech in court of a man accused of
exhuming a corpse. His defence is that he was overwhelmed by
the death of his mistress, by the thought that he would never
see her again, and mad with grief, tried to open the grave.
The following is part of his speech:

"Jamais aucun visage ne renaîtra semblable au sien. Jamais,
Jamais! On garde les moules des statues; on conserve des empreintes qui refont des objects avec les mêmes contours et les
mêmes couleurs. Mais ce corps et ce visage, jamais ils ne

[23] "Solitude," *Gaulois*, March 3, 1884; *Monsieur Parent* (Conard), pp.
261-270; LF, IV, 305-311.
[24] "Causerie triste," *Gaulois*, February 25, 1884.
[25] "La Tombe," *Gil Blas*, July 29, 1883; *Contes de la Bécasse* (Conard), pp. 253-260; LF, III, 313-317. Cf. *Bel-Ami* (Conard) p. 309.

reparaîtront sur la terre. Et pourtant il en naîtra des milliers de créatures, des millions, des milliards, et bien plus encore, et parmi toutes les femmes futures, jamais celle-là ne se retrouvera. Est-ce possible? On devient fou en y songeant." Compare this with the passage in *Bel-Ami*:

"Et jamais un être ne revient, jamais. . . . On garde les moules des statues, les empreintes qui refont toujours des objets pareils; mais mon corps, mon visage, mes pensées, mes désirs ne reparaîtront jamais. Et pourtant il naîtra des millions, des milliards d'êtres qui auront dans quelques centimètres carrés un nez, des yeux, un front, des joues et une bouche comme moi, et aussi une âme comme moi, sans que jamais je ne revienne, moi, sans que jamais même quelque chose de moi reconnaissable reparaisse dans ces créatures innombrables et différentes, indéfiniment différentes, bien que pareilles à peu près." The *Bel-Ami* passage is obviously a reworking and an expansion of the earlier one; Maupassant, even when setting forth his most cherished ideas, apparently took the trouble to look up his previous treatment of the subject, remembering no doubt the image of the "moules des statues." Having found the image, he took the paragraph, developed it and fitted it to his novel.

This whole discourse on death as it appears in *Bel-Ami* seems like an unnecessarily long digression which slows down the movement of the novel and is unrelated to the rest of the action. The original manuscript shows that Maupassant had made the speech even longer, including a passage on a text of Montesquieu developing the view that our senses are not accurate instruments of perception.[26] This he cut out before publication, as well as some of Duroy's later references to it. Norbert de Varenne's monologue seems out of place because it has apparently little effect on Duroy, whose view of life is utterly different from that of his colleague. His reaction is simple: "Bigre, ça ne doit pas être gai, chez lui. Je ne voudrais pas un fauteuil de balcon pour assister au défilé de ses

[26] *Bel-Ami* (Conard), p. 587.

idées, nom d'un chien."[27] The speech has no effect on him until Forestier's death, as he and Madeleine keep vigil over the body. He recalls some of the phrases, but the effect is simply a momentary gloom, which he throws off by proposing marriage to his dead associate's wife. It is difficult to justify the presence of this long digression in the novel; it serves only as a vehicle for some of Maupassant's favorite ideas, which he could well have left in their newspaper form, since he was eventually to dig them out again to put in *Sur l'eau*.[28]

Two other items should be mentioned. Duroy, it will be recalled, first won attention in Mme Walter's salon, by a little speech on the Academy: the oldest and most infirm of the candidates should be elected, since he would be most likely to die shortly and give the ladies of the salons the joy of picking a successor. The same idea is developed, retaining some of the same expressions, in an article, "Les Académies,"[29] written in December 1884. From the date it would seem that the article was concocted from a recollection of Duroy's speech in the manuscript of *Bel-Ami*, which was then almost completed. The second case is a lengthy, almost word for word, borrowing from the short story "Misti."[30] The passage describes a woman who insisted that her lover take her to "les endroits louches où s'amuse le peuple" so that she could experience a little thrill of danger and feel herself protected by her escort. In *Bel-Ami* the woman is Mme de Marelle and the story is clearly a preliminary sketch of her character and position even to the device of giving her as husband a railroad inspector who was often absent. Aside from shifting from the first person to the third the section is repeated intact save for a few changes in adjectives and the addition of several phrases.

---

[27] *ibid.*, p. 213.

[28] This same theme is picked up again and elaborated in *Fort comme la mort*; Norbert de Varenne is a preliminary sketch of Olivier Bertin.

[29] "Les Académies," *Gil Blas*, December 23, 1884.

[30] "Misti," *Gil Blas*, January 22, 1884; *Yvette* (Conard), pp. 273-283; LF, IV, 173-181. Cf. *Bel-Ami* (Conard), pp. 149-151.

Was "Misti," as well as some of the other borrowings, simply a by-product of Maupassant's early efforts to work out *Bel-Ami*? Was it inspired by the latter and were the passages in question written first in the novel or was the story composed first and then used in *Bel-Ami* as a kind of afterthought? Maupassant says in the letter quoted earlier that he began *Bel-Ami* in the summer of 1884. One would imagine he had been turning the subject over in his mind for some time before that, but we lack any early, dated manuscripts to settle the point. I suggest as a hypothesis that in general material published earlier than, say, June 1884, was composed independently of the novel; what appeared during the writing of the novel would most likely be simply a by-product of the longer work. Aside from the fact that Maupassant constantly went back to *chroniques* published years before for passages to insert in his current articles, there is one detail in *Bel-Ami* which is at least suggestive. Duroy, with Madeleine Forestier's help, wrote his first article "Souvenirs d'un chasseur d'Afrique," but never was able to finish the series. Some years later, when he was a well-established journalist, the African question was again the topic of the day and a feature article was needed in a hurry. Duroy recalled his first article, dug it out of the files, made a few necessary changes, published it, and then continued the series. The incident is powerfully suggestive of Maupassant's own method.

In spite of the patchwork method of composition there is a unity in *Bel-Ami* which comes from something more than the mere fact that everything concerns one central character. We have noted that Duroy is a far more positive character than the heroine of *Une Vie*, but Maupassant went further than that in his efforts to fuse together the various elements of his book. The main theme and purpose of the novel are emphasized and made clear by the recurrence of an image—not a figure of speech, but an actual reflection in a mirror, used as a conscious artistic device. Nor is this Stendhal's mirror which is carried along a road reflecting life; it is a reflection within the reflection of life that the novel is supposed to be. Maupassant observes his characters, but his characters rarely pause to consider themselves. Duroy, with all his activity, has no time for introspection, no desire even to judge himself or to meditate on the course he is following. Yet at every critical point in his career he is suddenly brought sharply to an awareness of himself and his position by catching a glimpse of himself as others see him in the sudden apparition of his own image in a mirror. With but one exception the image that he sees always comes as a pleasant surprise, bolsters his self-confidence, reveals to him that he is equal to the changed circumstances he is about to encounter as he moves steadily on to new conquests. It is perfectly clear from these abrupt encounters with his own image that Duroy's successful career represents not so much a rise in the world as a sudden realization from time to time that society is on his level, not above him as he had thought, and that he does not have to strive upward but has merely to accept things as they are. The portrait of a mediocrity who succeeds is inevitably an indictment of the society which has allowed him to flourish. By repeatedly making Duroy see that the road to success is so much easier than he had imagined, that those he had believed far above him are in reality indistinguishable from himself, Maupassant has enlarged the canvas of his novel, setting the individual against a social background which is revealed in all its falsity by the progress of Bel-Ami.

The second chapter of the book is constructed entirely within the framework of a mirror, and the same device is used, more subtly and with many variations throughout the novel. As Duroy climbs the stairs to Forestier's apartment, wearing for the first time in his life formal evening dress, hired with money borrowed from Forestier, he is timid, awkward and ill-at-ease. "Il montait lentement les marches, le cœur battant, l'esprit anxieux, harcelé surtout par la crainte d'être ridicule; et, soudain, il aperçut en face de lui un monsieur en grande toilette qui le regardait. Ils se trouvaient si près l'un de l'autre que Duroy fit un mouvement en arrière, puis il demeura stupéfait: c'était lui-même, reflété par une haute glace en pied qui formait sur le palier du premier une longue perspective de galerie. Un élan de joie le fit tressaillir, tant il se jugea mieux qu'il n'aurait cru."[31] He is naïvely and sincerely astonished that he could be so easily transformed from a scrimping clerk into an *homme du monde*, and with renewed assurance is able to act his part at the dinner and set his feet firmly on the road to conquest. The chapter ends with Duroy descending the same stairs, this time in a joyous rush, and again he is greeted by his image in the mirror: "il s'élança, enjambant les marches deux par deux; mais tout à coup il aperçut, dans la grande glace du second étage, un monsieur pressé qui venait en gambadant à sa rencontre, et il s'arrêta net, honteux comme s'il venait d'être surpris en faute.

"Puis il se regarda longuement, émerveillé d'être vraiment aussi joli garçon; puis il se sourit avec complaisance; puis, prenant congé de son image, il se salua très bas, avec cérémonie, comme on salue les grands personnages."[32]

Georges marvels that everything is so much simpler than it looks. Mme de Marelle becomes his mistress immediately without any long campaign:

"Il en tenait une, enfin, une femme mariée! une femme du monde! du vrai monde! du monde parisien! Comme ça avait été facile et inattendu!

"Il s'était imaginé jusque-là que pour aborder et conquérir une de ces créatures tant désirées, il fallut des soins infinis, des attentes interminables, un siège habile fait de galanteries, de paroles d'amour, de soupirs et de cadeaux. Et voilà que tout d'un coup, à la moindre attaque, la première qu'il rencontrait s'abandonnait à lui, si vite qu'il en demeurait stupéfait."[33] The great lesson that he draws from this first successful adventure is the reflection: "C'est plus facile que je n'aurais cru."[34] He is at his ease with Mme de Marelle because he

[31] *Bel-Ami* (Conard), p. 29.   [32] *ibid.*, p. 51.   [33] *ibid.*, p. 130.
[34] *ibid.*, p. 132.

senses that they are alike, "deux êtres de même caractère et de même race."[35] As their liaison continues, the kinship is more and more evident: "Leurs deux natures avaient des crochets pareils; ils étaient bien, l'un et l'autre, de la race aventureuse des vagabonds de la vie, de ces vagabonds mondains qui ressemblent fort, sans s'en douter, aux bohêmes des grandes routes."[36] He feels a similar kinship for the "courtisane connue," boldly driving in her carriage in the Bois among the "hypocrites aristocrates," proclaiming herself their equal; "Il sentait peut-être vaguement qu'il y avait quelque chose de commun entre eux, un lien de nature, qu'ils étaient de même race, de même âme, et que son succès aurait des procédés audacieux de même ordre."[37]

At every turning point, at every crisis, when Bel-Ami is impelled to examine himself, his impulse is not to look inward and analyze but to look outward at his reflected image. In the most serious crisis of his whole career, the night before the duel, when he is alone with himself tortured by fear, he naturally turns to a mirror, seeking the confidence it had given before. "Et un singulier besoin le prit tout à coup de se relever pour se regarder dans sa glace. Il ralluma sa bougie. Quand il aperçut son visage reflété dans le verre poli, il se reconnut à peine, et il lui sembla qu'il ne s'était jamais vu."[38] This time the mirror gave no comfort, his pale haggard face suggested only death, and his morbid fascination with his own image became a hallucination in which he saw himself in his own bed stretched out as if dead: "Il se retourna vers sa couche et il se vit distinctement étendu sur le dos dans ces mêmes draps qu'il venait de quitter. Il avait ce visage creux qu'ont les morts et cette blancheur des mains qui ne remueront plus."[39]

Later, as Duroy is about to marry Mme Forestier, it is Madeleine who provides him with a new image of himself, who opens up an entrancing perspective of what he could

[35] *ibid.*, p. 111.　[36] *ibid.*, p. 435.　[37] *ibid.*, p. 216.
[38] *ibid.*, p. 238.　[39] *ibid.*, p. 238.

easily become. She wanted to bear a name which would suggest nobility so she calmly changed the name of Georges' parents to "Monsieur et Madame Alexandre du Roy de Cantel" on the wedding announcements. Georges, only a little dazzled by thus being so suddenly ennobled, took the image for the reality and without hesitation conformed to this new view of himself:

"Quand il se retrouva dans la rue, bien déterminé à s'appeler désormais du Roy, et même du Roy de Cantel, il lui sembla qu'il venait de prendre une importance nouvelle. Il marchait plus crânement, le front plus haut, la moustache plus fière, comme doit marcher un gentilhomme."[40]

After the marriage Duroy installs himself in Madeleine's apartment, the same one she occupied with Forestier, and the same full-length mirrors on each landing constantly hold before Georges as he goes in and out a vision of the personage he is supposed to be. "A chaque étage de son nouvel escalier il se regardait complaisamment dans cette glace dont la vue lui rappelait sans cesse sa première entrée dans la maison."[41] Duroy's progress is the pursuit of his own image, which is repeatedly revealed to him in newer and more enticing forms. Lunching with the minister, M. Laroche-Mathieu, he suddenly sees himself in the other's place, a great political career appears possible to him, not because he feels he has ability and intelligence, but because precisely these qualities are not required: "Et comparant sa valeur à lui, à l'importance bavarde de ce ministre, il se disait: 'Cristi, si j'avais seulement cent mille francs nets pour me présenter à la députation dans mon beau pays de Rouen, pour rouler dans la pâte de leur grosse malice mes braves Normands finauds et lourdauds, quel homme d'Etat je ferais à côté de ces polissons imprévoyants.' "[42]

Maupassant uses the mirror-image again to mark Duroy's acquisition of the wealth he needed to launch himself on a grand scale. Georges had allowed Madeleine to accept the

---

[40] *ibid.*, p. 301.   [41] *ibid.*, pp. 336-337.   [42] *ibid.*, p. 428.

fortune bequeathed her by Vaudrec only on condition that he be given half to avoid "scandal," as he suggested. On their return from a dinner celebrating their good fortune, they go up the stairs with Georges lighting the way with matches: "En arrivant sur le palier du premier étage, la flamme subite éclatant sous le frottement, fit surgir dans la glace leurs deux figures illuminées au milieu des ténèbres de l'escalier.

"Ils avaient l'air de fantômes apparus et prêts à s'évanouir dans la nuit.

"Duroy leva la main pour bien éclairer leurs images, et il dit, avec un rire de triomphe:

—Voilà des millionnaires qui passent."[43]

Duroy has complete confidence in himself now; he deliberately plans his career which includes divorcing Madeleine so that he can marry Suzanne Walter. But always it is only in his reflected image that he sees himself fully; intoxicated with pride, he does not really appreciate how far he has come until the bishop who is marrying them describes in eulogistic terms the position Duroy holds:

"Du Roy l'écoutait, ivre d'orgueil. Un prélat de l'Eglise romaine lui parlait ainsi, à lui. Et il sentait derrière son dos, une foule, une foule illustre venue pour lui. Il lui semblait qu'une force le poussait, le soulevait. Il devenait un des maîtres de la terre, lui, lui, le fils des deux pauvres paysans de Canteleu."[44] And the novel ends with Duroy leaving the Madeleine on the day of his marriage to Suzanne, looking across the Place de la Concorde to the Chambre des Députés, thinking of his brilliant political future—and of Mme de Marelle.

In tracing this progression of Duroy, Maupassant skipped rapidly, too rapidly, over one phase of his career. At the end of Chapter IV, in a single page of bald summary he transforms Duroy from a fumbling apprentice into a clever, experienced reporter. The description amounts to little more than that old saw about the newspaper profession: "You meet such

43 *ibid.*, pp. 475-476.   44 *ibid.*, p. 569.

interesting people." He omits the whole development and hence deliberately rejects the opportunity to describe the milieu of the newspaper world; Maupassant is too eager to get on to Duroy's amorous adventures and his rise through them. It is mere accident that he is a reporter—almost any other calling would have done as well, as Maupassant himself pointed out in his reply to those critics who attacked the book as an unfair picture of the newspaper profession.[45] The picture that he paints in *Bel-Ami* is certainly not a favorable one, but it concerns not merely the journalistic milieu, but society as a whole, or what Maupassant thought was the whole of society. The social criticism implicit in the book is directed toward politics more than anything else; journalism as practiced at *La Vie française* is a mere subsidiary activity of politics, and it is only at the end of the book that Duroy emerges into the true sphere of his activity when he looks across the river and sees himself in the Palais-Bourbon.

Technically *Bel-Ami* represents a considerable advance over *Une Vie*, a development and a consolidation of the impersonal, objective, external method. Maupassant avoids the inflexibility inherent in his method by venturing to look below the surface occasionally to expose the thoughts of his characters, and by his use of a mirroring object, a looking-glass or another person, he is able to exteriorize Duroy's mental processes and show him in the very moment of self-discovery. Maupassant remains convinced that no one can really penetrate another's mind, as he frequently pointed out in essays written during this period. He still scorns the psychological novel, though his occasional plunges below the surface, objective and dispassionate as they are, can be considered as a hesitant step in that direction. They are used, however, simply as a method of lending flexibility to his technique. His attitude is made clear in *Bel-Ami* itself when Georges and Madeleine discuss whether the legacy from Vaudrec should be accepted or not: "Il s'arrêta

---

[45] "Aux critiques de *Bel-Ami*—Une Réponse," *Gil Blas*, June 7, 1885; *Bel-Ami* (Conard), pp. 576-581; LF, xv, 154-157.

en face d'elle; et ils demeurèrent de nouveau quelques instants les yeux dans les yeux, s'efforçant d'aller jusqu'à l'impénétrable secret de leurs cœurs, de se sonder jusqu'au vif de la pensée. Ils tâchaient de se voir à nu la conscience en une interrogation ardente et muette: lutte intime de deux êtres qui, vivant côte à côte, s'ignorent toujours, se soupçonnent, se flairent, se guettent, mais ne se connaissent pas jusqu'au fond vaseux de l'âme."[46]

Composed, as was *Une Vie*, by addition, of bits and pieces, *Bel-Ami* nevertheless achieves a unity of tone and a coherence that is lacking in the earlier novel. The patchwork method of composition, the urge to use earlier themes and fragments, is admirably concealed in *Bel-Ami* by the care and artistry with which each piece was refashioned to fit into the whole plan. The theme of the novel seems to be Balzacian in that it portrays the rise of an ambitious man; it is an apparent exception to the characteristic pattern of the realistic novel of the second half of the nineteenth century which preferred to "dessiner ironiquement des existences qui se défont."[47] *Bel-Ami* is an *Education sentimentale* in reverse, and as Thibaudet remarked, Frédéric Moreau with a few years service as a *sous-officier* in the cavalry could easily become a Bel-Ami.[48] Sartre, who has no fondness for the work of Maupassant and his contemporaries, came very close to hitting on the real force of the book when he wrote: "*Bel-Ami* ne prend pas d'assaut les redoutes de la bourgeoisie, c'est un ludion dont la montée témoigne seulement de l'effondrement d'une société."[49] But society does not fall as Duroy rises, nor, in fact, does he rise at all. The novel records soberly the discovery by a mediocre man, who is only mildly ambitious, that the world is on his own level, that he has only to shift his perspective to give himself the illusion of ascent.

[46] *Bel-Ami* (Conard), p. 466.
[47] Albert Thibaudet, *Gustave Flaubert*, Paris, Gallimard, 1935, p. 163.
[48] *ibid.*, p. 144.
[49] Jean-Paul Sartre, *Situations II*, Paris, Gallimard, 1948, p. 173.

MONT-ORIOL (1887)

Mont-Oriol, published early in 1887, was Maupassant's third and last attempt to build a novel by accumulation of detail and incident. It is by far the weakest of all his novels and brought to an end this first phase of his career as a novelist in which he used with varying success the technique most natural to an established *conteur*, that of assembling enough short stories to fill out a novel and adopting some method to give them unity and focus. He was only moderately successful in finding a unifying element for *Une Vie*, for Jeanne was too negative and too ineffectual a character to hold things together, and the Norman countryside could provide only a suggestion of unity. *Bel-Ami*, as we have seen, was far more successful, for Georges Duroy, with all his faults, was able to control the center of the stage. In *Mont-Oriol*, which is quite different in tone from *Bel-Ami*, Maupassant relies almost uniquely on the peculiar setting, a spa in Auvergne, to give unity to the varied incidents and stories he pours into his novel.

In August 1885 Maupassant, visiting Châtel-Guyon in Auvergne, was profoundly impressed by the natural beauty of the region, and determined to use this setting as a background for his next novel.[1] He outlined the novel while at Châtel-Guyon, then settled down in Antibes to write it, returning later to Auvergne to check on various geographic details. It was finished in December 1886 and appeared serially in the *Gil Blas* between December 23, 1886 and February 6, 1887, before its publication by Havard early in 1887.

Contemporary critics were immediately conscious of the strangely different note struck in *Mont-Oriol*; the tough, impassible Maupassant produced a sentimental love story against the poetically described backdrop of the Auvergne countryside. He had set out deliberately to acquire a new manner, but though the subject is handled differently, technically he not

---

[1] Maupassant, letter to Henri Amic, August 17 [1885]; LF, xv, 336.

only followed the method of *Une Vie* and *Bel-Ami* but exaggerated the defects of that technique. From the first he noted: "Ce sera une histoire assez courte et très simple dans ce grand paysage calme. Cela ne ressemblera guère à *Bel-Ami*."[2] Some time later he described his work in progress as follows: "Je fais une histoire de passion très exaltée, très ardente et très poétique. . . . Les chapitres de passion sont beaucoup plus raturés que les autres. Enfin ça vient tout de même. On se plie à tout, avec de la patience; mais je ris souvent des idées sentimentales, très sentimentales et tendres que je trouve, en cherchant bien! J'ai peur que ça ne me convertisse au genre amoureux, pas seulement dans les livres, mais aussi dans la vie. Quand l'esprit prend un pli, il le garde; et vraiment il m'arrive quelquefois, en me promenant sur le cap d'Antibes— un cap solitaire comme une lande de Bretagne—en préparant un chapitre au clair de lune, de m'imaginer que ces histoires-là ne sont pas si bêtes qu'on le croirait."[3] His new manner obviously gave him some trouble, but he seems to have been converted to the "genre amoureux" only too well. The ironical tone of the letter is missing from *Mont-Oriol*, especially from those places where it is most needed.

Although *Mont-Oriol* gives the impression of being assembled from bits and pieces, actually it contains fewer borrowings from previously published material than either of the first two novels, and these borrowings are in general rather thoroughly reworked. A. Guérinot has shown that three short pieces based on an earlier visit to Châtel-Guyon were re-used in the novel: "Petits voyages—en Auvergne," *Gil Blas*, July 17, 1883; "Malades et Médecins," *Gaulois*, May 11, 1884; and "Mes vingt-cinq jours," *Gil Blas*, August 25, 1885.[4] No other articles or stories were set directly into the framework of the

2 Maupassant, letter to his mother [August 1885]; LF, xv, 335.

3 Maupassant, letter to Mme Lecomte du Nouy, March 2, 1886; LF, xv, 337.

4 A. Guérinot, "Maupassant et la composition de *Mont-Oriol*," *Mercure de France*, June 15, 1921, pp. 597-623. The article "Malades et Médecins" is in part a repetition of the earlier "Un Vieux," *Gil Blas*, September 26, 1882.

novel, though there are many echoes of Maupassant's favorite tirades on diverse subjects.

The article "Malades et Médecins" is interesting not only for the sketches and scenes that are re-used but because it contains, in 1884, one paragraph which gives the essential framework of the future novel: "Dans chacune des stations thermales, qui se fondent autour de chaque ruisseau tiède découvert par un paysan, se joue toute une série de scènes admirables. C'est d'abord la vente de la terre par le campagnard, la formation d'une Société au capital, fictif, de quelques millions, le miracle de la construction d'un établissement avec ces fonds d'imagination et avec des pierres véritables, l'installation du premier médecin, portant le titre de médecin inspecteur, l'apparition du premier malade, puis l'éternelle, la sublime comédie entre ce malade et ce médecin."

Herein lies the germ from which the novel grew, for the establishment of a spa around a newly discovered spring forms the main axis of *Mont-Oriol*. But in the course of composition a great many diverse elements have been added, the most important of which is the love story, the supposedly tender but actually rather brutal affair between Christiane Andermatt and Paul Brétigny. The component parts of the novel can be enumerated rather easily since they are held together only by the mechanics of the plot and are never fully integrated into a single structure. Scattered through the novel are numerous set pieces on the geography of Auvergne and the beauties of its natural scenery. Along with these we have vignettes of life at a thermal station, heavily satirical, even caricatural sketches of patients and doctors, which are balanced by portraits of peasant types, old Oriol, his son Colosse, and the wily Clovis, who combines a career as a professional cripple with that of poacher. When old Oriol discovers a spring on his property, Andermatt, a wealthy Jewish businessman who is staying at the nearby spa of Enval with his wife Christiane, decides to form a company to create a rival establishment. His deals form a large portion of the book; he dickers with the shrewd and cautious peasant Oriol, and he induces his wife's spendthrift brother Gontran to marry one of Oriol's daughters for her dowry. Gontran is attracted to the younger daughter Charlotte, but when he learns that her dowry will be land of no immediate value to the company, he shifts his attentions to the older daughter Louise and marries her. Meanwhile, running parallel with these events is another almost separate story, the love affair between Christiane Andermatt and Paul Brétigny, which leads to a theme frequently treated by Maupassant, though it is handled here with unusual sentimentality. It is the old theme of the child born of a woman and her lover, accepted as his own by the husband, followed by the disappearance from the scene of the lover. *Pierre et Jean* will be a further exploitation of this theme, far more soberly and artistically handled and related from a quite different point of view. *Pierre et Jean*, so unlike *Mont-Oriol* in almost every respect, is in this sense a kind of transposed sequel to it, beginning where the earlier novel leaves off. In *Mont-Oriol* the lover, Paul Brétigny, removes himself from the scene because he loses interest in Christiane as soon as she becomes pregnant: "il était, cette homme, de la race des amants, et non point de la race des pères."[5] He ends by feeling sorry for Charlotte Oriol, abandoned by Gontran, and decides to marry her.

The loose organization of all these elements—plots, background, and sketches—allows Maupassant to introduce at will passages on his favorite subjects, set down in the style of his essays or *chroniques*: discourses by Paul Brétigny on the keenness of the senses, and on beauty, complete with verses from Baudelaire; on the art of music by the local orchestra-leader, Maestro Saint-Landri, and on the fallibility of medical science by Dr. Mazelli. Most of these, although no actual "sources" have been found, give every appearance of having been lifted bodily from some forgotten essay. In the first chapter Maupassant parodies at length Dr. Bonnefille's prescriptions, a

[5] *Mont-Oriol* (Conard), p. 256.

heavy-handed and long-drawn-out piece of doubtful humor that appears most inopportunely at the beginning of the novel when he has barely introduced some of his characters. Similarly, he reproduces the entire poster announcing a concert and a play to be presented at the spa; the announcement is utterly banal, and if there is anything amusing or significant in it, it escapes this writer.

The novel has certainly very little to recommend it: the best parts are the economical and evocative descriptions of natural scenery, and one can take a mild interest in the documentary accounts of life at a spa. The main characters are mere clichés, uninteresting as individuals. Andermatt is nothing more than the conventional rich Jew of stage and fiction, and the others are molded in exactly the same fashion into their own stock parts: Christiane's father, the penniless nobleman; Gontran, the young man-about-town, freely spending borrowed money; Christiane, the unawakened wife who had married not for love but to save her family from poverty. There is a hint of vitality in old Oriol, caricature though he is; Maupassant was undeniably more at his ease in dealing with peasants, and Oriol, his son, and the wily Clovis are shrewdly observed. Yet they remain peasant types, or rather the peasant type, and, if their accent is Auvergnat, they are otherwise indistinguishable from their Norman counterparts. The love story is mawkishly sentimental and is constantly getting mixed up with Andermatt's deals, with which it has no real connection. After a fumbling exposition, Christiane appears as the central character, but when she becomes pregnant, Maupassant, like Paul Brétigny, loses interest in her, and turns to Gontran's affairs with the Oriol sisters.

Paul Brétigny, although he is given more attention than any other character and is provided with more elaborate speeches to deliver, remains like the others a stock figure with no sharply defined individuality. This is rather curious because Maupassant seems to have used himself as a model for the character of his hero. He resembles the author physically, even to the celebrated round head which, according to Maupassant, assumed that shape at the time of his birth, when the doctor molded it into a perfect sphere. Here is his description of Brétigny: "Il avait des cheveux noirs, ras et droits, des yeux trop ronds, d'une expression presque dure, la tête aussi toute ronde, très forte, une de ces têtes qui font penser à des boulets de canon, des épaules d'hercule, l'air un peu sauvage, lourd et brutal."[6] Brétigny has Maupassant's physical love of the country: "Il aimait la campagne avec ses instincts ardents où transperçait toujours de l'animalité. Il l'aimait en sensuel qu'elle émeut, dont elle fait vibrer les nerfs et les organes."[7] He has the same sensitivity to odors, the same sensuality, physical strength, violence, the same attractiveness to women. Brétigny is based on Maupassant, if not as he was, at least as he liked to imagine himself: "C'était d'ailleurs un de ces hommes qui plaisent aux femmes, à toutes les femmes, par sa nature même, par l'acuité vibrante de ses émotions. Il savait leur parler, tout leur dire, et il leur faisait tout comprendre. Incapable d'un effort continu, mais intelligent à l'extrême, aimant toujours ou détestant avec passion, parlant de tout avec une fougue naïve d'homme frénétiquement convaincu, aussi changeant qu'il était enthousiaste, il avait à l'excès le vrai tempérament des femmes, leur crédulité, leur charme, leur mobilité, leur nervosité, avec l'intelligence supérieure, active, ouverte et pénétrante d'un homme."[8] The hero of *Mont-Oriol* seems to fall more nearly into the category of *l'homme-fille* which Maupassant once described,[9] than does his more vigorous predecessor, Georges Duroy. Brétigny, like Maupassant, has traveled in Italy and Sicily and he recites to his lady-love travelogues on Mount Aetna which repeat the ideas and the tone of some of Maupassant's own travel pieces.[10] Paul is composed of segments of Maupassant, just as

[6] *ibid.*, p. 31.   [7] *ibid.*, p. 100.   [8] *ibid.*, pp. 109-110.

[9] "L'Homme-Fille," *Gil Blas*, March 13, 1883; *Toine* (Conard), pp. 49-56.

[10] Cf. "L'Etna," *Gil Blas*, July 14, 1885 and *Mont-Oriol* (Conard), p. 150.

the novel is a collection of the author's observations; they have no focus or vital force that would endow them with life and coherence. The resemblance of the character to the author is interesting as a sidelight, but it is not enough to lift the hero above the level of the other puppets in the book.

The great defect in *Mont-Oriol* is, above all else, the absence of any irony or detachment. If the initial idea of the novel was a satirical treatment of "la sublime comédie" between patient and doctor, the injection of the love story made this unrecognizable. True, there is a ponderous mockery of medical science here and there, but in general what Maupassant presents to us in this book is offered with perfect seriousness, as if it all were undeniably worthy of our interest. When he describes for our edification the remarkable system of a "lavage d'estomac," one rather expects him to adopt an ironical tone, but he soon becomes so involved in the details of the apparatus that he describes it with all the loving care that one would expect from its inventor. Hardest to swallow, however, are Brétigny's speeches to Christiane on love and beauty; what is acutely embarrassing to the reader is that Maupassant seems to think that these mediocre banalities are brilliant pieces of seductive prose. Those moonlight strolls on the Cap d'Antibes have a thoroughly pernicious effect on the novel.

Victor Havard, Maupassant's publisher, foreseeing a sensational sale of the book among the *femmes de chambre,* was delighted with the new tone the master had found and enthusiastically wrote to the author: ". . . je déclare que ce livre est un chef-d'œuvre sublime et impérissable. C'est du Maupassant dans toute l'expansion et la plénitude de son génie et la pleine maturité de son merveilleux talent.

"Vous donnez là, avec une puissance inouïe, une nouvelle note que j'avais deviné en vous depuis longtemps." After this lyrical outburst Havard gets down to business, adding: "En résumé, il doit nous venir avec ce livre-là de vingt à vingt-cinq mille nouveaux lecteurs, car il est accessible aux âmes les plus

timorées de la bourgeoisie que vos premières productions per-
sistaient à effaroucher."[11]

Let us leave to Maupassant himself, however, the last word
on his novel. In 1890, writing to Havard about the collection
of stories, *L'Inutile Beauté*, he questioned Havard's judgment
and reminded him: "Rappelez-vous votre emballement pour
Mont-Oriol que je n'aimais pas, moi, et qui ne vaut point
grand'chose."[12]

[11] Victor Havard, letter to Maupassant, December 10, 1886; printed
in Lumbroso, *Souvenirs sur Maupassant*, pp. 416-418.

[12] Maupassant, letter to Victor Havard, March 17, 1890; *L'Inutile
Beauté* (Conard), p. 42; LF, xv, 377-378. LF incorrectly gives Ollendorf
as the addressee.

9

THE NOVEL BY EXTENSION

PIERRE ET JEAN (1888)

Mont-Oriol brought Maupassant to the end—a dead end—of his first conception of novelistic technique. He saw the inadequacy of this novel in spite of his publisher's lavish praise, and began to reflect deeply on the nature of his art. He could continue to turn out short stories with facility, and he did, but he had to write novels as well, and here there was no "natural" method of producing them, for his instinctive technique had taken him as far as he could go. His reflections on the novel as a form resulted in the celebrated preface to *Pierre et Jean,* called simply "Le Roman." This little essay is not, however, a chart of the road he is about to follow, and he specifically denies that the theories set forth in the preface apply to the novel with which it was printed. "Le Roman" is rather a summary of the artistic and novelistic credo, derived from Flaubert, on which all his past work had been based. There is nothing new here; all the ideas had been expressed and developed much earlier in his newspaper articles, as we have shown in Part One. He had reached a critical point, he recognized that he could not go on as before, compiling novels out of various fragments, but before pushing on, he felt the necessity of putting on paper the basic tenets of his creed as a novelist, hoping to obtain from this exposition a hint as to the direction he should follow. As a result, "Le Roman," which is drawn up at a crucial period mid-way in his career as a novelist, points backward to *Une Vie, Bel-Ami,* and *Mont-Oriol,* and applies specifically to them. The last three novels, *Pierre et Jean, Fort comme la mort,* and *Notre Cœur,* do not represent a denial of the principles of the preface, but are rather an extension of them. The purely objective method he advocates was adequate to treat the rather primitive characters and situations of the three early novels, but, given other situations and more complex and reflective people, some other way had to be found to present them fully. The problem was to penetrate deeply into the psychology of his characters, since the basic action of the novel was henceforth to be internal, and yet do this without compromising the objectivity he so highly prized. *Pierre et Jean* is the result of this effort to extend the objective technique to make it supple enough to deal with a purely psychological drama.

The starting point of *Pierre et Jean*, the shortest and undoubtedly the best of his novels, was very different from his earlier works. Instead of composing by addition or accumulation, he operated this time by expansion and development. The earlier linear structure of a number of separate incidents strung out in time and attached to a character or a place gives way to the centripetal structure of a single situation among a restricted group of characters, wherein every action and word drives inward to the center which is the mind of Pierre. Coming after *Mont-Oriol* which was larded with extraneous incidents and superfluous documentation, *Pierre et Jean* provides a sharp contrast with its severe economy, its concise but evocative description, its exclusion of all padding. As he frees himself from the stringent limitations of objectivity and moves into the dimension of psychology, he finds the substance of his novel not in extent but in depth, not by padding but by probing.

It is obvious from his earliest essays that Maupassant considered the psychological novel a rather absurd form, and although in his more generous moments he granted authors the right to work in that form, he frequently expressed his own antipathy to it. He repeats the same strictures in the very preface to what is generally considered a psychological novel, and insists that no man can penetrate the mind of another and explain all his secret thoughts and motives. Yet the contradiction between the theories of the preface and the practice of the novel itself is more apparent than real, if one examines

Pierre et Jean closely. He has not turned away from the objective technique but has extended it, at the same time keeping it within very definite limitations. It is these limitations, in fact, which lend sobriety and power to the novel. Given the nature of his subject, a purely objective presentation, revealing the inner motive by an artistic description of the externals, would be too cumbersome: what goes on in the mind of a man seated on a dock may revolutionize his whole life without revealing anything of the nature of his conflict to the most discerning bystander. Maupassant is impelled therefore to expose for us what goes on in the mind of his character, but this presentation operates within precisely defined limits which are a logical result of Maupassant's preoccupation with objectivity. The author never makes his presence felt in the story, his role is that of the skilled observer, ubiquitous but not omniscient. Much of the action is revealed by this careful, unobtrusive, objective reporter, which is Maupassant's favorite technique. But frequently the author is obliged to relate what Pierre is thinking, and these excursions into "psychology" represent simply a shifting of the point of view: he tells what goes on in Pierre's mind, without comment, as if he were merely reporting what Pierre had revealed to him. At no point does the author assume a superior position and analyze his character's thoughts; he knows no more about Pierre than Pierre knows of himself; it is exactly as if a confession or journal written in the first person singular had been transformed into a narrative in the third person by a self-effacing scribe. Pierre's motives are not explained except insofar as he himself explains them; we fumble in hypotheses based on the subconscious only when Pierre becomes aware of them. There is no external analysis; in this framework, the author can never be more subtle or penetrating than his character, and for Maupassant's purposes in this book that is sufficient.

The central idea of the novel is the theme of paternity, a theme that seems to have obsessed Maupassant. René Dumesnil, who made an interesting classification by subject of all of Maupassant's stories, writes: "Maupassant est hanté par certains sujets et principalement par celui qui trouvera dans *Le Champ d'Oliviers* son expression définitive et parfaite; l'enfant, l'enfant ignoré de son père, l'enfant abandonné sciemment ou non, et qui a poussé comme une mauvaise graine livrée aux caprices des saisons. Sous ses formes les plus diverses, ce problème de la responsabilité morale du père revient plus de trente fois dans les quelque deux cent cinquante nouvelles que Maupassant a laissées."[1] In *Pierre et Jean* the situation is studied not from the point of view of one of the principals, father or son, but from the point of view of the brother, or rather the half-brother, of the son whose parentage is questioned. The focus of the book is on Pierre Roland and his anguish as the truth is gradually revealed to him that his brother Jean is not Roland's son, but the fruit of an adulterous liaison of Mme Roland and an old friend of the family, Léon Maréchal. The crisis develops when the calm bourgeois life of the Roland family in Le Havre is shattered by news of Maréchal's death and by the fact that he has left his fortune to Jean. Pierre accepts the news of his brother's good fortune calmly and with only a twinge of jealousy at first. He is indignant at the suspicions of some of his acquaintances who are surprised that the money was not left to both sons equally, especially since Pierre was the older. From his initial concern over his mother's reputation, not doubting her innocence, and the propriety of accepting the legacy under such conditions, he arrives after painful analysis and investigation at the moral certainty that the implication is all too true and that Jean is Maréchal's son. In a crucial scene all his pent-up anger and distress burst forth and he tells Jean the truth. Jean is shocked, but stands by his mother—and the legacy—and the situation is resolved by Pierre's leaving home and accepting a post as ship's doctor.

The entire book is tightly constructed around this single situation, the effect of a legacy, and further, everything is

[1] *Chroniques, Etudes, Correspondance* (Gründ), p. xv.

seen from a single angle, that of Pierre. His reactions are the real subject of the book, and all the other characters are seen through him. There is simply no place for the leisurely superfluities of the earlier novels. *Pierre et Jean* is therefore much closer to his usual short story technique, and, by its brevity and simplicity more a *nouvelle* than a novel. The framework of the short story is filled out, not by multiplication of events but by the enlargement of the psychological dimension. Since this excursion into psychology is controlled by his preoccupations with objectivity, it is worth making a close analysis of this masterpiece in order to try to reveal the nature and limits of Maupassant's art.

The first chapter is a remarkable example of concise and economical exposition, presenting the characters, laying the groundwork of the entire novel and at the same time moving through a dramatically presented scene. It opens abruptly with an exclamation "Zut!" uttered by M. Roland, annoyed that the fish are no longer biting. By a skillful mixture of dialogue and exposition we see the chief characters, grouped here in Roland's sail boat, and are given a glimpse of their past. The party includes M. Roland, a retired jeweler with a passion for sailing; his wife, "une femme d'ordre, une économe bourgeoise un peu sentimentale, douée d'une âme tendre de caissière";[2] their older son, Pierre, who had tried various professional studies and now, having won his degree as a doctor, was ready to begin his practice; the younger son, Jean, who had just completed his law studies; and finally, their neighbor, Mme Rosémilly, a young and attractive widow. The two brothers are quite different, and there has always been a certain rivalry between them, which has become more marked in the presence of Mme Rosémilly. Their contrasting natures and their latent jealousy are discreetly established to foreshadow the real subject of the book: "Mais une vague jalousie, une de ces jalousies dormantes qui grandissent presque invisibles entre frères ou entre sœurs jusqu'à la maturité et qui éclatent

[2] *Pierre et Jean* (Conard), p. 6.

à l'occasion d'un mariage ou d'un bonheur tombant sur l'un, les tenait en éveil dans une fraternelle et inoffensive inimitié."[3]

Having set forth his background and outlined his characters, Maupassant refers back to the conversation during which the fishing trip was planned, then brings us again to the "Zut!" and we are once more in the present as the party starts home. On the way we get a further sketch of Mme Roland, her sentimental, poetic nature, "sa taille autrefois très souple et très mince,"[4] and we see the rivalry of the two brothers expressed in their juvenile efforts to outrow one another. Details of the setting, the boats, the coast-line, the port of Le Havre, are filled in as we proceed.

That evening the local notary brings the news of Léon Maréchal's death and announces that Jean is named his sole heir. From this point on every element of the writing is charged with intensity and significance; each person reacts in his own way, normally, precisely as one would expect from what we know of them, yet each phrase that is uttered, simple though it is, has a resonance that carries through the rest of the novel. One detail, the significance of which is not immediately apparent, is the stipulation in Maréchal's will that if Jean refuses the inheritance, the estate will pass to the "enfants abandonnés." M. Roland is overjoyed by the unexpected good fortune and cavorts about the room, but his wife is reserved, as if in a dream, and says simply, "Cela prouve qu'il nous aimait." In this simple scene, simply reported without comment, innocent remarks, pregnant with meaning no one is aware of as yet, mark the beginning of the drama and prefigure what is to ensue. Pierre breaks in with a perfectly natural question, but it is the first step on the long and tortuous path he is to follow: "Vous le connaissiez donc beaucoup, ce Maréchal?"[5] Roland replies with his usual empty effusion, relating how Maréchal went for the doctor when Jean was about to be born, and naïvely quotes what he supposes Maréchal must have said: "Tiens, j'ai contribué à la naissance de ce

3 *ibid.*, p. 5.   4 *ibid.*, p. 13.   5 *ibid.*, p. 34.

petit-là, je vais lui laisser ma fortune."[6] Mme Roland, again
with an apparently guileless remark, goes right to the heart
of the matter when she says of this fortune: "Elle tombe du
ciel pour Jean . . . mais Pierre?"[7] Her husband retires and the
chapter ends: "Mme Roland se remit à songer devant la lampe
qui charbonnait."[8]

This first chapter gives an admirable exposition, starting in
the present and weaving in the past with extreme economy.
Nothing is superfluous: every word plays its part in presenting
the scene or in evoking what we should know of the past and
the nature of the people involved. Every development in the
rest of the novel is a natural outgrowth of elements contained
in the first chapter: the rivalry over Mme Rosémilly, and
Pierre's jealousy over her seeming preference for Jean; the fact
that both Pierre the doctor and Jean the lawyer are looking
for offices, which will bring them into conflict at a crucial
moment later; the central problem, Pierre's suspicions, are
suggested unobtrusively, for he has begun his investigation
without being aware of it. The point of view throughout the
chapter is that of the omniscient author, or, more exactly, the
ubiquitous author. He knows something of the past of these
characters and he acts as observer, giving no more information than could an alert witness, adding a few shrewd deductions of his own. He is in a privileged position but he does not
analyze; he gives either his observations directly, or deductions based on his observations.

From this point on our attention is centered almost entirely on Pierre, and we find him restlessly strolling about the
port of Le Havre, finally sitting down on a bench on the quai
to examine himself, wondering why he feels a certain "malaise." We are told directly that "Il avait l'esprit excitable et
réfléchi en même temps, il s'emballait, puis raisonnait, ap-
prouvait ou blâmait ses élans; mais chez lui la nature première
demeurait en dernier lieu la plus forte, et l'homme sensitif
dominait toujours l'homme intelligent."[9] This brief analysis is

[6] *ibid.*, p. 35.   [7] *ibid.*, p. 36.   [8] *ibid.*, p. 37.   [9] *ibid.*, p. 40.

repeated by Pierre himself as he meditates on the dual nature of man, on the conflict between "l'être instinctif" and "l'être pensant," and he concludes that the reason for his restlessness can only be his subconscious jealousy of Jean, especially since the fortune would allow his brother to marry Mme Rosémilly. He probes further, deciding that since he has a low opinion of the widow and does not want her anyway, his envy is all the more base, "C'est donc de la jalousie gratuite."

Woven into Pierre's examination of conscience is a description of the background: the harbor, the lights of ships and lighthouses, the sights and sounds of the port. These brief descriptive notes do more than merely set the stage, however; certain elements possess a symbolic value which accompanies and reinforces the evolution of Pierre. The fog, especially, whirls and eddies through the novel as a discreetly handled "objective correlative." The fog in Pierre's mind as he tries to see his way clear through the chain of circumstances is matched by the haze and fog of the harbor setting. As he meditates here on the quai, only slightly troubled about himself and without suspecting anything untoward in the legacy, the night is clear and lights are visible, but there is nevertheless a "brume nocturne" which filters the light of the stars. Once engulfed in the fog, Pierre will never be able to emerge completely or dispel it entirely.

He meets his brother on the quai, congratulates him on his good fortune, and muses on the ships entering and leaving. He expresses his nostalgia for foreign lands: ". . . j'ai des désirs fous de partir, de m'en aller avec tous ces bateaux, vers le Nord ou vers le Sud . . . mais voilà il faudrait de l'argent, beaucoup . . . ,"[10] a banal idea but it prepares the final resolution of the situation that is being built up.

From this slight feeling of "malaise" Pierre is driven to suspicion and speculation by two major incidents, aided by a series of lesser but nonetheless significant annoyances. The first is occasioned by his visit to his friend Marowsko, a Polish

[10] *ibid.*, p. 45.

refugee pharmacist. When he tells Marowsko of his brother's fortune, the old pharmacist repeats several times: "Ça ne fera pas un bon effet," and refuses to explain other than by saying: "Dans ce cas-là, on laisse aux deux frères également, je vous dis que ça ne fera pas un bon effet."[11]

Pierre does not reflect much on this statement, but sets off next morning in search of an apartment and office, and is annoyed that the family began lunch without him in their eagerness to arrive at the notary's office to accept the legacy. Finding just the apartment he needs, he hopes his brother can advance him the rent. Then the second incident: his conversation with the waitress in a café whom he knew casually. He tells her of his brother's inheritance and her remark reinforces Marowsko's: "Vrai, ça n'est pas étonnant qu'il te ressemble si peu!"[12] Now it is suddenly clear to him what others are suspecting and he concludes that Jean should refuse the inheritance for the sake of his mother's reputation, although Pierre himself does not believe for a moment that the suspicion could be founded in fact. He is however upset enough to spoil the dinner in celebration of the legacy by his warnings to his father about over-indulgence.

After a night's sleep he feels better, more kindly disposed, and thinks that perhaps the waitress, like all prostitutes, was eager to tear down the reputation of any honest woman. He reflects that he would not even have understood the implications of her remark had it not been for the "levain de jalousie qui fermentait en lui."[13] Or perhaps she had had no such evil thought at all. There is a certain ambiguity in this examination of Pierre's mind at the beginning of Chapter IV; it seems at first that Maupassant himself is analyzing Pierre's reactions, but actually what we have is clearly Maupassant's summary of Pierre's self-examination, and the author remains strictly within the limits of Pierre's knowledge of himself. Consequently it is Pierre, not the author, who takes us briefly into the subconscious when it occurs to him that all his suspicions

[11] *ibid.*, p. 51. [12] *ibid.*, p. 67. [13] *ibid.*, p. 83.

have been dredged up from the depths of his mind: "Il se pouvait que son imagination seule, cette imagination qu'il ne gouvernait point, qui échappait sans cesse à sa volonté, s'en allait libre, hardie, aventureuse et sournoise dans l'univers infini des idées, et en rapportait parfois d'inavouables, de honteuses, qu'elle cachait en lui, au fond de son âme, dans les replis insondables, comme des choses volées; il se pouvait que cette imagination seule eût créé, inventé cet affreux doute. Son cœur, assurément, son propre cœur avait des secrets pour lui; et ce cœur blessé n'avait-il pas trouvé dans ce doute abominable un moyen de priver son frère de cet héritage qu'il jalousait. Il se suspectait lui-même, à présent, interrogeant comme les dévots leur conscience, tous les mystères de sa pensée."[14] The only function of the author here is to turn the results of Pierre's self-examination into indirect discourse.

Immensely cheered and relieved by his reflections, Pierre goes for a sail, and through him Maupassant, who was probably happiest when afloat, describes the joyous sensation of sailing a small boat. Pierre is happy and dreams of a brilliant future in his newly-found apartment. But this joyous interlude is cut short by the intrusion of the fog, the physical fog from the sea which is the concomitant of the misty uncertainty of his mother's position. The old sailor with him says suddenly, "V'là d'la brume, m'sieu Pierre, faut rentrer."[15] He returns to find his mother and Jean enthusiastic over the office-apartment they have just rented for Jean's law practice. It is the same one Pierre had wanted, but he lacked money for a deposit. He is furious but manages to conceal it. Then in the middle of the meal he asks abruptly, "Comment l'aviez-vous connu, ce Maréchal?"[16] Troubled by jealousy and anger, his suspicions are rekindled, although this is conveyed simply by an objective report of the conversation. What he learns is not reassuring: he was three years old when the family first knew Maréchal, who, a little later, had been extremely helpful when Pierre had scarlet fever. Why then did he leave all his money

[14] *ibid.*, pp. 83-84.   [15] *ibid.*, p. 88.   [16] *ibid.*, p. 91.

to Jean? Pierre goes out into the fog which is still thick. He calls on Marowsko but senses the old man's suspicions and his hesitancy to push the subject very far. He leaves, pondering the motive behind Maréchal's legacy; it is not jealousy that stirs him now, but the fear lest he himself believe that Jean is Maréchal's son. He must know for certain, must remove all suspicion. The fog still surrounds him: he leaves Marowsko "et se replongea dans le brouillard de la rue."[17]

He goes toward the jetty to settle down to examine the facts. He is startled by the lament of a fog-horn, "le cri des navires perdus dans la brume . . . ce cri de détresse qu'il croyait avoir jeté lui-même."[18] The horns of other ships add a chorus of blasts, and closer at hand the port siren wails in reply. Seated on the jetty, "dans ces ténèbres lugubres et mugissantes,"[19] he tries to recall all he ever knew of Maréchal: he recalls his elegance and refinement, realizing Maréchal could never have been the friend of M. Roland, "pour qui le mot 'poésie' signifiait sottise."[20] Suddenly he remembers that Maréchal was blond, like Jean, and that there used to be a portrait of him in the house. Had his mother hidden it because of too striking a resemblance? He groans: "Et soudain, comme si elle l'eût entendu, comme si elle l'eût compris et lui eût répondu, la sirène de la jetée hurla tout près de lui. Sa clameur de monstre surnaturel, plus retentissante que le tonnerre, rugissement sauvage et formidable fait pour dominer les voix du vent et des vagues, se répandit dans les ténèbres sur la mer invisible ensevelie sous les brouillards."[21] He half convinces himself that his mother could never have been Maréchal's mistress, but bitterly reviewing the situation, he asks, why not? In a rage he turns to go and the siren goes off almost in his face. Shapes appear in the fog, ships entering the port, their names announced by the pilot—the *Santa Lucia* from Naples, an English ship from India. Again he dreams of

17 *ibid.*, p. 95.   18 *ibid.*, p. 97.   19 *ibid.*, p. 98.
20 *ibid.*, p. 102.   21 *ibid.*, pp. 103-104.

foreign countries, unconsciously seeking the only way out of the fog.

By now Pierre's concern is not so much that his mother's reputation will be damaged by acceptance of the legacy but rather that his suspicions may be proven valid. It is no longer a question of public opinion: "Il aurait voulu que tout le monde accusât sa mère pourvu qu'il la sût innocente, lui, lui seul!"[22] Looking at his brother closely, he fails to find any resemblance between Jean and M. Roland. He asks his mother to find the portrait of Maréchal and, unable to endure the presence of his family, goes off to Trouville for the day, which he spends on the beach. Disgusted by all the women there who adorn themselves not for their husbands but for their present or future lovers, he sees the beach only as "une halle d'amour."[23]

At dinner in the evening he again refers to the portrait of Maréchal; his mother a little reluctantly goes to look for it and finds it immediately. Pierre takes it, notes the resemblance between Jean and Maréchal, almost blurts it out, and rather ostentatiously looks from Jean to the picture and back again. After dinner there follows a dreadfully intense silent scene, Pierre striding up and down looking first at the picture on the mantel, then at his mother. When Mme Rosémilly is announced, Mme Roland seems even more troubled, and Pierre guesses that his mother fears a woman will be quick to see the resemblance. He hides the picture, which alarms his mother still more, and disappears without a word.

In the weeks that follow, Pierre's suspicions, so obvious to his mother, bring about a daily crisis of dumb suffering between them. He cannot refrain from torturing her by his actions or by thinly veiled references. During this protracted tension the whole family goes for a day's outing to Saint-Jouin, where Jean comes to a decision and proposes to Mme Rosémilly. Here there is a shift of point of view: Pierre leaves the center of the stage and is replaced by Jean. Jean's thoughts

[22] *ibid.*, p. 112.   [23] *ibid.*, p. 124.

are disclosed without commentary by the author, followed by the admirably objective scene of the proposal, culminating in the practical-minded Mme Rosémilly's "exposé net de la situation." Pierre and his mother witness the scene from a distance and his bitter remark, "J'apprends comment on se prépare à être cocu,"[24] sends her flying in anguish to her other son.

On their return to Le Havre they inspect Jean's new apartment. During the absence of the others, the two sons find themselves together in the salon, where Pierre's slighting remarks about "the widow" involve them in a dispute which leads to Jean's announcement that he is going to marry her. Pierre has reached the breaking point; exasperated, he flings at his brother that it is dishonorable to accept "la fortune d'un homme quand on passe pour le fils d'un autre," and reveals what is common gossip. He pours it all out, "la tumeur venait de crever," and he rushes out blindly. Here the author intervenes with a comment on Jean: "Il était de la race des temporiseurs qui remettent toujours au lendemain . . . ,"[25] one who had never faced any problems in his life and who was now overwhelmed by this catastrophic revelation. His mother, who has overheard everything, confesses to Jean her guilt and in a long speech she divulges the history of the Maréchal affair. She agrees not to run away, but meanwhile what can be done about Pierre?

Maupassant, after presenting almost entirely in dialogue this long crucial scene in Jean's apartment with a profoundly dramatic effect, turns to an analysis of Jean's reaction, so different from that of Pierre, who had been hurt "dans la pureté de son amour filial." Jean is more concerned with the effect on "ses intérêts les plus chers." Maupassant goes on to explain that the suddenness of the shock had swept away any moral prejudices he might have had and that he was not, in any case, "un homme de résistance" but one who preferred above all to escape embarrassing complications. But some solution is necessary. All of this analyzing by the author, explaining Jean by

<hr>

[24] *ibid.*, p. 162.   [25] *ibid.*, p. 177.

deductions and comparisons which Jean himself does not make, is rarely applied to Pierre. This serves to keep Pierre the central figure since we have the illusion of being told the story as if directly by him, from his point of view. The shift of point of view in the scene between Jean and his mother is necessary to impart to the reader that knowledge which Pierre seeks, but which he can never find. He can never completely dispel the fog.

Jean debates whether he should not refuse the legacy and has about convinced himself that he should renounce all claim, when a steamer whistle in the port gives him an idea. At breakfast the surface of things has been glossed over and the brothers behave as if nothing had happened. Jean leads the conversation to a discussion of a new ship, the *Lorraine*, which is about to make its maiden voyage, and reports what salary is earned by the captain, the purser, and the ship's doctor. Pierre, already intent on the idea of getting away, understands the drift of the conversation, and it is generally agreed than an effort should be made to get him the post of doctor on the *Lorraine*.

Jean and his mother pay a visit to Mme Rosémilly. Maupassant takes over with a survey of her apartment from his own point of view, a merciless portrait of a sentimental bourgeois décor, with a particularly heavy-handed irony in the description of the pictures on the wall. This and the distressingly coy conversation on the coming marriage strike what sounds like a false note, though there is some justification for the scene at this point. From the moment that Pierre understands that the post of ship's doctor provides a solution to his problem, there is a marked decrescendo, the affair is settled, only a few threads remain to be gathered, and perhaps the acid description of Mme Rosémilly's apartment has at least the function of marking this *détente*.

Everything is in fact settled: Pierre gets the position as doctor on the *Lorraine*, yet he alone is still uncertain about Jean's birth. He does not know whether his mother confessed or denied to Jean, nor does he know with absolute certainty himself that she is guilty, although he is almost sure that she is. He makes his preparations for departure, and as he waits for the sailing date we are shown two scenes which parallel those at the beginning which had set off the whole train of action. The whole dénouement in fact matches exactly the opening scenes and marks the return to an equilibrium that is however not quite the same. Again Pierre visits Marowsko, this time to say good-bye, which fills the old man with consternation for he was counting on Pierre's practice to build up his pharmacy. As he leaves him Pierre thinks, "Personne n'aura pour moi un regret sincère."[26] Again he remembers the waitress ("Elle avait raison, après tout.") but the *brasserie* is full, the waitress busy and totally indifferent to his departure.

On the day of the sailing the family gathers in his cabin for an intolerably awkward scene. There being nothing left to say, Pierre lectures on the pharmaceutical properties of the contents of his medicine chest to fill up the silence. The family leaves him at last to wave good-bye to him from their small boat. Here we are effectively back at the beginning again, with the Rolands and Mme Rosémilly in the boat, only this time Pierre has been eliminated. It is only after they wave and the steamer passes that M. Roland ("le bonhomme comptait si peu") learns by accident that Jean is to marry Mme Rosémilly.

It is no accident that the fog symbol reappears at the very end. The last words of the novel as Mme Roland turns again to the sea as the steamer fades into the distance, are: "Mais elle ne vit plus rien qu'une petite fumée grise, si lointaine, si légère qu'elle avait l'air d'un peu de brume." Maupassant in his manuscript wrote: "si légère qu'elle semblait un nuage," but changed it in proof. Pierre is pursued by "un peu de brume," never able to rid himself of it completely for he never *knows* the truth absolutely as does Jean or the reader. This bit of haze that remains carries back through the book to the first sign of it which was "la lampe qui charbonnait" at the end of the

26 *ibid.*, p. 226.

first chapter as Mme Roland mused over the news of the inheritance.

The theme of *Pierre et Jean* was deeply rooted in Maupassant's consciousness and one that he treated in short stories and novels from every possible angle. He appears to have been obsessed by speculation on what happens to children who are the product of illicit or adulterous love affairs, especially children who grow up unaware of their true parentage. In a short story "Le Testament," written in 1882, he used the device of a will to reveal that the third son of a family was really the son of the lover, all the mother's fortune being left to this younger son, who then assumed the family name of his true parent. Yet this story, while it is obviously linked to *Pierre et Jean,* is actually a by-product of his work on *Une Vie,* the mother in the shorter work being a curious combination of Jeanne's mother and Jeanne herself. "L'Attente," also written in 1882, is perhaps closer to the treatment of *Pierre et Jean,* since it deals with the effect on a son when he discovers his mother has a lover. But it is idle to look for a single "source" in a short story for the novel. Dumesnil's classification of the stories by subject shows this single theme treated an extraordinary number of times both before and after *Pierre et Jean.* Mme Lecomte du Nouy's statement that the idea for the novel was suggested by the fact that a friend of his was left a large fortune by "un commensal de la famille," may be true or simply a pleasant fiction, but does not in any case add anything to our knowledge of the novel.[27]

What is probably more instructive is a glance at what has been left out of the novel, sources that Maupassant wisely refrained from utilizing, which is essentially what distinguishes *Pierre et Jean* from the earlier novels. We have been particularly struck by the tight structure of this novel, its concentration, its unique concern with the subject at hand,

[27] Mme H. Lecomte du Nouy et Henri Amic, *En regardant passer la vie,* Paris, Ollendorf, 1903, p. 46.

eliminating any extraneous material. The first three novels are crammed with anecdotes and sketches which sometimes fill out the background and enrich it but which most often, in *Une Vie* and *Mont-Oriol*, are simply gratuitous padding. In *Pierre et Jean* he happily overcame this desire to pad, not that materials were lacking, but by definite artistic choice. One very revealing example of this is contained in the episode of the Roland family's trip to Saint-Jouin. They lunch at the inn there, are provided by the proprietress with clothing and equipment for crayfishing. The proprietress of the inn, who is known as "la belle Alphonsine" is but briefly described and plays her role at the edge of the scene. Now Maupassant had written in the *Gil Blas* of August 1, 1882 a sketch of the curious and picturesque innkeeper of Saint-Jouin, "la belle Ernestine," and in the course of the article remarked three times what a wonderful character she would be in a novel. In view of his past record, it is remarkable that Maupassant was able to bring in this personage without lingering over her at all; for he saw that though she was splendid material for a novel she had no function whatsoever in *Pierre et Jean*.

As far as one can see, there are no real textual borrowings from earlier works. Certain favorite ideas or leit-motivs recur but are generally brief and quite different in form from previous versions. For example, the theme of man's solitude and his desire for the companionship of marriage is expressed by Pierre as he wanders on the quai early in the story. The nearest thing to a textual borrowing is a description of the ship leaving for Trouville, which resembles the account of the same scene as given earlier in a story "Découverte."[28] In the story he began thus: "Quand on fut sorti du port, le petit bâtiment fit une courbe rapide, dirigeant son nez pointu sur la côte lointaine entrevue à travers la brume matinale. . . ." In *Pierre et Jean* we read: "Le petit paquebot sortit des jetées, tourna à gauche et soufflant, haletant, frémissant, s'en alla vers la

---

[28] "Découverte," *Gaulois*, September 4, 1884; *Monsieur Parent* (Conard), pp. 249-257; LF, v, 247-252.

côte lointaine qu'on apercevait dans la brume matinale. . . ."[29]
This may be nothing more than a new evocation of a familiar
scene rather than a rewriting of an earlier text, but, in any
event, Maupassant refrained from dumping into the novel his
ready-made description.

One more item of source material should be mentioned since
the connection has apparently not been made before. Pierre
Borel and Léon Fontaine have written: "Pour essayer de se
faire expliquer le secret de ses effroyables migraines, il ques-
tionnait invariablement le pharmacien de la localité où il se
trouvait. À Etretat, que de soirées il a passées dans l'arrière-
boutique du pharmacien Leroy! À Bezons, il avait d'interminables conversations avec un pharmacien polonais."[30] Undoubtedly this Polish pharmacist is the base on which he built
Marowsko.

The real source of *Pierre et Jean*, however, remains hidden
in Maupassant's mind, in the circumstances, whatever they
were, which drove him to treat again and again in his fiction
the theme of doubtful paternity. That obsession produced
many fine stories and this tight little masterpiece of a novel.
He had freed himself from the limitations of the novel by addition, had extended and made more supple his technique, re-
sisting the temptation to develop extraneous incidents which
so vitiated the earlier novels. He had produced a novel virtually
without a blemish, but he could not stop there. He continued
the process of liberation in his next two novels, but he moved
falteringly, without the absolute control he showed in *Pierre
et Jean*, and he moved into an alien field, as if against his will.

[29] *Pierre et Jean* (Conard), p. 122.
[30] Pierre Borel et Léon Fontaine, "Maupassant avant la gloire," *Revue
de France*, October 1, 1927, p. 398.

THE NOVEL BY INTROSPECTION

FORT COMME LA MORT (1889)

AFTER the publication of *Pierre et Jean* in January 1888 there was a marked decline in Maupassant's creative ability. The year 1888 is a remarkably thin one, in terms of total literary production, and although he wrote during that time what would represent a respectable accomplishment for an average writer, it is in no way comparable to the extraordinary output of novels, articles, and stories that marked his earlier years. Moreover, much of what did appear in 1888 (and in 1889) was merely a reissue of pieces written much earlier. The great creative force was undeniably running out. *Sur l'eau*, published in 1888, was a mere scrap-book of old articles, and *Le Rosier de Madame Husson*, a collection of fourteen short stories, all previously published, contained only one which had appeared in 1888; of the others, four had come out in 1887 and nine were of the period 1883 to 1885. The one preface he wrote, for *La Grande Bleue* of René Maizeroy, had in fact already seen service as "Pêcheuses et Guerrières" in the *Gil Blas* of March 15, 1887. In short, while working on *Fort comme la mort*, Maupassant turned out only a half-dozen short pieces, none of them of very high quality.

The novel itself gave him a good deal of trouble. He began work on it in the spring of 1888 and wrote to his mother in May: "Je prépare tout doucement mon nouveau roman, et je le trouve très difficile, tant il doit avoir de nuances, de choses suggérées et non dites. Il ne sera pas long, d'ailleurs, il faut qu'il passe devant les yeux comme une vision de la vie terrible, tendre et désespérée."[1] Progress was exceedingly slow and in September he wrote to Madame Strauss from Etretat that he had been troubled by severe migraine headaches and that the

[1] LF, xv, 360.

novel was no further advanced than when he had left Paris.[2] About the same time he informed the publisher Havard in a business letter that things were going badly: "Je ne vais pas du tout. Depuis deux mois je n'ai pu travailler une heure. Je pars pour Aix demain afin d'essayer de soigner les affreuses migraines dont je souffre."[3]

There were other factors besides his ill health which made the year a distressing one for Maupassant. His brother Hervé had become insane and it was Guy's painful task to take him to an asylum recommended by Dr. Blanche. This was, understandably, a severe shock, and no doubt contributed to the migraine which kept him from working. Maupassant's most recent biographer, Mr. Francis Steegmuller, describes in a chapter titled "Paul Bourget, High Life and Other Calamities" additional disturbing elements in Maupassant's life at this time: the pernicious effect on his work of his introduction to "high life" by Bourget, his efforts to pattern his own work along the psychological lines followed by his fellow novelist, and the mysterious "grande passion" Maupassant had for Marie Kahn, or some strange "Madame X," which is reflected in his last two novels.[4]

The decline in his creative powers is evident not only in the quantity of works produced but in their quality as well. What is more interesting, however, is that his last novels do more than reflect the growing impotence; in essence their subject is really the theme of the sterility of the artist, the blunting of the creative force by old age and by the diversions of society. *Fort comme la mort* has been both praised and scorned by critics but all agree that the theme of the novel is the fear of growing old, a theme that is illustrated by the machinery of the plot. So considered, the novel is only mediocre and trivial. It acquires greater depth, however, when viewed as a portrait

[2] Artine Artinian, ed., *Correspondance inédite de Guy de Maupassant*, Paris, Wapler, 1951, p. 257.

[3] LF, xv, 363.

[4] Francis Steegmuller, *Maupassant, a Lion in the Path*, New York, Random House, 1949, pp. 287-305.

of an artist whose creative powers are on the decline: not old age so much as the inability to create, sterility striking the man who had formerly produced works of art so effortlessly. It is not a question of age—Maupassant was only thirty-eight and Olivier Bertin of the novel was not much older and certainly far from senile. The novel, when it is concerned with the peculiar plight of a mature man in love with the daughter of his mistress, is more than a little hollow; but insofar as it portrays an artist tortured by his inability to go on and questioning all he has done, it is marked by a depth and a sincerity which come from Maupassant's own puzzled awareness that his machine was running down. Consequently this novel and, a little later, *Notre Cœur*, are of particular interest in this study of Maupassant where we have been following the technical efforts of the *conteur* to turn himself into a novelist. In this context his last two novels have more value than they would otherwise have if considered simply as successful or unsuccessful examples of the novelist's art.

With *Fort comme la mort*, published in June 1889 after having run serially in the *Revue Illustrée*, Maupassant turns in a new direction in his search for a novelistic technique. His first three novels were essentially faithful to the cherished principle of the "objective" technique, as outlined in the preface to *Pierre et Jean*. But *Pierre et Jean* itself was an extension of the objective method into the psychological domain; it is objective in the sense that the author does not intervene directly, nor can he be identified with the characters. Maupassant remains outside the system of *Pierre et Jean*; he personally is not involved. In his last two novels his position and accent are unlike anything he had done before. He is not an observer relating a story, but a sufferer who has transmuted his own feelings and preoccupations into fiction. Maupassant is not outside the system of *Fort comme la mort* and *Notre Cœur*. He is not merely sympathetic, he suffers with his characters. This does not mean that Maupassant *is* Olivier Bertin, but that Bertin was created in part out of Maupassant's own preoccupations with old age, with a disillusioned examination of his own career, and, above all, with a haunting fear of artistic sterility. In the first four novels he is relating stories which came to him from outside himself, and he treats them because they seem to him to be good stories, hence the objective position is easy to maintain. But in the last two the starting point of the story may be something outside him, but he writes from within himself, informing his novels with his own anguish.

Maupassant held that the psychological novel was possible only in terms of the author's own mind; we cannot penetrate the mind of another. And here, in the last novels, which are apparently more directly psychological than *Pierre et Jean,* Maupassant, whether consciously or not, holds to his principle, for the psychology he lays bare in his characters is specifically his own. Thus *Pierre et Jean,* for all its exposition of the workings of Pierre's mind, tells us very little about Maupassant; but *Fort comme la mort* and *Notre Cœur* reveal much of Maupassant the man, particularly a portrait of the artist as an old man, conscious of his ebbing powers, and haunted by the thought that he had squandered his talent. The two novels represent a poignant "summing-up" for Maupassant that is far from the self-satisfied tone of Somerset Maugham's reflections on his own career.

In *Fort comme la mort* Maupassant sets out to write a psychological novel à la Bourget dealing with the upper level of society; it is a study of the relations of Olivier Bertin, a painter, and Countess Any de Guilleroy, whose liaison has lasted a long time and grown calm with the years. They are getting older and are troubled by the thought of old age with its attendant loss of beauty for her and loss of vitality and artistic power for him. Into this well-established, orderly situation a catalyst is introduced by the arrival of Any's daughter, Annette, young, beautiful, strikingly like her mother, the very image of the portrait of Any painted by Bertin long before. The painter confuses the two women in his mind and thanks to the mother's extremely inept actions, comes to realize that he is really in love with the daughter. Once this is clear to him, the only solution is death, and he wanders about until he is run over by an omnibus.

This story provides the frame on which the novel is hung, but the machinery of the plot does not begin to work until the second half of the book. Part I does, of course, set the stage for what is to follow, but it is by no means simple exposition: Maupassant was not one to spin out an introduction for half of the book. Part I is deeply and ardently concerned with the elaboration of two themes: sterility, the artist who feels his creative powers drying up; and solitude, the loneliness of a bachelor existence which is intensified as he grows older. The second theme recalls Norbert de Varenne in *Bel-Ami* and other pieces where, early in his career, Maupassant gave expression to this feeling; but it takes on greater force here where it is played against the theme of the decline of creativity, which I take to be the dominant note of the novel, fully expressed in the first part, and reverberating throughout the second.

The novel opens with a description of Bertin's atelier which not only evokes the material aspect of the room but states directly and through the style and choice of words the basic theme of the novel. The objects of the décor lack life, the daylight itself becomes filtered and attenuated when the moment of creation has passed. "En ces murs que la pensée habite, où la pensée s'agite, s'épuise en des efforts violents, il semble que tout soit las, accablé, dès qu'elle s'apaise. Tout semble mort après ces crises de vie." The opening passages are filled with an overwhelming fatigue, the feeling of having reached a *point mort*, "comme si le logis entier avait souffert de la fatigue du maître."[5]

Bertin, though a highly successful artist, is unsure of himself, is troubled by a feeling of having missed the true path,

[5] *Fort comme la mort* (Conard), p. 2.

of having been turned aside by external forces. "Ce n'était point d'ailleurs un artiste résolu et sûr de lui, mais un inquiet dont l'inspiration indécise hésitait sans cesse entre toutes les manifestations de l'art."[6] He had undeniable technical competence, but there were forces which may have kept him from fully realizing his potentiality: "Peut-être aussi l'engouement brusque du monde pour ses œuvres élégantes, distinguées et correctes, avait-il influencé sa nature en l'empêchant d'être ce qu'il serait normalement devenu. Depuis le triomphe du début, le désir de plaire toujours le troublait sans qu'il s'en rendît compte, modifiait secrètement sa voie, atténuait ses convictions."[7]

It is difficult not to see in these opening pages a transposition of Maupassant's feelings toward his own career, a bewilderment, a sense of having got off the track somewhere, and of finding things more complicated than he had thought. His declining productivity, his rather desperate reuse of old material, his inability to create, and his weariness with the old forms and patterns he had used are suggested by a bleak paragraph describing Bertin's search for a new subject which leads him to review his whole work: "Il ne trouvait rien! Toutes les figures entrevues ressemblaient à quelque chose qu'il avait fait déjà, toutes les femmes apparues étaient les filles ou les sœurs de celles qu'avaient enfantées son caprice d'artiste: et la crainte encore confuse, dont il était obsédé depuis un an, d'être vidé, d'avoir fait le tour de ses sujets, d'avoir tari son inspiration, se précisait devant cette revue de son œuvre, devant cette impuissance à rêver de nouveau, à découvrir de l'inconnu."[8]

The secondary theme of old age, of the threatened decline of physical power and beauty is introduced just after this in a description of Olivier Bertin's appearance: "Il avait été célèbre dans les ateliers pour sa force, puis dans le monde pour sa beauté. L'âge maintenant pesait sur lui, l'alourdissait."[9]

[6] *ibid.*, pp. 2-3.   [7] *ibid.*, p. 3.   [8] *ibid.*, p. 5.   [9] *ibid.*, pp. 5-6.

Along with the exposition of these two themes in the first chapter, Maupassant lays the groundwork of the action of the plot, and as in *Pierre et Jean* he has his characters make seemingly innocent casual remarks which have overtones and significance that are not fully understood until much later. In the idle badinage of the first conversation between Bertin and Any he says gallantly, "Oh . . . on ne fait pas deux fois un portrait d'Any," to which she remarks simply, "Je l'espère bien." Obviously when Bertin wants to do a portrait of Any's daughter some time later, it is a denial of his casual phrase here, for in a real sense he is trying to do Any's portrait again and recapture and relive his youthful past. Similarly, she teases him about the coquettishness of his current sitters, but ends on a note of confidence: "Je suis tranquille d'ailleurs. Vous n'aimerez plus que moi maintenant. C'est fini, fini pour d'autres. Il est trop tard mon pauvre ami."[10] In their relations an equilibrium has been established, although it is soon to be broken.

Both Any and society have had a pronounced effect on Bertin's work and career; Any's influence is emphasized by Maupassant directly in his own words: "Depuis douze ans elle accentuait son penchant vers l'art distingué, combattait ses retours vers la simple réalité, et par des considérations d'élégance mondaine, elle le poussait tendrement vers un idéal de grâce un peu maniéré et factice."[11] Yet there is something disturbing and perhaps symbolic about Bertin's rejecting Any's suggestion that he attempt a portrayal of Christ and seizing instead on the more congenial idea of "un pied de femme au bord d'une robe." He adds: "On peut mettre tout là-dedans, de la vérité, du désir, de la poésie. Rien n'est plus gracieux, plus joli qu'un pied de femme, et quel mystère ensuite: la jambe cachée, perdue et devinée sous cette étoffe."[12]

Having got his novel under way, Maupassant goes back to give in some detail the history of the liaison of Bertin and Any, from its beginning when she posed for her portrait to

10 *ibid.*, p. 11.   11 *ibid.*, p. 10.   12 *ibid.*, p. 15.

the present tranquillity of an "amitié amoureuse."[13] What
emerges clearly from this evocation of the past is a view of
the relations of the artist to the social world, a successful
artist who is more than a little intimidated by high society;
though he is drawn into this world and is accepted, he remains something of an outsider and suffers a real inferiority
complex. "Les femmes du monde l'inquiétaient un peu, car
il ne les connaissait guère." Much more at home in the "demi-
monde," where he had had "des aventures rapides dues à sa
renommée, à son esprit amusant, à sa taille d'athlète élégant
et à sa figure énergique et brune," he was never quite sure of
himself with women of established social position. He felt,
and was made to feel the barrier, "cette disparité de race qui
empêche de confondre, bien qu'ils se mêlent, les artistes et
les mondains."[14] His reaction was to adopt a stiff politeness
which rather disconcerted Any at first, although once the ice
was broken, their affair moved rapidly enough.

This discussion of the artist and "le monde" is interpolated
directly by Maupassant, and this kind of analysis by the
author occurs with some frequency in *Fort comme la mort*.
He nevertheless makes an effort to have his characters do
their own analyzing, as Pierre did in the previous novel, and
tries to establish both Any and Bertin as people given to self-
analysis. As part of his courtship, Bertin describes and an-
alyzes minutely for her benefit everything he does, including
his thoughts while away from her;[15] and when Any, looking
at her husband, ponders her relations with him, we get no
more than her own examination of herself. Maupassant clings
to the extension of the objective method used in *Pierre et
Jean*, which forces him into constant use of phrases such as
"elle crut . . . ," "il lui semblait" to indicate a kind of psychological indirect discourse.

[13] *ibid.*, p. 56. (*Amitié amoureuse* is the title of a book published in
1896 by Madame Lecomte du Nouy in which Maupassant figures prominently.)
[14] *ibid.*, p. 23.　　[15] *ibid.*, p. 38.

After giving the history of the Any-Bertin liaison in Chapter I and bringing us again into the novelistic present, we expect Maupassant to pick up the events of his story and carry
them forward. Instead he seems to wander uncertainly and
feels the need of developing certain ideas which have little
relation to the plot, though they reenforce what I take to be
his main preoccupation during the writing of the novel. He
describes the Guilleroy salon, gives vivid pen-portraits of the
people who assemble there, and faithfully records their conversation. The portraits are sharp and tinged with irony and
criticism, but he gives the banal conversation with a straight
face as if it were significant and worth reporting; it is dull,
but Maupassant's "objectivity" makes us think that he is not
aware how dull it is: "Ce point-là fut encore discuté et par-
tagea la société. Tout le monde, cependant, se trouva à peu
près d'accord sur ceci: qu'une personne très grasse ne devait
pas maigrir trop vite."[16] But all this, one discovers, is a rather
heavy-handed preparation for Bertin's outburst against the
ignorance and futility of the conversation of the "gens du
monde." This is merely a restatement of a favorite Maupassant subject which he had treated as early as 1882 in "Les
Causeurs" (Gaulois, January 20, 1882) and had recently reworked as a by-product of Fort comme la mort in "Comment
on cause" in the Gil Blas (November 29, 1887). Bertin's conclusion takes some of the sting from his criticism but re-
enforces his position as an artist caught up and dissipated by
the frivolous forces of society. Once drawn in, he cannot escape because, as he admits, he likes it, but adds, "Je me mé-
prise un peu comme un métis de race douteuse."[17] This is
passed off by the others as a mere pose, but read in the context of the whole first part this impresses one as the only
sincere and valid statement made during the entire scene.
Chapter II contains only this rather flat-footed condemnation of le monde and a necessary piece of information that

[16] ibid., p. 75.   [17] ibid., p. 80.

plans are afoot for the marriage of Annette to the Marquis de Farandal.

One has the feeling that Maupassant is groping rather awkwardly for a way to develop his novel, and he throws in a series of disconnected scenes and discussions, most of which echo strongly pieces that he had used before. Lacking inspiration and direction, he turns, as he so often did, to an older inspiration and reworks it into his current novel. The ride in the Bois in the third chapter recalls the similar scene in *Bel-Ami* even including the elegant *courtisane* with whom Duroy had recognized a kinship. The conversation at Bertin's club turns about themes familiar to Maupassant, and the fear of old age which underlies the boasting comments of these older members, the "grisons," reiterates, though somewhat idly, one of Maupassant's main concerns in this book. The music played at the club sends Bertin into an agreeable revery in which he evokes the ride in the Bois with Any and Annette, tying together after a fashion these various scenes and displaying Bertin's (and Maupassant's) sensitivity to music which prepares us for the effect on Bertin of the opera *Faust*.

The next day is one of joyful artistic creation for Bertin, the only period in the book when he is really able to work: "Ce fut une journée excellente, une de ces journées de production facile, où l'idée semble descendre dans les mains at se fixer d'elle-même sur la toile."[18] Happy and creative, he enjoys his walk in the park with Annette and is moved by seeing a young girl, a book in her hand and lost in thought, to suggest that Annette pose for him in precisely that attitude. It is here that Maupassant sounds his first note of warning to Bertin in a passage curiously suggestive of Proust: "Bertin sentait en lui s'éveiller des souvenirs, ces souvenirs disparus, noyés dans l'oubli et qui soudain reviennent, on ne sait pourquoi. Ils surgissent rapides, de toutes sortes, si nombreux en même temps, qu'il éprouvait la sensation d'une main remuant la vase de sa mémoire."[19] We have seen that Maupassant had

[18] *ibid.*, p. 114. [19] *ibid.*, p. 121.

a certain sensitivity to the workings of the subconscious,[20] but he was content to place in *Fort comme la mort* a lengthy discussion of the suggestive powers of sounds and odors, rephrasing without extending them, the same ideas set forth in his earlier pieces.[21] In his novel all this is merely a device to show what is happening to Bertin before he is himself aware of it. The whole passage is inserted as an essay, and, while interesting, though not profound in itself, has so small a function in terms of the novel that it seems like padding. It has a labored effect, for it leans too heavily on a subject which is not further developed, and its very length makes the otherwise sensitive and perceptive Bertin seem strangely obtuse. The first part of the passage would have been enough to show Bertin's malaise at a passing evocation of the *déjà-vu*, but the expansion of the idea and the naïve questions that follow reveal the incongruity of this development in the structure of the novel. It is all the more incongruous in that it reveals Maupassant venturing timidly into an alien field and withdrawing hastily. The real action that follows in the novel takes place in Olivier Bertin's subconscious, his love for Annette grows without his being aware of it; but aside from this little essay on Proust before the fact, Maupassant treats the subconscious of Bertin as an area that is out of bounds. His subconscious ferment is generally observed from without, from Maupassant's favorite position of the external observer, but in any case the author never penetrates more deeply than the painter's own conscious reflections. Bertin soon finds that the source which has awakened his memory is Annette, whose voice is exactly that of her mother, and he wonders, "Comment n'avait-il pas remarqué plus vite cet étrange écho de la parole jadis si familière qui sortait à présent de ces lèvres nouvelles?"[22] It is a question which the reader may well have asked in the same wondering tone somewhat earlier.

20 See above, Chapter 5.
21 *Fort comme la mort* (Conard), pp. 121-122.
22 *ibid.,* pp. 123-124.

In the course of the aimless wanderings of the first half of the novel, the constant recurrence of the themes of senility, sterility, and solitude provide the only articulation. After his walk with Annette, Bertin feels that he is bursting with energy, that his vision is renewed, the world is full of subjects to paint. "Dire qu'il y a des moments où je ne trouve pas de sujets à peindre!" But when faced with a blank canvas, his energy drains away and the inspiration vanishes, "cette ardeur qui lui brûlait le sang tout à l'heure s'apaisa tout à coup. Il se sentit las, s'assit sur son divan et se mit à rêvasser."[23]

Sterility produces a meditation on solitude, particularly on the lack of a wife or a mistress to live with him, to be with him at all times, to provide company and comfort in his moments of discouragement. Bertin feels acutely what he has lost in this liaison, "ne pouvant rencontrer qu'avec des précautions de voleur celle qu'il aimait."[24] Part of his joy in his relation with Any came from the fact that it provided a partial fulfillment of his desire for a home: "Le désir de la famille, d'une maison animée, habitée, du repas en commun, des soirées où l'on cause sans fatigue avec des gens depuis longtemps connus, ce désir du contact, du coudoiement, de l'intimité qui sommeille en tout cœur humain, et que tout vieux garçon promène, de porte en porte, chez ses amis où il installe un peu de lui, ajoutait une force d'égoïsme à ses sentiments d'affection. Dans cette maison où il était aimé, gâté, où il trouvait tout, il pouvait encore reposer et dorloter sa solitude."[25] But as time goes on, it is apparent that this is but a makeshift solution. The feeling is intensified by the appearance of Annette on the scene, but it had long existed, and, Any, well aware that it represented a danger, was in constant fear lest he marry. Unable to paint, he lets himself go in contemplation of his solitude: "Il se releva, ne pouvant plus tenir en place, et se mit à marcher en songeant de nouveau que, malgré cette liaison dont son existence avait été remplie, il demeurait

[23] *ibid.*, p. 126.   [24] *ibid.*, p. 128.   [25] *ibid.*, pp. 90-91.

1 3 1

bien seul, toujours seul."[26] Words swirl and echo in Maupassant's sharply felt evocation of the cold loneliness of a bachelor's flat: "Il sentait sa maison vide, et désert son grand atelier; . . . son hôtel désert, immobile, silencieux, froid." The third chapter does introduce Annette into her rôle in the plot, but is mainly given over to the long cry of a lonely man. Aware of the nullity of his club, desiring company, a wife, a house, he feels a resurgence of tenderness for Any which is not passion but an urge to find a companion to dispel his loneliness.

The fourth and last chapter of Part I revolves entirely about an exhibition of paintings, the "Salon" of the year. Maupassant presents a large scene, the movements of the crowd, the comments of painters and critics, a scene which serves mainly to bring out again Bertin's uneasiness about his own work. Here he echoes a series of articles called "Au Salon" which he wrote for *Le XIXe Siècle* in April and May 1886. There is no direct cribbing of sentences or phrases from these articles, but he carries over into the novel the same notions he had expressed, though more blatantly and mockingly, in the articles. Maupassant's art criticism, if it can be called that, in *Le XIXe Siècle*, though violent and crude, is nevertheless colored by a generally good-natured attitude. In the novel this becomes more sombre, more deeply felt, a nihilistic pessimism, which tends to sweep all away, to deny every value; it is the artist sensing that he is coming to a dead end. In the midst of all the faithfully reported chit-chat of the spectators and artists, this note is struck again and again. Bertin is, first of all, dissatisfied with his own work exposed in the Salon. "Un malaise l'oppressait, une inquiétude sur son œuvre exposée, dont, malgré les félicitations empressées, il ne sentait pas le succès."[27] He is reassured when Any expresses her approval, but Maupassant intervenes directly with a comment: "Il oubliait, pour rassurer ses craintes, que depuis douze ans il lui reprochait justement d'admirer trop les mièvreries, les délicatesses élégantes, les sentiments exprimés,

[26] *ibid.*, p. 127.   [27] *ibid.*, pp. 145-146.

les nuances bâtardes de la mode, et jamais l'art, l'art seul, l'art dégagé des idées, des tendances et des préjugés mondains."[28]

Fort comme la mort, considered as a novel, gives the impression that Maupassant's powers were waning. His own subconscious awareness of this decline finds an echo in the utterly despairing words he puts into the mouth of Olivier Bertin. The painter, sensing his own sterility, sees no possibility of renewal for himself or for others or for Art. Looking at the paintings displayed in the Salon he sees only ". . . des échantillons enfin de tout ce qu'ont fait, de tout ce que font et de tout ce que feront les peintres jusqu'au dernier jour du monde."[29] The conversation of the artists themselves no longer has any meaning for him: ". . . on discutait, comme tous les ans, en soutenant ou en attaquant les mêmes idées, avec les mêmes arguments sur des œuvres à peu près pareilles"; and Bertin, normally an eager participant in such discussions is bored and weary, "sachant d'avance tout ce qu'on dirait sur ces antiques questions d'art dont il connaissait toutes les faces."[30]

Some of his malaise, without his realizing it, springs from an obscure jealousy of Annette and the Marquis de Farandal, her suitor; and he takes exception to "la tenue déplaisante du marquis auprès d'Annette." Any is aware that Bertin finds her daughter attractive, but is not displeased at this development. She makes a serious effort to grow slim like her daughter, and spends considerable time caring for her complexion. Though she enjoys the inevitable comparisons of mother and daughter, she makes sure that such comparisons are made in the flattering softness of artificial light. The result of all this is that Any and Annette begin to merge and become confused in Bertin's mind.

The stage is now set for the working out of the plot of the novel in Part II; Bertin begins by confusing the two women but eventually succeeds in separating them again in his mind,

[28] *ibid.,* p. 148.   [29] *ibid.,* p. 145.   [30] *ibid.,* p. 155.

which means he rejects the older Any and accepts the younger Annette as a reincarnation of her mother's youth. This transformation is brought about mainly by Any's inept and hysterical actions.

The second part of the novel, which moves more rapidly than the first, is less dominated by the fear of sterility, though this remains the secondary theme, and illustrates rather the creeping terror of old age. Maupassant, after considerable backing and filling, has at last got into his novel and is ready to work out his story; he has, in a sense, done what Bertin tries to do and fails; he throws off some of his dejection through creative work.

Part II opens with a series of letters between Any and Bertin, revealing an event with serious consequences. Prostrated with grief at the death of her mother, Any suffers a nervous breakdown. Broken, too, is her beauty, her face ravaged by her protracted and uncontrolled grief, and from this point on it is easier for Bertin to see in Annette rather than in her mother the image and idealized memory of his beloved. Maupassant has made all this abundantly clear indirectly and objectively through well-observed details. Yet, since he intends almost in spite of himself to write a psychological novel, he stops for a long analysis[31] of Any's growing awareness of her age and the devastation of her beauty caused by her mother's death. The analysis, unfortunately, adds nothing to what we know, for Maupassant explains ponderously what he has already skillfully suggested.

Bertin's awareness of his solitude is intensified by Any's absence. He is completely lost, unable to do anything, even take a walk, and he writes to her: "C'est extraordinaire comme je vous sens loin et comme vous me manquez. Jamais, même aux jours où j'étais jeune, vous ne m'avez été *tout*, comme en ce moment."[32] He is unable to paint, to create: "Mais, je n'ai plus rien dans l'esprit, rien dans l'œil, rien dans la main. Je ne suis plus un peintre! . . . Cet effort inutile vers

[31] *ibid.*, pp. 188-191.   [32] *ibid.*, p. 167.

le travail est exaspérant." He is fatigued, gone stale: "Vrai, je ne puis plus rien voir de neuf, et j'en souffre comme si je devenais aveugle. Qu'est-ce que cela? Fatigue de l'œil ou cerveau, épuisement de la faculté artiste ou courbature du nerf optique? Sait-on! il me semble que j'ai fini de découvrir le coin d'inexploré qu'il m'a été donné de visiter."[33] Bertin's lament on the loss of his "eye" suggests that Maupassant, who had so highly developed his visual acuity under Flaubert's guidance, is here speaking in part for himself, or at least out of himself. Some of Bertin's complaint expresses a complete nullification of Maupassant's prized faculty of seeing and describing a concierge or a coachman so individually that he was distinct from any other concierge or coachman anywhere; all this is gone: "Je n'aperçois plus que ce que tout le monde connaît; je fais ce que tous les mauvais peintres ont fait; je n'ai plus qu'une vision et qu'une observation de cuistre. Autrefois, il n'y a pas encore longtemps, le nombre des motifs nouveaux me paraissait illimité, et j'avais, pour les exprimer, une telle variété de moyens que l'embarras du choix me rendait hésitant. Or, voilà que, tout à coup, le monde des sujets entrevus s'est dépeuplé, mon investigation est devenue impuissante et stérile. Les gens qui passent n'ont plus de sens pour moi; je ne trouve plus en chaque être humain ce caractère et cette saveur que j'aimais tant discerner et rendre apparents."[34] There is left only one spark of interest or inspiration, which points out, perhaps too sharply, the direction he is taking, for he adds in his letter: "Je crois cependant que je pourrais faire un très joli portrait de votre fille. Est-ce parce qu'elle vous ressemble si fort, que je vous confonds dans ma pensée? Oui, peut-être."[35]

The cry of solitude is heard again and again, but here it is coupled with the expression of his staleness and sterility. "Oui, ma chère amie, je suis à l'âge où la vie de garçon devient intolérable, parce qu'il n'y a plus rien de nouveau pour moi, sous le soleil." He repeats in more pathetic tones his longing

[33] *ibid.*, p. 171.   [34] *ibid.*, pp. 171-172.   [35] *ibid.*, p. 172.

for a home and constant companionship, a community of interests, hopes and sorrows; he would eagerly give up his bachelor's freedom: "La liberté pour un vieux garçon comme moi, c'est le vide, le vide partout."[36] When Any's husband envies him his freedom, Bertin confides to him his melancholy and his isolation, so earnestly that the husband is moved to discover the advantages of marriage: "Quand il eut tout dit, récité jusqu'au bout la litanie de ses mélancolies, et raconté naïvement, poussé par le besoin de soulager son cœur, combien il eût désiré l'amour et le frôlement d'une femme installée à son côté, le comte, à son tour, convint que le mariage avait du bon."[37] The scene with the husband simply repeats, though mercifully in a condensed form, all that Bertin had expressed in his letters. Maupassant is plagued by his belief that he is writing a psychological novel, but again what he sets forth as analysis turns out to be merely repetition and summary.

The transfer of Bertin's affections is outlined step by step. He is struck by the appearance of Annette in mourning and her extraordinary resemblance to the portrait of Any, painted when she too was in mourning. He is in love with both mother and daughter, identifying them, considering them as one: "N'était-ce pas une seule femme que cette mère et cette fille si pareilles? et la fille ne semblait-elle pas venue sur la terre uniquement pour rajeunir son amour ancien pour la mère?"[38] But gradually he begins to separate them; "il confondait moins à présent la comtesse avec Annette, mais il confondait de plus en plus la fille avec le souvenir renaissant de ce qu'avait été la mère."[39] The change in Bertin is conveyed in somewhat ambiguous terms; it is described, though not shown directly, by the author, who uses a kind of indirect discourse that leaves us wondering to what extent Bertin himself is aware of what goes on, since Maupassant's manner gives the impression that he is not so much analyzing Bertin as reading his mind.

[36] *ibid.*, p. 174.　　[37] *ibid.*, p. 180.　　[38] *ibid.*, p. 206.　　[39] *ibid.*, p. 218.

The action moves swiftly toward a dramatic scene after Any's return from the country to the softer lights of Paris and the flattering ministrations of couturières and cosmeticians. More and more troubled, however, she calls in a doctor whose bedside manner is temporarily reassuring, and in an unaccustomed visit to a church she even invokes the aid of God to preserve her beauty. The crisis occurs when Bertin has Annette pose for him in his studio as the mother looks on. There is a fine economy in the scene; Bertin is obviously moved by the sight of Any: "il retrouvait soudain devant cette apparition, devant cette résurrection, dans ce même endroit, après douze ans, une irrésistible poussée d'émotion." Trembling he turns to the countess and murmurs "Dieu, qu'elle est belle." The scene and the novel reach a climax in the one sentence: "Mais il demeura stupéfait devant le visage livide et convulsé de Mme de Guilleroy."[40] What follows is a natural extension of that line. Any suffers a *crise de nerfs*, and hysterically insists that Annette not pose again. She sees the situation clearly now for the first time, but Bertin, though thoroughly upset, is still unaware of the true nature of the development that has taken place below the level of his conscious mind. He goes to see her, still puzzled, and she finally speaks plainly: "Prenez garde, mon ami, vous allez vous éprendre de ma fille."[41] They have it out in a curious scene which lacks vigor mainly because, though Any's words are quoted directly, Bertin's speeches are for the most part merely summarized. It gives the effect that weariness has set in again, and the author, having decided everything in advance, is simply getting done with it as rapidly as possible.

She has at least convinced him that he is confusing Any and Annette and that the feeling he has for Farandal is in fact jealousy. He indulges in a long self-analysis, which is reported without further comment by the author. Bertin explains to his own satisfaction that he has only a natural affection for Annette, but, once the matter has been brought into

40 *ibid.*, p. 242.   41 *ibid.*, p. 247.

the open he is even more acutely troubled, and ill-at-ease in his relations with the two women. He reflects: "Any est stupide de m'avoir dit ça. Elle va me faire penser à la petite à présent."[42] Bertin's jealousy of Farandal, who is now installed as Annette's fiancé, breaks out unmistakably. His obvious ill-temper provokes Any to another hysterical scene in which she insists that he admit he is in love with Annette. Reflecting on the scene afterward, he realizes that he does love Annette, that this is the only adequate explanation of his own recent conduct.

The situation has reached a complete impasse: Bertin recognizes his love for Annette and is terrified by it; Any makes frantic efforts to retain her beauty, but admits the battle is a losing one by smashing her mirror, which afforded her none of the assurance conveyed by Georges Duroy's mirror in *Bel-Ami*. Some resolution is obviously required, the intolerable situation can be eased only by the removal of Bertin; but Maupassant fumbles for a solution although he had found an adequate artistic answer to the similar problem in *Pierre et Jean*. One last dramatic scene foreshadows the necessary ending; it is a performance of Gounod's *Faust* attended by Any, Bertin, Annette, and Farandal. Here the painter feels the pull of the music, not the words, "les paroles banales du livret,"[43] and thinks he understands how Goethe conceived Faust, and even is able to see himself as Faust. Death alone is the solution for him: "il écoutait au fond de lui-même l'écho des lamentations de Faust; et le désir de la mort surgissait en lui, le désir d'en finir aussi avec ses chagrins, avec toute la misère de sa tendresse sans issue."[44] His indifference to the words of the songs is wiped out by a phrase that strikes deep within him: "Je veux un trésor qui les contient tous. Je veux la jeunesse," sung by the handsome tenor, Montrosé. Added to the impact of these words is his intense jealousy aroused by Annette's undisguised admiration for the singer; it is not merely a jealous rage but the anger felt by the creative artist toward

[42] *ibid.*, p. 265.   [43] *ibid.*, p. 321.   [44] *ibid.*, p. 322.

the mere interpreter, and in this case by the impotent creator for the successful interpreter. His violent condemnation includes not only Montrosé and his kind but the enthusiastic audience as well, and springs directly from Maupassant's own troubled soul: "Un artiste! Ils l'appelaient un artiste, un grand artiste! Et il avait du succès, ce pitre, interprète d'une pensée étrangère, comme jamais créateur n'en avait connu! Ah! c'était bien cela la justice et l'intelligence des gens du monde, de ces amateurs ignorants et prétentieux pour qui travaillent jusqu'à la mort les maîtres de l'art humain. Il les regardait applaudir, crier, s'extasier; et cette hostilité ancienne qui avait toujours fermenté au fond de son cœur orgueilleux et fier de parvenu s'exaspérait, devenait une rage furieuse contre ces imbéciles tout-puissants de par le seul droit de la naissance et de l'argent."[45]

One last blow awaits him, a blow which touches not his love but his art. It is a slighting reference in an article on some younger painters to "l'art démodé d'Olivier Bertin."[46] Nothing now remains but the off-stage catastrophe: news is brought to the Guilleroy family that the painter has been struck down by an omnibus and he dies in Any's arms, "apaisé soudain par l'Eternel Oubli."[47]

The ending has a peculiar irony when we recall Maupassant's remark in his essay on *Le Roman* of but a short time before: "Le nombre des gens qui meurent chaque jour par accident est considérable sur la terre. Mais pouvons-nous faire tomber une tuile sur la tête d'un personnage principal, ou le jeter sous les roues d'une voiture, au milieu d'un récit, sous prétexte qu'il faut faire la part de l'accident?"[48] To be sure, Bertin commits suicide, and dies not in the middle but at the end of the book; but there is something a little odd about the fact that Maupassant, who so readily reached back into his earlier works for material, this time, almost at the end of his

---

[45] *ibid.*, p. 331.   [46] *ibid.*, p. 337.   [47] *ibid.*, p. 372.
[48] *Pierre et Jean* (Conard), p. xv.

creative ability, reached back to find a solution which he had previously declared to be unjustifiable.

As a novel, *Fort comme la mort* suffers from a confusion of method: uncertain of the path to follow after *Pierre et Jean,* driven by those around him toward the psychologizing of high life à la Bourget, Maupassant was unwilling to cut loose completely from his own objective technique and combined the two, or rather, overlaid one on the other. Again and again in this novel, after having portrayed his characters through closely observed action and dialogue, he seems to remember that he is writing a psychological novel and goes back over the ground already covered and gives pages of analysis which add nothing. He insists on commenting on what has already been completely conveyed by his familiar methods. One cannot help feeling that with this subject he could have written a remarkable novel, the equal of *Pierre et Jean*, had he limited himself to his natural technique of understatement, suggestion, and objective but artistic presentation. The weakness, of course, is that the psychology is laid on, and contributes nothing more because his own particular tools were adequate to the task. Yet it is the desire to psychologize, the need to speak directly, which leads him to lay bare his own private concerns as he had never done before in his fiction in so desperate a way.

It has been frequently pointed out that the objective method has its limitations, that it cannot deal with complicated characters such as Proust's or Gide's. Yet the deliberately limited point of view often used by Dostoevsky has a powerful effect in a novel like *The Brothers Karamazov*, where the undeniable complexity of the characters is intensified and enriched by putting on the reader the burden of resolving apparently conflicting actions and speeches. Maupassant's people, however, even in *Fort comme la mort* are not especially complex or even exceptionally introspective; they are more than a little shallow. Maupassant lays out in his novel all the psychological equipment for plumbing the depths, but he soon gets tangled in it because he is not sure how to use it, and also because this deep-sea gear is not suited to the shoals over which he runs.

Fort comme la mort is yet another stage in Maupassant's long and conscious search for the proper novelistic technique, and represents an effort to push beyond what he had done in *Pierre et Jean*. But his extraordinary creative ability had already begun to run out, and haunted by his own fear of impotence, he was impelled to make that the essential subject of his book; the deep irony of the novel, for us, lies in our awareness that his failing powers were not adequate to the task of portraying that decline in a novel. Sterility of the artist and fear of old age are the main themes of this novel, which derives its force from them, although this force is diminished by his inability to integrate these themes into the structure of the whole. His last complete novel, *Notre Cœur*, springs from the same preoccupations, reflects even more surely his own anguish, for it deals not with the intransigence of old age but essentially with the effect of society on the artist, the forces which cause him to deviate from the narrow path of art.

NOTRE CŒUR (1890)

BY 1890 Maupassant could still summon up something of his old powerful creative ability, but very little of it distinguishes his last novel, *Notre Cœur*. Four stories published that year, *Mouche*, *Le Champ d'Oliviers*, *l'Inutile Beauté*, and *Qui Sait?*, can stand unchallenged among the best of his *contes* of any period, but the novel is a hollow piece that ranks among his worst efforts in the longer genre, only slightly above *Mont-Oriol*. *Notre Cœur* is the product of two motives: one, the conscious desire to pursue further what he believed to be the psychological technique; the other, of which he was probably not fully conscious, the need to express his own preoccupation, the decline of his creativity, the sense of having somehow wasted his talent. It is a thesis novel, an attempt to show a new kind of woman, the product of "modern" society, and the ravages her type causes among creative artists; but the direct elaboration of the thesis is flatly done, awkwardly handled, and, in fact, far less worthy of our attention than the less conscious, more indirectly revealed portrait of the artist.

The germ of the novel is found in a newspaper essay written in 1886, where he developed at some length, around a review of Loti's *Pêcheur d'Islande*, the idea which was to be the central thesis of *Notre Cœur*. The article bore the title "L'Amour dans les livres et dans la vie,"[1] and discussed the effect of literature on the attitude toward love and sentiment in various periods: "les tendances littéraires d'une époque déterminent presque toujours les tendances amoureuses." Contemporary literature has rid us of the tender, sentimental Larmartinian view of love, according to Maupassant, and he looks on Loti's book as an outmoded and false survival, criticizing his "méthode de poétisation continue," and preferring two books of a more documentary nature, both about India: a novel, *Le Baiser de Maïna*, by Robert de Bonnières, and a factual personal history, *L'Inde à fond de train* by the Comte de Pontevès-Sabran. At the end of the article, expounding the theme that will underlie his last novel, Maupassant attempts to deal with the sensibility of his own day, particularly with the development of the "modern" woman: "Et l'on peut dire, on peut affirmer que l'amour n'existe plus dans la jeune société française.

"La faculté d'exaltation, mère des tendresses passionnées et de tous les enthousiasmes, a disparu devant les envahissements de l'esprit d'analyse et de l'esprit scientifique. Et les femmes atteintes par contagion, plus frappées même que les hommes, s'agitent, souffrent d'un malaise singulier, d'une inquiétude harcelante, qui n'est au fond que l'impuissance d'aimer.

"Plus elles apartiennent au monde, plus elles ont l'esprit cultivé et les yeux ouverts sur la vie, plus se manifeste en elles cette maladie étrange et nouvelle. . . .

[1] "L'Amour dans les livres et dans la vie," *Gil Blas*, July 6, 1886.

"Nous voyons des femmes coquettes, ennuyées, irritées de ne rien sentir, qui s'abandonnent par ennui, par désœuvrement, par mollesse; d'autres qui restent sages uniquement par désillusion; d'autres qui tentent de se tromper, qui s'exaltent sur les souvenirs d'autrefois et balbutient sans les croire les paroles ardentes que disaient leurs mères."

From this conception grew the idea of a book on "modern" women, on the society coquette incapable of real love, an idea fortified no doubt by his own amorous adventures in salon society. The heroine of *Notre Cœur*, Michèle de Burne, is just such a woman, and an important scene in the novel is a discussion in her salon of the very subject Maupassant had treated earlier in his article. André Mariolle, chief sufferer at the hands of Madame de Burne, makes this contribution to the conversation, echoing Maupassant's essay: "Au temps où les romanciers et les poètes les exaltaient et les faisaient rêver, disait-il, elles cherchaient et croyaient trouver dans la vie l'équivalent de ce que leur cœur avait pressenti dans leurs lectures. Aujourd'hui, vous vous obstinez à supprimer toutes les apparences poétiques et séduisantes, pour ne montrer que les réalités désillusionnantes. Or, mon cher, plus d'amour dans les livres, plus d'amour dans la vie. Vous étiez des inventeurs d'idéal, elles croyaient à vos inventions. Vous n'êtes maintenant que des évocateurs de réalités précises et derrière vous elles se sont mises à croire à la vulgarité de tout."[2]

Built on this idea, the plot is of the simplest. André Mariolle, a rich and talented young man who has no profession or art that he practices seriously, meets and falls in love with a young widow, Michèle de Burne, whose salon is a gathering place for artists and men of distinction. She becomes his mistress, but it is soon apparent that love is subordinate to her social preoccupations. He disappears for a time, takes a less complicated mistress, an attractive waitress at an inn, and when Madame de Burne comes to fetch him back to Paris, he yields, but takes his newest acquisition with him. Gathered around Madame de

[2] *Notre Cœur* (Conard), pp. 145-146.

Burne are a collection of suitors, all apparently unsuccessful but all faithful to the attractions of the widow and her salon, and they include a number of artists: Lamarthe, a novelist; Massival, a musician; and for one occasion only Prédolé, a sculptor.

Notre Cœur was first published in the *Revue des Deux Mondes* in May and June 1890, a new departure for Maupassant, who had previously scorned the publication as a semi-official organ of the Academy. But he abandoned his scruples in his search for a wider audience, or the kind of public who would appreciate his new subject and manner. This was a miscalculation, he noted shortly after in a letter to his mother in July 1890: "La publication dans la *Revue* fait tout de même du tort à la vente. Les gros libraires de Paris me disent que parmi mes acheteurs fidèles 6 sur 10 l'ont lu dans la *Revue* et ne prennent pas le volume. Un autre inconvénient est celui-ci. Tout le bruit—et il a été énorme—se fait au moment de l'apparition dans la *Revue des Deux Mondes*; et on a fini d'en parler quand le volume arrive."[3] In spite of a slow start, sales of the book mounted and it had reached the fortieth edition by the end of the year.

I have already noted that Maupassant's best work of this period, his last surge of creative energy, is to be found in a few short stories, some of which bear an interesting relation to the novel that was in his mind at the time. Together the stories published in 1890 are a kind of summing-up, each of them representing a different facet of the author's talent. *Mouche* is a brilliantly written poetic evocation of the old days of boating on the Seine, full of nostalgia for a vigorous, rowdy, uncomplicated life. If *Mouche* looks backward, the story *Qui Sait?* seems to look forward, describing the hallucinations of a man who has voluntarily entered an asylum to escape them; it is of course in the same line as *Le Horla*, *La Peur*, and other terrifying stories. *LeChamp d'Oliviers*, one of his best stories, sharply drawn and dramatic, picks up

[3] LF, xv, 387.

once again that favorite theme of paternity tardily revealed, which was the subject of *Pierre et Jean* and so many short stories. *L'Inutile Beauté* is a successful attempt to deal with aristocratic society, and is directly connected to *Notre Cœur*, for the movement of this story, too, is based on the theme of the "modern" woman as a new type; she is revealed to her husband only in a brief moment at the end of their drama: "Alors, il sentit soudain, il sentit par une sorte d'intuition que cete être-là n'était plus seulement une femme destinée à perpétuer sa race, mais le produit bizarre et mystérieux de tous nos désirs compliqués, amassés en nous par les siècles, détournés de leur but primitif et divin, errant vers une beauté mystique, entrevue et insaisissable. Elles sont ainsi quelques-unes qui fleurissent uniquement pour nos rêves, parées de tout ce que la civilisation a mis de poésie, de luxe idéal, de coquetterie et de charme esthétique autour de la femme, cette statue de chair qui avive, autant que les fièvres sensuelles, d'immatériels appétits."[4] An even more specific echo is found in *Notre Cœur* of another story, *Le Rendez-vous*, of 1889 which develops a situation which reappears in the novel. It is a sketch of a woman, bored by the monotonous regularity of her frequent rendez-vous, for whom adultery has become mere drudgery. Michèle de Burne, on her way to one of her now regular meetings with Mariolle, goes through the same mental processes as her earlier prototype, though, unlike her, she does keep her appointment.

Of all the stories written about the time he was working on his last novel, one is particularly suggestive of what lies at the heart of the book and points up sharply the real subject, which is not the "modern" woman, but rather Maupassant's own bewilderment at the loss of his powers, his haunting preoccupation with old age and sterility. The story, *Le Masque*, published in the *Echo de Paris* on May 10, 1889 is a symbolic link between *Fort comme la mort* and *Notre Cœur*. It tells of an old man who, refusing to admit the loss of his youth, goes

4 *L'Inutile Beauté* (Conard), pp. 40-41; LF, VIII, 24.

to all the *bals costumés* wearing the elaborate mask of an elegant young man; there he dances with youthful ardor until he falls exhausted and is carried home to his wife. It is she who utters the phrase which, like so many of Maupassant's, has a symbolic significance for us, who with hindsight can view the double tragedy of his last years, his loss of extended creative power and his final madness. *Qui Sait?* is for us a dreadful premonition of his death in an asylum, but *Le Masque* suggests the even more tragic loss of the power he identified with youth, as the old woman says: "Voyez-vous, c'est le regret qui le conduit là et qui lui fait mettre une figure de carton sur la sienne. Oui, le regret de n'être plus ce qu'il a été, et puis de n'avoir plus ses succès!"[5]

Regret for what he had been, regret for what he might have been, both form the real substructure on which the novel is built, endowing it with an interest it cannot claim on novelistic grounds alone.

Notre Cœur is an unhappy last stage on the road of the *conteur* who so desperately sought the best method of expressing his genius in the novel form. Here he has cut loose from everything that was his own—objectivity, reticence, dramatic narrative—to flounder helplessly in a morass of his own making which he naïvely believed to be psychological analysis. Setting out to present Madame de Burne as a new feminine type, as the "modern" woman incapable of deep and simple love, he attempts to analyze her and those affected by her. But where *Fort comme la mort* was essentially objective in technique with an overlay of psychological discussion, *Notre Cœur* is all "psychological analysis," which appears as merely undramatic summarizing. The characters have little life or movement, the author keeps talking *about* them, but we rarely see them move, and the total effect is essentially non-novelistic. We are seldom in the novelistic present; the book is mainly a summary of events which occurred in the past filled out by generalized observations which bear no time relation to the

[5] "Le Masque," *L'Inutile Beauté* (Conard), p. 168; LF, viii, 86.

movement of the novel. The result is a formless mass of what seems like excerpts from essays, occasionally applied to one of the characters or uttered by one of them.

As a portrait of a modern Célimène, the novel is only trivial. It may be more useful for us to examine it rather as a portrait of the artist, of the artist at the moment of his decline. *As A Man Grows Older*, Joyce's title for Svevo's *Senilità*, would be an apt collective title for Maupassant's last two novels, and an ironic one when we recall the profound differences between the Norman and the Triestine, for the latter found in old age the very substance of his art.

No critic of *Notre Cœur* has failed to identify Maupassant with the novelist, Gaston de Lamarthe, and the passage describing Lamarthe has invariably been taken as a self-portrait of Maupassant: "Armé d'un œil qui cueillait les images, les attitudes, les gestes, avec une rapidité et une précision d'appareil photographique, et doué d'une pénétration, d'un sens de romancier naturel comme un flair de chien de chasse, il emmagasinait du matin au soir des renseignements professionnels. Avec ces deux sens très simples, une vision nette des formes et une intuition instinctive des dessous, il donnait à ses livres, où n'apparaissait aucune des intentions ordinaires des écrivains psychologues, mais qui avaient l'air de morceaux d'existence humaine arrachés à la réalité, la couleur, le ton, l'aspect, le mouvement de la vie même."[6] Yet, if we look at Lamarthe as he appears in the context of the novel and in his relations with Mariolle and others, there is something more than a simple identification of the author with his character. Lamarthe represents Maupassant as he saw himself and as he judged himself: the portrait is critical and ironical, a disillusioned comment on himself and his own career. Lamarthe is roughly analogous to Gide's Édouard or Joyce's Stephen Dedalus (in *Ulysses* as well as in *A Portrait of the Artist as a Young Man*), both of whom have the same curious relationship to their author: the character represents the author, but

[6] *Notre Cœur* (Conard), pp. 17-18.

the author is himself present as well, though off-stage; and his detached critical attitude toward his creation is clearly felt— even without the *Journal des Faux-Monnayeurs*. But the analogy ends there. *Notre Cœur* can in no other sense be compared to *Les Faux-Monnayeurs* or to *Ulysses*; it has nothing of the breadth and complexity of these two extraordinary novels. Maupassant simply was forced by his technique and his temperament to conceal his own feelings as much as possible, yet was not nearly so successful as he thought. He is often present in his work: his attitude toward his characters is evident, as in *Une Vie* and *Pierre et Jean*. So, when he creates a character out of his own substance, he still retains his privileged position as the author and is free to express indirectly his criticism or his sympathy.

In 1890, the year in which *Notre Cœur* was published, Maupassant wrote in a letter: "On me pense sans aucun doute un des hommes les plus indifférents du monde. Je suis sceptique, ce qui n'est pas la même chose, sceptique parce que j'ai les yeux clairs. Et mes yeux disent à mon cœur: Cache-toi, vieux, tu es grotesque, et il se cache."[7] This skepticism he turned on himself, when, weary and tormented by illness, he wrote what was to be his last novel. Lamarthe represents only a part of Maupassant; he is Maupassant as the latter saw himself as an artist, looking back at his career and at what he had accomplished. To get the full portrait of the author in *Notre Cœur* we must go beyond Lamarthe: André Mariolle, whose desperate love for Mme de Burne is the subject of the novel, expresses Maupassant as he saw himself as a man, separate from the artist; and, finally, the sculptor Prédolé symbolizes the artist uniquely devoted to his art, indifferent to the world of society which had absorbed Mariolle completely and had enfeebled Lamarthe. He is to Maupassant the unrealized ideal. Let us examine the novel from this point of view and attempt to see what significance these characters had for Maupassant.

[7] LF, xv, 384.

Lamarthe is introduced and described directly by the author in the passage quoted above. He is seen again a few pages later when we observe him through the eyes of Mme de Burne. She is vexed by his belief that women are incapable of discerning true excellence in art, a theme which Maupassant was fond of elaborating, and she adds: "Quand il a prononcé ce mot, l'art, il n'y a plus qu'à le mettre à la porte."[8] While this reveals something about Mme de Burne, there is more than a hint of irony on the part of Maupassant, irony directed at himself, an awareness of the position he held in the salons, a grim appreciation of the minor rôle assigned to what he held all-important. Yet Lamarthe is so involved in this milieu that his perspicacity deserts him, especially when he attempts to analyze Mme de Burne; he speaks "en homme intéressé, entraîné par son sujet, un peu dérouté aussi, ayant l'esprit plein d'observations vraies et de déductions fausses."[9] Lamarthe, in spite of his literary and social success, is to some extent a failure, for he has not fully realized his potentialities, he has deviated from the narrow path of art. His sincere admiration for Prédolé, the note of frank envy that is always present when he speaks of the sculptor, reveal his awareness of his own limitations. Maupassant presents him as a *raté*, echoing in the novel the indictment expressed in his correspondence: "Le monde fait des ratés de tous les savants, de tous les artistes, de toutes les intelligences qu'il accapare. Il fait avorter tout sentiment sincère par sa façon d'éparpiller le goût, la curiosité, le désir, le peu de flamme qui brûle en nous." Saddened, embittered, and ill, Maupassant is haunted by a sense of failure, of having wasted something in the futile diversions of the salons. As a novelist he sees what material this milieu offers him; "Ah! j'en vois des têtes, des types, des cœurs et des âmes! Quelle clinique pour un faiseur de livres!" But he recognizes his inability to deal with this wealth of material, and adds: "Le dégoût que m'inspire cette humanité me fait regretter plus encore de n'avoir pu devenir ce que j'aurais voulu être avant tout: un

---

[8] *Notre Cœur* (Conard), p. 28. [9] *ibid.*, p. 34.

satirique destructeur, un ironique féroce et comique, un Aristophane ou un Rabelais."[10]

The case of Massival, the musician, presents a parallel to that of Lamarthe, and suggests that the impotence that Maupassant felt is general and in some obscure way the fault of society. After two successful and highly promising works, "il avait subi cette espèce d'arrêt qui semble frapper la plupart des artistes contemporains comme une paralysie précoce. Ils ne vieillissent pas dans la gloire et le succès ainsi que leurs pères, mais paraissent menacés d'impuissance, à la fleur de l'âge. Lamarthe disait: 'Aujourd'hui il n'y a plus en France que des grands hommes avortés.' "[11]

In the manuscript of *Notre Cœur* is a passage which, although it was cut out before publication, furnishes a key to Maupassant's conception of the character of Lamarthe. It was intended to be part of the celebrated description of Lamarthe in the first chapter, and reads thus: "Après avoir affirmé pendant des années qu'il ne ferait jamais partie de l'Académie Française, il s'était présenté et avait été élu. Depuis lors il ne pardonnait cette défaillance de principe ni à lui-même ni à ses collègues de l'Institut. Il avait baptisé cet endroit sa Ratière parce que c'était, disait-il, une cage de Ratés, où on se laissait prendre au trébuchet, comme un Rat."[12] Maupassant removed this paragraph because he realized it would be interpreted as jealous vexation that he was not himself a member of the Academy. But it seems likely that this outburst represents a transposition of his thoughts: membership in the Academy is confirmation of social rather than literary success, and it is *le monde* which dissipates talent and makes *ratés*. In *Notre Cœur* Maupassant wrote not a social satire, but a self-portrait, drawn in a period of despair. It is easy enough to equate Lamarthe with Maupassant, but we are surely leaving out a good deal if we see the portrait as that of a confident naturalist

[10] LF, xv, 422.
[11] *Notre Cœur* (Conard), p. 19.
[12] *ibid.*, p. 302 (Variantes).

equipped with a photographic eye imperturbably recording his observations.

If we can see in Lamarthe a critical self-portrait of the artist, André Mariolle represents Maupassant the man, distinct from the artist. Having no art to cling to, Mariolle is completely engulfed by the society in which he moves, and is unable to achieve even the partial salvation of a Lamarthe. Maupassant made his chief character a dilettante, a dabbler in the arts rather than an artist, in order to show more forcefully the destructive power of this society. Mariolle is gifted; he has written travel sketches of considerable charm, has won praise for his sculpture, and is an excellent amateur violinist; but he has no drive, no incentive. If he had been poor, he might have become something, says Maupassant. He is the artist without an art, an "artiste infécond," and hence completely helpless when caught up in the meaningless movement of Michèle de Burne's life. His enslavement to her is enslavement to *le monde* which she symbolizes. Even more than Lamarthe he is a *raté*: "Il n'avait rien fait, rien réussi, rien obtenu, rien vaincu. Les arts l'ayant tenté, il ne trouva pas en lui le courage nécessaire pour se donner tout à fait à l'un d'eux, ni l'obstination persévérante qu'il faut pour y triompher. Aucun succès ne l'avait réjoui; aucun goût exalté pour une belle chose ne l'avait anobli et grandi. Son seul effort énergique pour conquérir un cœur de femme venait d'avorter comme le reste. Il n'était au fond qu'un raté."[13] In a letter to Madame de Burne he laments that if he were an artist he could at least have eased his torment by infusing it in a work of art, which was apparently just what Maupassant himself was trying to do. "Si j'étais un artiste et si mes émotions pouvaient être exprimées de manière à m'en soulager vous m'auriez peut-être donné du talent,"[14] writes Mariolle. This pious hope is contradicted, both for Mariolle and for Maupassant, by the very premise of the book, which establishes the destructive effect of *le monde* on the artist. Michèle de Burne is a nineteenth-century Célimène, but the

[13] *ibid.*, p. 205.   [14] *ibid.*, p. 224.

Alceste of the piece is neither Mariolle nor Lamarthe, but both—that is to say, Maupassant, who sought the *désert* on his yacht the *Bel-Ami* and never quite succeeded in finding it.

Mariolle suffers more than Lamarthe because, having no real interests beyond his love, he is completely absorbed by Mme de Burne and the forces of society. Lamarthe, who had gone through a crisis similar to Mariolle's, was able to free himself partially at least and fall back on his writing. He is, in a sense, dehumanized by literature, and his reactions are those of a man of letters. Maupassant shows a curious preoccupation throughout the book with "literature," meaning anything artificial, arbitrary, or false-sounding. Now Maupassant is himself, as Abel Hermant pointed out in an admirable essay, "l'écrivain français le plus dépouillé de littérature,"[15] who refused to admit that there should be any distinction between truth in literature and truth in life; but throughout *Notre Cœur* he seems worried lest he fall into the falseness of "literature." When Mariolle writes his first letter of adieu to Mme de Burne, she remarks: "Il écrit mieux que Lamarthe: ça ne sent pas le roman."[16] Yet Maupassant merely summarizes the letter, as if fearing it too might sound novelistic. Almost never does he show us a line of Mariolle's letters, but contents himself with stating that they are excellent, different from those of Lamarthe "qui marivaude littérairement."[17] Maupassant had noted the duality set up within himself by the fact that he was a writer; the novelist was constantly observing the man, analyzing his emotions even at the moment he was experiencing them. The man of letters, he wrote in 1882, "semble avoir deux âmes, l'une qui note, explique, commente chaque sensation de sa voisine, de l'âme naturelle, commune à tous les hommes." He is "acteur et spectateur de lui-même et des autres."[18] In *Notre Cœur* he reveals both parts of his nature:

[15] Abel Hermant, "Guy de Maupassant," *Essais de Critique*, Paris, Grasset, 1912, p. 384.
[16] *Notre Cœur* (Conard), p. 45.   [17] *ibid.*, p. 64.
[18] "L'Homme de lettres," *Gaulois*, November 6, 1882; used again in "La Femme de lettres," *Figaro*, July 3, 1884, and in *Sur l'eau* (Conard), pp. 81-83.

Mariolle, who feels and suffers; Lamarthe, who notes and observes, and is in turn observed and criticized by Maupassant. At this period of his life, when his physical and mental torment was greatest, Maupassant looks back with longing at the time when he was able to cut himself off from the world by erecting a wall of indifference. He had no illusions, he is resigned to the "néant de cette vie," as he says in a letter; but he is tortured by memories: "Je ne peux avoir aucune espérance, je le sais, mais je sens obscurément et sans cesse le mal de cette constatation et le regret de cet avortement. Et les attaches que j'ai dans la vie travaillent ma sensibilité qui est trop humaine, pas assez littéraire."[19] Lamarthe has escaped suffering by being "littéraire," by remaining the clinical observer of women: "De cette façon je ne serai jamais vraiment pincé par elles."[20] Mariolle is too human, uniquely so, and can never free himself.

Maupassant, the least "literary" of writers, is torn by inner contradictions in writing *Notre Cœur*: his suffering is real and human, but he is afraid to transpose it directly into his novel lest it sound merely "literary." He therefore puts something of himself into both Mariolle and Lamarthe, yet retains an objective critical attitude toward both, and, unwilling to betray himself, or perhaps uncertain of his own ability at the moment, summarizes letters, conversations, and actions, instead of giving the reader the material and letting him draw his own conclusions as he did in his earlier works. It is extraordinary how much of the action in *Notre Cœur* is skipped over, generalized, or summed up.

The sculptor Prédolé is a highly significant figure in this interpretation of the book, for he alone is saved, and his salvation is his singleness of purpose, his unswerving devotion to his art. He is not presented until near the end of the novel[21] and is the central figure in a rather long scene, discoursing eloquently but simply on his art, ignoring the coquetry of dress and manners of the elegant Mme de Burne and her

[19] LF, xv, 423.   [20] *Notre Cœur* (Conard), p. 145.
[21] *ibid.*, p. 209.

friends. When *Notre Cœur* appeared in 1890, Augustin Filon[22] thought that the scene itself was admirably done but detrimental to the action, a "merveilleux hors-d'œuvre." But the scene is essential to Maupassant's purpose. He was deeply concerned with his presentation of Prédolé, and in the original manuscript mentioned him in the first part of the book (p. 32, line 9), when Mariolle and Lamarthe leave Mme de Burne's together. In the manuscript they go to Prédolé's studio, but Maupassant changed this before publication and reserved the appearance of Prédolé until he could develop the scene most effectively. Prédolé was in his mind from the beginning of the book, and the scene is no hors-d'œuvre. Mme de Burne condemns herself with her judgment of Prédolé: "Assez intéressant, mais raseur,"[23] while Lamarthe points the moral: "Quel homme heureux, ce Prédolé. . . . Il n'aime qu'une chose, son art, ne pense qu'à cela, ne vit que pour cela, et cela emplit, console, égaye, fait heureuse et bonne existence . . . il ne s'inquiète guère des femmes, celui-là. . . ."[24] And as Lamarthe launches into a familiar condemnation of the "modern" woman, his speech is marked by an accent of envy—envy of Prédolé, envy of the man he might have been.

Nowhere, not even in *Sur l'eau* and in his articles, where he speaks directly for himself, has Maupassant revealed himself more poignantly than in *Notre Cœur*. But there is more to the matter than a simple identification of the author with the novelist in his story. Neither Lamarthe nor Mariolle is Maupassant, but each expresses a part of him, while Prédolé represents the unrealized ideal. He is separate from his characters, for his method of presenting them reveals a critical self-examining mind outside of them. He is objective only in the sense in which Abel Hermant applies the term to him; for, while Hermant sees Maupassant's personality in all of his works,

[22] Augustin Filon, "Courrier littéraire," *Revue bleue*, August 2, 1890, p. 134.
[23] *Notre Cœur* (Conard), p. 218.
[24] *ibid.*, p. 220.

"Il demeure entendu que Maupassant évite de se mettre en scène, à l'inverse des lyriques, dont l'œuvre n'est jamais qu'une confession franche ou déguisée; Maupassant est objectif; mais avec cela, comme il nous est impossible de concevoir l'objet indépendamment de notre sensibilité, nous sommes bien obligés de reconnaître que le plus objectif des artistes n'exprime encore en fin de compte que soi."[25] *Notre Cœur* is the least objective of his works, yet even here the artist transmutes his own reality into fiction, nourishing with his own substance the characters he has created, while remaining independent of them, critical of them—and of himself.

In an article called "Les Amateurs d'artistes" (later used in *Sur l'eau*), Maupassant wrote with some feeling about women who cultivate artists in order to display them proudly in their salons, and he warned that the novelist may take his revenge by putting them into his novels, saying: "Certes, il est aussi dangereux pour les gens du monde de choyer et d'attirer les romanciers, qu'il le serait pour un marchand de farine d'élever des rats dans son magasin. Et pourtant ils sont en faveur. Donc, quand une femme a jeté son dévolu sur l'écrivain qu'elle veut adopter, elle en fait le siège au moyen de compliments, d'attentions et de gâteries. . . ."[26] In Chekhov's play *The Seagull*, the actress Arkadina reads from *Sur l'eau* the same passage and, closing the book, remarks that nothing of the sort ever happens in Russia, for the woman who sets out to capture a writer usually falls in love with him herself first; and she cites her relations with Trigorin as an example. In his discussion of the play, Francis Fergusson writes: "In the context the irony of her remark is deep. . . . Chekhov with his subtle art of plotting has caught her in a situation, and at a brief moment of clarity and pause, when the falsity of her career is clear to all, even to herself."[27] The same deep irony under-

[25] Abel Hermant, *op. cit.*, p. 403.

[26] "Les Amateurs d'artistes," *Gil Blas*, June 30, 1885; *Sur l'eau* (Conard), p. 31.

[27] Francis Fergusson, *The Idea of a Theater*, Princeton University Press, 1949, pp. 164-165.

lies Maupassant's last two novels, particularly *Notre Cœur*, for here he takes as his subject the themes of artistic sterility, dissipation of talent, failure; yet not through the novelist's art but by the very inadequacies of the novels themselves is the essential falsity of the last years of his career made clear to all, perhaps even to himself.

11

CLOSING THE CIRCLE

FROM *Une Vie* to *Notre Cœur* Maupassant had been groping his way toward a valid technique in the novel, and these six published novels preserve the record of his struggle. He made two more efforts, but there was little time left to him. One of these he abandoned; the second, which promised much, was cut short by his final madness. Of these last attempts at the novel form we have only a few pages of manuscript, but enough to give us some idea of the goal he set for himself.

The first of these, called *L'Ame étrangère*, he worked on sporadically between July 1890 and February 1891, as far as the increasingly alarming state of his health would permit. The novel was to continue, in subject and technique, the pattern established in *Fort comme la mort* and *Notre Cœur*. It was to be again a study of "high-life," the world of the rich, the idle, the socially elect, set this time in Aix-les-Bains, where a cosmopolitan society gathered for the "cure" or merely for diversion. All that survives of the novel is the opening chapter and a part of the next. The central character is a wealthy young man, an idle amateur of art, much like André Mariolle of *Notre Cœur*, even to the extent of having the same last name as his prototype. Robert Mariolle, after finally breaking off a long and stormy liaison with a *demi-mondaine* who had frequently deceived him, has come to Aix simply to amuse himself and to shake off old habits. It is obvious that the novel will deal chiefly with his new affair with a Rumanian widow, Madame Mosska.

In early July 1890, Maupassant, with the idea of his novel already in mind, went to Aix to gather material for it. His valet François writes: "Mon maître nous installe dans un pavillon dépendant de l'Hôtel de l'Europe . . . M. de Maupassant prend ses repas à l'hôtel, puisqu'il n'est pas venu ici pour

écrire mais pour glaner des notes en vue de *L'Ame étrangère*."[1]
To reinforce his impressions Maupassant followed a Russian
princess around, observing her closely, and François struck up
an acquaintance with her valet de chambre to provide further
details about this exotic personality. After an excursion
through the countryside around Aix Maupassant remarked to
François: "Vous avez bien vu? Eh bien, tout cela, vous le
retrouverez dans mon roman. Aix et ses environs me donneront
un cadre merveilleux pour faire mouvoir mes personnages. Je
suis satisfait. C'était beau et je sens que tout ce que j'ai vu
est bien imprimé là." And he tapped his forehead as he made
this last remark. By the end of July he felt he had found all
the documentation he needed and had firmly settled his characters: "Je vois mon affaire très claire, absolument nette."[2] On
August 5 he told François that he had begun *L'Ame étrangère*
and that "il croyait que ce serait un bon roman, un peu sen-
sationnel peut-être."[3] Such is the external history of the novel,
and however thoroughly he had developed it in his mind, he
was able to get very little of it down on paper in the six months
or so that he was involved with it.

After Maupassant's death these fragments were published,
on November 15, 1894, in the *Revue de Paris*, and drew from
Paul Bourget some rather extravagant praise: ". . . ces vingt
pages suffisent pour donner au lecteur une sensation intense de
réalité, ce frisson de la vie qui fut le don incomparable du
malheureux et grand écrivain . . . le récit commencé en chef-
d'œuvre s'arrête brusquement."[4] Bourget believed that the
subject of *L'Ame étrangère* was to be the conflict between two
races, two people who love, but who are separated by barriers
of race and heredity, so that the same words have different
meaning for each; "un malentendu invincible sépare toujours
un homme et une femme venus de deux extrémités du monde

---

[1] François Tassart, *Souvenirs sur Guy de Maupassant*, Paris, Plon,
1911, p. 230.
[2] *ibid.*, p. 234.   [3] *ibid.*, p. 248.
[4] Paul Bourget, "Un Roman inachevé de Maupassant," *Nouvelles
Pages de critique et de doctrine*, Paris, Plon, 1922, p. 65; written in
November 1894.

historique et physiologique." And beneath this lies "la plainte profonde de la mésintelligence éternelle, cette torture que, même dans la plus complète et la plus tendre communion des cœurs, ces cœurs ne soient pas un seul cœur, qu'ils restent deux, irréparablement, immortellement."[5]

Bourget credits this one chapter with all the best qualities of Maupassant's other works, so that his essay is probably more valuable as a general appraisal of the art of his contemporary than as a balanced appreciation of the work in question. One is forced to conclude after reading what is left of *L'Ame étrangère* that Bourget's praise is exaggerated, and that he was influenced by the fact that the subject is one he himself would have found congenial. In any case this novel was to follow the same barren path Maupassant had been pursuing in his last two novels, a path toward which Bourget himself had helped to steer him. Whether or not the author of *L'Ame étrangère* recognized that he was heading into a dead end, something happened to make him drop the whole subject in February 1891 and concentrate on a new inspiration, a novel to be called *L'Angélus*.[6]

This last work of Maupassant, likewise unfinished, brings us full circle. The line begun with *Fort comme la mort* and projected through *Notre Cœur* to *L'Ame étrangère* ended abruptly; it could not be prolonged. He apparently felt the need to make a fresh start, to break with what he had been doing, and *L'Angélus* represents in effect a last desperate effort to go back to the beginning and start over. In the beginning was *Boule de Suif*, Normandy and the Franco-Prussian war; it was with these that he began his career, and it was with these same materials that he ended it. *L'Angélus* was to be a very different story from *Boule de Suif*, but it is set against the same background. What is most striking about his urge to return to his origins is the fact that the last novel begins at precisely the same moment as his first and most famous *nouvelle*. As *Boule de Suif* opens, "Les Prussiens allaient entrer

[5] *ibid.*, p. 73.   [6] François Tassart, *op. cit.*, p. 265.

dans Rouen, disait-on. . . . Les derniers soldats français venaient enfin de traverser la Seine pour gagner Pont-Audemer par Saint-Sever et Bourg-Achard. . . .”[7] And in the early pages of *L'Angélus* we read: “On dit que les Prussiens sont entrés à Rouen aujourd'hui. L'armée du général Briant s'est repliée sur le Havre par la rive gauche. Elle doit être maintenant à Pont-Audemer. Une flotte de chalands et de bâteaux à vapeur l'attend à Honfleur pour la transporter au Havre.”[8] A little later in *Boule de Suif* we witness the entrance of the Prussians into Rouen: “. . . une masse noire descendit de la côte Sainte-Catherine, tandis que deux autres flots envahisseurs apparaissaient par les routes de Darnetal et de Boisguillaume. Les avant-gardes des trois corps, juste au même moment, se joignirent sur la place de l'Hôtel-de-Ville. . . .”[9] In the first chapter of the novel the news of the same event is reported, in phrases that are strangely close to those we have just quoted: “Les trois corps de l'armée envahissante se sont présentés, juste au même moment, à trois portes de la cité, et les avant-gardes se sont rencontrés place de l'Hôtel-de-Ville, presqu'à la même minute.”[10] Consciously or unconsciously he was going back to the beginning of his glory in a vain desire to retrace the route with a surer knowledge of where the pitfalls lay. He had gone back to the beginning, but it was not granted him to pursue his course any farther; the circle was complete.

From February 1891 on, when he was composing his novel, references to it in his correspondence are coupled with serious complaints about his health: “. . . aussitôt que j'ai travaillé une demi-heure, les idées s'embrouillent et se troublent en même temps que la vue, et l'action même d'écrire m'est très difficile, les mouvements de la main obéissant mal à la Pensée.”[11] The novel was not going forward very rapidly, so he planned to go to Nice for a rest and to finish it there in the

[7] *Boule de Suif* (Conard), p. 5.
[8] *Œuvres posthumes II* (Conard), p. 202.
[9] *Boule de Suif* (Conard), p. 6.
[10] *Œuvres posthumes II* (Conard), p. 207.
[11] Maupassant, letter to his mother, February 22, 1891; LF, xv, 393.

spring. By the end of March he knew the novel would not be done before autumn, but in June, according to François, he talked of it with enthusiasm, having found in Avignon a model to furnish some aspects of his heroine's character and appearance.[12] Though the book was to be a short one,[13] his rapidly worsening condition prevented him from getting very far with it. Little more is heard of the work, except an oblique reference in October 1891, which reflects his obsession with the novelistic genre which gave him so much trouble: "Depuis que j'ai vu M. de Fleury, j'ai réfléchi et je me suis absolument décidé à ne plus faire de contes ni de nouvelles. C'est usé, fini, ridicule. J'en ai trop fait d'ailleurs. Je ne veux travailler qu'à mes romans, et ne pas distraire mon cerveau par des historiettes de la seule besogne qui me passionne. Je pourrai vous donner, lorsque l'œuvre à laquelle je travaille depuis deux ans sera terminée, quelques récits de voyages mouvementés."[14]

L'Angélus, consisting of a fairly long first chapter and some fragments of later scenes, was published in the *Revue de Paris* on April 1, 1895. The writing is vigorous and powerful, contrasting sharply with the anemic, half-hearted style of *L'Ame étrangère*. His return to the beginning did bring a renewal of strength, and infused his last effort with the same visual clarity and the contained, but deeply felt emotion that are found in *Boule de Suif*. The chapter we have tells of a woman, alone in her château except for some elderly servants and her small son, while her husband is with the now defeated French army. A detachment of the invaders, led by a gross and brutal officer, occupies her house, and, because she refuses to play the rôle of the vanquished and stands up to them with great force and dignity, she is obliged, on the eve of her confinement to leave her own house. From the later fragments it is clear that the son that is born that night, crippled from birth by the brutality of the Prussians, is to be the chief character of the novel. Mau-

12 François Tassart, *op. cit.*, pp. 270-271.
13 Maupassant, letter to his mother, March 1891; LF, xv, 394.
14 Maupassant, letter to Monsieur X . . . , October 1891; LF, xv, 408.

passing, one evening in August 1891 at Champel-les-Bains, outlined the novel to Auguste Dorchain and Doctor Cazalis (who was the poet Jean Lahor); the following is Dorchain's account of what the novelist told them: "Voici les cinquante premières pages de mon roman: *L'Angélus*. Depuis un an, je n'ai pu en écrire une seule autre. Si, dans trois mois, le livre n'est pas achevé, je me tue.... Je vais vous raconter *l'Angélus*." Dorchain went on: "Il le conta, avec une lucidité, une logique, une éloquence, une émotion extraordinaires. C'était, si ma mémoire est fidèle, l'histoire d'une femme à la veille d'être mère, et que son mari, soldat, a laissée seule dans le château de famille, pendant l'Année Terrible. Un soir d'hiver, le soir de Noël, les Prussiens envahissent la maison; sur une résistance ou une plainte, ils rélèguent la malheureuse dans une étable, après l'avoir maltraitée et même blessée; et, sur la paille, tandis qu'au loin sonnent les cloches de l'église, elle met au monde un fils, comme autrefois la Vierge Marie. Mais quel fils! un fils blessé, estropié à jamais par le coup qu'a reçu sa mère, un fils aux jambes brisées et qui jamais ne marchera, et qui jamais ne sera un homme pareil aux autres hommes. Les années passent sur lui, sans le guérir, mais en affinant son âme à l'amour infiniment tendre de sa mère, comme pour qu'il puisse souffrir encore davantage. Est-ce que, vraiment, Jésus est venu au monde pour y apporter de la joie? . . . Un jour, quand il est devenu un jeune homme, une jeune fille passe, et l'infirme l'adore, de son grand et tendre cœur, mais sans qu'il puisse le lui dire et sans qu'elle puisse l'aimer. C'est son frère aîné, son frère valide et beau qu'elle aime, et tous deux donnent au misérable le torturant spectacle de leur bonheur.

"—Va, mon chéri, lui disait la mère en le berçant comme un petit enfant, je t'emmènerai dans de beaux pays, je te lirai de beaux livres, tu oublieras, tu seras heureux aussi, je le veux, je le veux. . . .

"Et le pauvre enfant secouait la tête. Et l'on s'en allait; et partout, et toujours, il devait voir passer devant ses yeux, jusqu'au jour où il les fermerait à la lumière, ce fantôme charmant dont il n'approcherait jamais, jamais: une jeune fille."[15]

The fragments of a later chapter are closely related to the violent interpolation in *L'Inutile Beauté* on the nature of God as a blind creative force, "come un monstrueux organe créateur inconnu de nous, qui sème par l'espace des milliards de mondes, ainsi qu'un poisson unique pondrait des œufs dans la mer. Il crée parce que c'est sa fonction de Dieu; mais il est ignorant de ce qu'il fait, stupidement prolifique, inconscient des combinaisons de toutes sortes produites par ses germes éparpillés. La pensée humaine est un heureux petit accident des hasards de ses fécondations. . . ."[16] In *L'Angélus* this thought is extended; God is incomprehensible, says a priest in the novel: "Il est trop épandu et trop universel pour nos esprits. Le mot Dieu représente une conception et une explication quelconques, un refuge contre les doutes, un asile contre la peur, une consolation contre la mort, un remède contre l'égoïsme. C'est une formule de la phraséologie religieuse. Dieu, ce n'est pas un Dieu. Nous autres hommes, nous ne pouvons aimer qu'un Dieu tangible et visible. L'autre, l'inconnu, l'inconnaissable, l'immense je ne sais quoi ne nous ayant pas donné un sens pour le comprendre, par pitié pour nos cœurs nous envoya le Christ."[17] The figure of Christ was to play a major rôle in this story of a crippled child born in a stable on Christmas night, Christ as sent by God but deceived by God: "—Oui, reprit le prêtre, le Christ doit être aussi une victime de Dieu. Il en a reçu une fausse mission, celle de nous illusionner par une nouvelle religion. Mais le divin Envoyé l'a accomplie si belle, cette mission, si magnifique, si dévouée, si douloureuse, si inimaginablement grande et attendrissante, qu'il a pris pour nous la place de son Inspirateur."[18]

[15] Auguste Dorchain, "Notes de la semaine: Quelques Normands," *Les Annales politiques et littéraires*, June 3, 1900, p. 339; reprinted in A. Lumbroso, *Souvenirs sur Maupassant*, Rome, Bocca frères, 1905, pp. 63-64. For another recollection of the plan of *L'Angélus*, see Mme H. Lecomte du Nouy and Henri Amic, *En regardant passer la vie . . .*, Paris, Ollendorf, 1903, pp. 50-62.

[16] *L'Inutile Beauté* (Conard), p. 28; LF, xv, 17.

[17] *Œuvres posthumes II* (Conard), p. 229.

[18] *ibid.*, pp. 229-230.

L'Angélus, fragmentary as it is, gives far more the measure of what was lost when darkness closed in on the author than do his last two completed novels. Tautly and beautifully written, it reveals the essential qualities of Maupassant's best work, economy and superb visual impact, without any of the flabbiness found in the "society" novels. But he could not finish it; the idea of the whole was clear, but the body failed and then the mind, "les mouvements de la main obéissant mal à la Pensée."

CONCLUSION

THIS brings to an end the story of a search, the conscious search of a *conteur* who strove persistently after the form of the novel that would best serve his own mode of expression. He made various experiments, explored different paths, worried about the problem in essays and in letters, all the while writing remarkable short stories without any anxiety over theory or technique.

His essays and *chroniques*, which we have pulled out of the limbo of newspaper files, are intimately connected with his novels, are in fact inseparable from them. In the columns of the *Gaulois* and the *Gil Blas* he found a medium which forced him to expose his ideas directly, to clarify and make explicit many beliefs which were strongly felt but difficult of expression. These same columns allowed him as well to try out chapters and sketches from his work in progress, and, one is bound to believe, provided him with a backlog of material, written independently of any novelistic enterprise, which nevertheless could be made to fill out a scene or an incident in a later novel.

His course led him full circle, from *Boule de Suif* to *L'Angé-lus*, which was, we have seen, an effort to return to the beginning for a fresh start fortified by the wisdom of experience. He was, in 1891, perhaps on the threshold of a great new period of creative activity, for *L'Angélus* is a powerful fragment, but his time was up, darkness closed in, and he was not permitted to finish. Yet what remains is considerable. In the field of the short story he is still "a lion in the path," as Henry James said in 1888 and as Francis Steegmuller reaffirmed in a slightly different sense more recently; he is some one to be reckoned with. Here we have been concerned only with his accomplishments in the novel, where his position is more disputed. My own examination of the six novels, the two fragments, and their relation to his stories and essays, leads me to believe that

Maupassant wrote two very great novels, *Bel-Ami* and *Pierre et Jean*; an extremely interesting first effort, *Une Vie*; two painful human documents, *Fort comme la mort* and *Notre Cœur*, in which the surface of impassible objectivity is shattered by the author's inner conflicts, self-examination, and obsessions. *Mont-Oriol* can only be recorded as a flat failure.

Bel-Ami is, to my mind, a great social novel; it is certainly the novel of Maupassant in which the structure and functioning of society bulk largest, and in which that society is most roundly condemned. Maupassant railed at the foibles of his time in his articles, often with excessive bitterness or grim mockery, but in *Bel-Ami* he does not raise his voice, does not expostulate, but lets that society, at least the part of it that he was concerned with, write its own condemnation. *Bel-Ami* is a terribly unsentimental *Education sentimentale*; Duroy's rise in the world results from his discovery that education, experience, wisdom, and ability are neither necessary nor important; he is as good as the next man, only because the next man is not very good, and he has only to glance in his mirror to have this fact reaffirmed.

Bel-Ami was written at a point when Maupassant was sure of his technique, was confident that the objective principle was incontrovertible. He had learned much from *Une Vie* about the organization of the material of a novel and he was able to work with skill and assurance. When the method disintegrated in *Mont-Oriol* he was unable to use it again with confidence. He struck out in a new direction, and *Pierre et Jean* was the result, the expansion of a *nouvelle*; the tightly controlled framework of the shorter form was infused with a soberly objective presentation of the workings of a troubled mind. There is hardly a flaw in this story, dominated by the recurring symbol of the fog as *Bel-Ami* is articulated on the series of reflected images that are Duroy's real education. On these two works his fame as a novelist will rest; they represent his best efforts within the limitations he imposed on himself: *Bel-Ami* is the finest example of the objective technique he so earnestly advocated in the preface to *Pierre et Jean* and elsewhere; *Pierre et Jean* is an extension of the method, yet a development that did not take him into fields that were alien to him. Henry James, in 1888 after the publication of *Pierre et Jean*, wrote of Maupassant: "A writer is fortunate when his theory and his limitations so exactly correspond, when his curiosities may be appeased with such precision and promptitude."[1] But that was before *Fort comme la mort* and *Notre Cœur*, which were efforts to adapt himself to a theory not his own which he had frequently decried as invalid; here he went beyond his limitations, and, in fact, made clear very precisely what his limitations were. The last two novels survive, if they can survive at all, only as somber portraits of the artist as an old man.

Although of the six novels, only *Bel-Ami* and *Pierre et Jean* can be considered as fully successful achievements, these two must be ranked high in any assessment of the nineteenth-century novel in France. Maupassant, clearly, was not a born novelist, but a man of undeniable literary gifts for whom the longer genre represented a definite challenge. Consequently his novelistic production is limited and in no way comparable in scope to the vast structures of Balzac and Zola; nor was he ever able to create with the apparent ease and grace of Stendhal, for whom the novel was the most congenial of forms; and he lacked the freedom from financial concerns which permitted Flaubert to dedicate himself with such single-mindedness to the art of the novel. Maupassant, as a novelist, is not of the stature of these four giants, but his best novels can bear comparison with many examples of their creative genius. *Bel-Ami* lacks the rich texture of *L'Education sentimentale* but it strikes with a directness of impact that the more` highly wrought work of the master cannot achieve. Maupassant, like any novelist, has his own peculiar qualities, which makes comparisons difficult; *Pierre et Jean* is admirable for its tight construction, for its deeply etched portrait of a narrowly circum-

---

[1] Henry James, "Guy de Maupassant," *Fortnightly Review*, March 1, 1888, p. 372.

scribed group; but fluidity and looseness, which in *Lucien Leuwen* and the *Chartreuse* are positive elements in the charm and genius of Stendhal, produce, in the hands of Maupassant, only something as unhappy as *Mont-Oriol*.

His measure can best be taken if we reread the works of some of his once highly-regarded contemporaries like the Goncourts or Bourget. *Germinie Lacerteux*, hailed by Maupassant himself as a great work, is now almost unreadable, interesting only historically as an effort to broaden the range of the novel by treating seriously, though very self-consciously, the life of a servant. The elegant psychological analysis of *Cruelle Enigme* impresses the present-day reader as neither subtle nor profound, and like *Le Disciple*, which recorded the tensions of a particular moment, is definitely dated. *Pierre et Jean*, on the other hand, with its clarity of style and freedom from mannerisms, can still affect powerfully the sensibilities of the modern reader, and, like *Bel-Ami*, it is a record of spiritual and material adventures that are far from being outmoded. As a novelist, Maupassant is not "a lion in the path," as he is in the domain of the short story; nevertheless he remains a figure to be reckoned with, one whose novels must be taken into account, not only in any study of novelistic technique, but also in any true appraisal of our literary heritage from the nineteenth century.

APPENDIX

Three *chroniques* of Maupassant

(The three essays that follow are reprinted for the first time since their initial appearance in *Le Gaulois* and the *Gil Blas*.)

AUTOUR D'UN LIVRE

(*Le Gaulois,* October 4, 1881)

J'ai reçu de Bruxelles, l'autre jour, par la poste, un livre dont je connaissais l'histoire et dont la lecture m'a vivement surpris en me faisant beaucoup réfléchir. Cette œuvre contient, du reste, des qualités de premier ordre. Elle a pour titre: *Un Mâle,* et pour auteur M. Camille Lemonnier. C'est l'histoire très simple d'un braconnier, une espèce de bête humaine, de plante vivante grandie dans les bois, pleine de la sève des arbres, brute magnifique qui devient amoureuse de la fille d'un fermier. La fille se laisse toucher par l'emportement passionné de ce mâle terrible; elle cède. Puis la lassitude arrive; elle cherche à rompre; mais le braconnier veille sur son amour avec une fureur jalouse; il assomme un des prétendants de sa maîtresse, et finit lui-même par mourir dans un fourré, comme un gibier blessé, abattu par la balle d'un gendarme. La donnée est donc fort simple. C'est l'éternelle histoire, l'éternel drame de l'amour.

La grande valeur de cette œuvre vient de l'atmosphère champêtre et sauvage dans laquelle l'auteur a eu le talent d'envelopper ses personnages et son action. On est grisé par l'odeur des bois, par les bouillonnements des sèves, par toutes les fermentations des campagnes.

Mais il y a une chose surprenante dans l'histoire de ce roman, c'est qu'il a excité de grosses colères lorsqu'il parut en feuilleton. On l'a traité d'œuvre naturaliste ou réaliste remuant les passions basses et sales. Or, s'il y a une critique à adresser à ce livre (critique que je suis tenté de faire), c'est qu'il est, au contraire, conçu et exécuté comme un poème: il est épique. Les paysans y apparaissent grandis à l'égal de héros; les petits faits de l'existence campagnarde prennent des proportions d'épopée. Il est vu enfin à travers l'optique spéciale et grossissante des poètes, et non avec l'œil froid du romancier.

* * *

Alors comment s'est-il trouvé des gens pour qualifier de réaliste ce poème exalté des sèves frissonnantes! Comment une aussi monstrueuse confusion a-t-elle pu se produire!

Que s'est-il passé dans l'esprit du public? Une chose bien simple.—Le public n'attache pas aux mots "idéalisme" et "réalisme" le même sens que les romanciers. Une confusion persistante a lieu qui empêche les uns et les autres de se comprendre.

Pour le public, il n'y a en cette affaire aucune question d'*art* ni de *littérature*. Pour les artistes, les idéalistes sont des rêveurs dont le métier consiste à présenter la vie déformée par une espèce de prisme grossissant qu'on nomme la Poésie.

Les réalistes, au contraire, sont des gens qui ont la prétention de rendre la vie telle qu'elle est, dans sa vérité brutale.

Les deux écoles sont logiques, bien qu'à mon sens le véritable romancier ne doive être ni idéaliste ni réaliste de propos délibéré. Ou plutôt il a le devoir d'être l'un et l'autre.

Il me semble clair comme le soleil que son unique prétention doit être d'exprimer la vie telle qu'elle apparaît à ses yeux d'artiste, sans parti pris d'école ni pactisations d'aucune sorte. Il sent avec le tempérament spécial que la nature lui a donné! Qu'il exprime donc avec toute l'habileté, tout l'art, toute la conscience dont il est capable; qu'il fasse de son mieux, enfin. Que peut-on exiger de plus?

Avons-nous d'autres modèles que la vie? Non. Possédons-nous les moyens de connaître autre chose que ce qui est? Non. Alors quoi? aurions-nous donc la prétention de représenter ce qui existe, mieux que la nature ne l'a fait? De corriger la création? Cet orgueil serait gigantesque! Et voilà pourtant ce que le public ose demander! Art, littérature, style, conscience d'écrivain, il s'en moque: par littérature idéaliste il entend uniquement de la littérature *invraisemblable, sympathique et consolante.*

Toute cette grosse question littéraire se borne là, à mon avis. Rien de plus. Donc que l'auteur, l'action, les personnages soient *sympathiques* au lecteur: qu'on sente même que l'auteur, lui aussi a de la *sympathie* pour ses bonshommes. Enfin de la sympathie dans le titre, de la sympathie entre les lignes, de la sympathie partout. Tarte à la crême! Vous serez, grâce à cette simple recette, un idéaliste.

Le lecteur veut être attendri; il consent à être remué doucement; il ne se refuse pas au larmoiement, à la petite émotion bourgeoise. Tout cela ne sort point du sympathique.

Mais, si un écrivain de grande race, âpre, sincère et désabusé, planant au-dessus de toutes les rengaines sentimentales, de toutes les fausses poésies, de toutes les illusions intéressées où se berce la pauvre humanité, saisit le lecteur tranquille et le traîne, éperdu, à travers la vie telle qu'elle est, empoignante, sinistre, empestée d'infamies, tramée d'égoïsme, semée de malheurs, sans joies durables, et aboutissant fatalement à la mort toujours menaçante, à cette condamnation de tous nos espoirs que nous nous efforçons, par lâcheté, de ne pas croire sans appel; s'il montre à chacun son image sans la farder, sans l'embellir; chacun alors se fâche à la façon des enfants pris en flagrant délit, et crie: "Ce n'est pas moi, ce n'est pas moi! Ce n'est pas vrai, ce n'est pas vrai!"

Les uns ajoutent: "Eh bien! si la vie est si triste, je veux être *consolé*, et non pas désespéré; je veux qu'on voile mes misères, qu'on me donne des illusions, qu'on me trompe enfin."

Cela veut dire: "Je sais bien que je ne suis guère bon, guère honnête, guère vertueux; que les autres ne le sont pas davantage; mais faites-moi croire que je suis parfait au milieu de voisins irréprochables!—Quand je reviens de mon cabinet d'affaires, où j'ai le plus possible filouté mes clients; quand je reviens de la Bourse où j'ai tâché de ruiner mes confrères pour m'enrichir à leurs dépens, où j'ai joué à la hausse, à la baisse afin de tromper le public, de faire vendre ou acheter les naïfs; quand je reviens de mon magasin où j'ai tenté de réaliser beaucoup de gains, même exagérés et illicites; quand je reviens de chez ma maîtresse pour laquelle je ruine ma femme légitime, je veux être consolé de mon improbité, de mes subterfuges inavouables, du sentiment intime de mes pactisations avec ma conscience, de mon infidélité, de mes faiblesses, etc., par la lecture saine d'un livre honnête où tous les commerçants seront irréprochables, les financiers probes, les maris fidèles, etc. Je veux enfin sentir mon âme purifiée par le spectacle d'un monde idéal, par le reflet trompeur d'une existence de convention!

*   *   *

Alors qu'arrive-t-il? Des écrivains de talent, des romanciers fort respectables répondent à ce goût du lecteur pour la littérature sympathique et consolante; et ils créent une humanité d'étagère, en sucre colorié, qui fait pâmer les femmes du monde dans leurs boudoirs.

C'est toujours la jeune fille pauvre qu'épouse un jeune ingénieur riche et plein d'avenir; des cousins qui s'aiment et se marient, ou bien un jeune homme ruiné que choisit une riche héritière, et cela se passe avec des surprises, des héritages inattendus pour équilibrer les situations, et des aventures dramatiquement attendrissantes dans le parc d'un vieux château breton. Il y a la scène de la tour, la scène de la chasse, la scène du duel et la scène de l'aïeule invariablement. Mais où triomphe le romancier mondain, c'est quand il touche au vice; Oh! le vice aimable, ganté, parfumé comme il faut! Comme les femmes l'aiment, ce grand seigneur criminel, blasé, sceptique et charmant! Et comme le milieu où se déroule l'action est choisi avec goût! Quel monde d'élite, dont toutes les pensées semblent des poésies et toutes les attitudes des poses de gravures de modes! Tarte à la crême!

De cette littérature "sirop" à l'usage des *dames,* on tombe bien vite dans la littérature mélasse à l'usage des petites bourgeoises; et de la littérature mélasse on dégringole dans la littérature tord-boyaux (pardon!) à l'usage des portières. Lisez plutôt les romans des petits journaux.

Voilà à quoi aboutissent les acquiescements au goût du public.

* * *

Employons enfin les grands mots, qui sont les mots justes; cette vieille querelle littéraire n'est, au fond, que la querelle de l'hypocrisie contre la sincérité. L'art n'a rien à y voir.

Et voilà notre grande plaie toujours purulente: l'hypocrisie. Nous sommes hypocrites dans les moelles, comme on est scrofuleux. Toute notre vie, toute notre morale, tous nos sentiments, tous nos principes sont hypocrites; et nous le sommes inconsciemment, sans le savoir, comme M. Jourdain était prosateur, cela s'appelle: l'art de sauver les apparences!

C'est tellement passé dans notre sang que ce phénomène monstrueux a lieu:—tout ce qui n'est plus hypocrite nous blesse comme un outrage à notre honnêteté de parade, à nos conventions mondaines, à nos usages de fausses paroles, de fausses protestations, de faux visages.

Oh! si l'on découvrait les dessous de la vie! si l'on ouvrait les consciences des hommes qui crient à l'immoralité! les alcôves des femmes qui s'évanouissent d'un mot un peu vif! Oh! Les bonnes pudeurs qu'ont celles-ci! Oh! Les belles indignations qu'ont ceuxlà! Quelle amusante colère de singes à qui l'on présente une glace!

* * *

N'ai-je pas entendu un homme connu et respecté dire, au milieu d'un cercle d'auditeurs: "Non, certainement, je ne crois pas; la foi n'est plus faite pour les hommes; Mais je pratique par devoir . . . quand ce ne serait que pour *notre monde.*" Et il ne songeait guère, en vérité, à l'abîme d'hypocrisie que contenait cet aveu.

Et toutes ces gens veulent, à leur image, une littérature hypocrite.

Oui, ces romans parfumés, ces mariages d'amour sans discussions de dot, ces dévouements sans récompenses, ces services tout désintéressés, cela n'est, en réalité, que de l'hypocrisie commandée à l'écrivain par le public. Tout le monde le sait: les lecteurs ne l'ignorent point; et les auteurs le savent si bien, qu'on voit à tout moment les plus honorables faire des concessions à ce besoin de fausseté, et introduire en des œuvres vraiment belles, artistiques et viriles, des épisodes attendrissants, à la manière anglaise, afin qu'on pardonne le reste à la faveur de ce tour de passe-passe.

Et le public se délecte à la lecture des aventures invraisemblables de fantoches niaisement parfaits, toujours les mêmes; et, dans sa joie, il déclare le livre "bien écrit," ce qui est, en ce cas, la pire insulte que la plupart des lecteurs puissent adresser à l'écrivain.

* * *

N'avons-nous pas inventé cet odieux adage: "Toute vérité n'est pas bonne à dire"? Nous l'appliquons à la littérature. Alors il faut mentir?—Vous répondrez: "Non! se taire."—Ce qui est encore mentir par le silence. Mais quand il s'agit d'un écrivain, il n'y a pas de milieu: il faut qu'il dise ce qu'il croit être la vérité ou qu'il mente.

Donc, en résumé, les querelles littéraires se bornent à ceci: lutte de l'hypocrisie humaine contre la sincérité du miroir, ou exaspération du lecteur contre le tempérament particulier de l'écrivain.

En général, nos vices ou nos défauts préférés sont ceux dont l'image nous blesse le plus, vérité constatée par cet autre adage: "On ne parle pas de corde dans la maison d'un pendu."

Je pourrais citer beaucoup d'exemples. Je m'en abstiendrai. Je reviens au livre de M. Camille Lemonnier.

J'ai dit que ce livre était un poème. Tout se passe, en effet, dans une atmosphère poétique très sensible et très puissante. Les arbres deviennent des espèces d'êtres; la forêt semble une sorte de monde animé; les sèves parlent et chantent; la chasse acharnée du braconnier est un symbole; il grandit comme une de ces créations quasi-fantastiques de Victor Hugo. Ce sont des luttes d'idées, de puissances animales, de créatures éternelles dans ce bois qui est plus vaste que la création même, et non les simples embuscades d'un petit paysan qui guette un lapin.

Alors comment a-t-on qualifié ce roman de réaliste?

1 7 5

Uniquement parce qu'on y sent un peu la bête humaine au milieu des senteurs forestières.

L'amour simple de ces deux êtres simples se déroule d'une façon normale, passe de l'exaltation à la fatigue chez l'un, tandis qu'il demeure toujours ardent chez l'autre, ainsi que cela a lieu dans la plupart des créatures. La vie est grossie, grandie, étendue, mais non fardée. C'est un chant, soit; mais il dit tout, ce chant; les paysans deviennent épiques, mais restent vraisemblables cependent; il n'ont point de morale à la Florian, ni de tendresses champêtres à la Deshoulières. Les personnages, enfin, ne sont ni *sympathiques* ni *consolants,* ainsi que l'entend le bon public.

Guy de Maupassant

ROMANS

(*Gil Blas,* April 26, 1882)

En tête de son nouveau volume intitulé *"Quatre petits romans,"* notre confrère Jean Richepin a placé une intéressante préface que les lecteurs de *Gil Blas* connaissent déjà.

Cette préface est une sorte d'analyse du livre, analyse faite sur un ton plaisant de débiteur de boniment.

Elle renferme beaucoup de choses très justes à mon gré; mais elle contient aussi la phrase suivante: "La belle malice de m'inventorier un appartement avec une minutie d'huissier. Le puissant effort de me noter comment M. Chose a le nez tordu, comment Mme Machin a la nuque tournée, comment des gens quelconques gesticulent, crachent, mangent, et s'acquittent de toutes leurs fonctions ordinaires!"

Et bien, cette phrase m'inquiète. Elle contient en résumé toutes les critiques adressées aux écoles dites réalistes, naturalistes, etc., qu'on peut, je crois, comprendre en bloc sous cette dénomination: "Ecoles de la vraisemblance."

Oh! je ne nie point qu'on ait souvent abusé de la description à outrance; je ne conteste pas qu'on ait fait souvent le principal de l'accessoire; je ne mets pas en doute que la psychologie soit la chose essentielle des romans vivants, mais je crois que retrancher la description de ces ouvrages, ce serait en supprimer l'indispensable mise en scène, en détruire la vraisemblance palpable, enlever tout le relief des personnages, leur ôter leur physionomie caractéristique, et négliger volontairement de leur donner le fameux coup de pouce artistique. Ce serait, en un mot, supprimer tout le travail de l'artiste pour ne laisser subsister que la besogne du psychologue.

Dans tout roman de grande valeur il existe une chose mystérieusement puissante: *l'atmosphère* spéciale, indispensable à ce livre. Créer l'atmosphère d'un roman, faire sentir le milieu où s'agitèrent les êtres, c'est rendre possible la vie du livre. Voilà où doit se borner l'art descriptif; mais sans cela rien ne vaut.

Voyez avec quel soin Dickens sait indiquer les lieux où s'accomplit l'action et il fait plus que les indiquer, il les montre, les rend familiers, rendant ainsi plus vraisemblables, nécessaires même les péripéties du drame qui, exposé en un autre cadre, perdrait son relief et son émotion.

Quand il nous présente un personnage il le décrit jusque dans ses tics, dans les moindres habitudes de son corps, dans ces mouvements ordinaires; et il insiste, il se répète.

J'ai cité Dickens, parce qu'il est aujourd'hui un maître incontesté, qu'il n'est pas Français, et que ce romancier a poussé aussi loin que possible l'art de donner une vie extérieure à ses figures, de les rendre palpables comme des êtres rencontrés, en poussant jusqu'à l'exagération ce besoin du détail physique.

La partie psychologique du roman, qui est assurément la plus importante, n'apparaît puissamment que grâce à la partie descriptive. Le drame intime d'une âme ne me tordra le cœur que si je vois bien nettement la figure derrière laquelle cette âme est cachée.

Il me semble qu'on pourrait classer les romans en deux catégories bien distinctes: ceux qui sont nets et ceux qui sont vagues. Les premiers sont les romans bien mis en scène, les seconds les romans expliqués simplement par la psychologie. Quelque extrême que soit le mérite de ces derniers, ils restent toujours confus pour moi, et lourds, comme indigestes et indistincts. Ils ont leur type dans les remarquables œuvres psychologiques de Stendhal dont la valeur n'apparaît que par la réflexion, dont les qualités semblent cachées au lieu de sauter aux yeux, d'être lumineuses, colorées, mises en place par la main d'un *artiste*.

Les dedans des personnages ont besoin d'être commentés par leurs gestes.

Les faits ne sont-ils pas les traductions immédiates des sentiments et des volontés? Expliquer l'âme par l'inflexible logique des actions n'est-il pas plus difficile que de dire:—M. X. . . . pensait ceci, puis cela, faisait cette réflexion, puis cette autre, etc., etc.? Décrire le milieu où se passera l'aventure, d'une façon si nette que cette aventure y vive comme en son cadre naturel; montrer les personnages si puissamment que tout leurs dessous soient devinés rien qu'à les voir; les faire agir de telle sorte qu'on dévoile au lecteur par les actes seulement tout le mécanisme de leurs intentions, sans entreprendre en eux un voyage géographique avec la carte des désirs et des sentiments, ne serait-ce pas là faire du vrai roman, dans la plus stricte et, en même temps, la plus grande acception du mot?

Je vais plus loin. Je considère que le romancier n'a jamais le droit de qualifier un personnage, de déterminer son caractère par des motifs explicatifs. Il doit me le montrer tel qu'il est et non me le dire. Je n'ai pas besoin de détails psychologiques. Je veux des faits, rien que des faits, et je tirerais des conclusions tout seul.

Quand on me dit: "Raoul était un misérable," je ne m'émeus point, mais je tressaille si je vois ce Raoul se conduire comme un misérable.

Chez le romancier, le philosophe doit être voilé.

Le romancier ne doit pas plaider, ni bavarder, ni expliquer. Les faits et les personnages seuls doivent parler. Et le romancier n'a pas à conclure; cela appartient au lecteur.

Cette question d'art, très confuse en beaucoup d'esprits, donnerait peut-être l'explication de bien des haines littéraires. Il est des gens qui ne peuvent comprendre que si on leur dit: "La pauvre femme était bien malheureuse," ceux-là ne pénétreront jamais les grands artistes dont la mystérieuse puissance est tout intentionnelle, et sobre de commentaires. L'œuvre porte leur indéniable marque par sa matière et sa contexture; mais jamais on ne voit surgir leur opinion, ni leurs desseins profonds s'expliquer par des raisonnements. Et quand ils décrivent, on dirait que les faits, les objets, les paysages se dressent, parlent, et se racontent eux-mêmes; car il faut une géniale et tout originale impersonnalité pour être un romancier vraiment personnel et grand.

*　　*　　*

Laissons cette question qui demanderait à elle seule un volume de développements. Je me suis laissé prendre par une phrase au lieu de parler uniquement, comme je le voulais faire, du très remarquable volume de Jean Richepin.

La première œuvre, *Sœur Doctrouvé*, est la simple et poignante histoire d'une pauvre fille de noble famille qui se sacrifie à son nom, laisse à son frère sa part d'héritage, et entre au cloître à l'heure du premier frisson des sens. Faite pour l'amour, elle devient bientôt une sorte d'extatique, d'exaltée volontaire, sauvagement religieuse; mais voilà qu'elle apprend soudain le mariage de ce frère chéri avec la fille, deux fois millionaire, d'un banquier juif; et tout s'écroule en elle, tout, jusqu'à sa croyance en Dieu; et elle meurt désespérée, victime de son héroïque et inutile sacrifice.

Sobre et puissante, cette nouvelle fait froid au cœur dans sa vérité nue.

Le second récit, *M. Destrémeaux*, est la curieuse histoire d'un pauvre clown enrichi qui devient amoureux d'une jeune fille, et, ruiné soudain à la veille du mariage, s'éloigne en demandant trois ans pour refaire sa fortune détruite.

Il réussit. Mais, aveuglé par l'amour, il n'avait point révélé au père de sa fiancée l'humiliante profession d'où venait son argent.

Alors, au moment de s'emparer du bonheur promis, il se confesse dans une longue et fort belle lettre, pleine d'orgueil et d'humilité, mais la famille indignée, le repousse.

Puis, un soir, comme la jeune fille, maintenant mariée, assistait aux divertissements du cirque, elle le reconnaît au moment où il va exécuter un saut vertigineux. Elle pousse un cri; il la voit, jette un baiser de son coté et, s'élançant dans le vide, vient se briser la tête à ses pieds.

J'aime moins le troisième conte: "Une Histoire de l'autre monde." Mais, j'ai ce défaut, car ce doit être un défaut, d'être rebelle aux extraordinaires aventures qui me laissent le seul étonnement qu'on ait pu imaginer des choses aussi invraisemblables.

Le volume se termine par un remarquable roman historique, qui est vrai dans le fond, bien que surprenant, car les personnages s'appellent les Borgia.

C'est le récit des débuts du fameux César Borgia, ce fils de pape qui, amant de sa sœur Lucrèce, fut le rival de son père, et l'assassin de son frère, et bien autre chose encore.

Cette épouvantable histoire, racontée sur un ton tranquille d'historien et de romancier qui regarde avec intérêt ces êtres singuliers, prend une intensité naturelle dans les faits mêmes.

Et c'est là, à mon humble avis, le plus excellent morceau du livre nouveau de Jean Richepin.

MAUFRIGNEUSE

LES SUBTILS

(Gil Blas, June 3, 1884)

Autant d'hommes, autant de manières de comprendre et de regarder la vie.

Les uns ne font que voir, à la façon des animaux. Les faits, les choses, les visages, les événements semblent ne se réfléter que dans leurs yeux, sans produire de répercussions dans l'intelligence, sans éveiller cette suite infinie de raisonnements, d'idées enchaînées, de réflexions, de déductions qui se prolongent indéfiniment comme les vibrations d'un son, ou les ondes dans l'eau où vient de tomber une pierre.

Les autres, au contraire, s'acharnent à pénétrer toujours le mystérieux mécanisme des motifs et des déterminations.

Quand une fois l'esprit se met à chercher le secret des causes, il s'enfonce, il s'égare, se perd souvent dans l'obscur et inexplicable labyrinthe des phénomènes psychologiques et physiologiques.

Depuis tant de siècles que le monde existe et qu'on l'observe, c'est à peine si les esprits les plus pénétrants ont pu saisir quelques-uns des secrets cachés dans l'homme et autour de l'homme. Ceux qui sont autour de nous, d'ailleurs, nous échapperont toujours en grande partie, car, ainsi que l'a dit Gustave Flaubert dans *Bouvard et Pécuchet*: "La science est faite suivant les données fournies par un coin de l'étendue. Peut-être ne convient-elle pas à tout le reste qu'on ignore, qui est beaucoup plus grand et qu'on ne peut découvrir."

Mais la recherche des seuls phénomènes psychologiques a préoccupé de tous temps les chercheurs. Jadis les philosophes avaient le monopole de ces études, qu'ils exposaient en des livres graves. Aujourd'hui, ce sont surtout les romanciers observateurs qui s'efforcent de pénétrer et d'expliquer l'obscur travail des volontés, le profond mystère des réflexions inconscientes, les déterminants tantôt plus instinctifs que raisonnés, et tantôt plus raisonnés qu'instinctifs; d'indiquer la limite insaisissable où le vouloir réfléchi se mêle, pour ainsi dire, à une sorte de vouloir matériel sensuel, à un vouloir animal; de noter les actions de l'un sur l'autre, etc. Un des hommes dont je vais m'occuper tout à l'heure, M. Paul Bourget, dit à la première page de sa remarquable nouvelle, *l'Irréparable*: "Par dessous l'existence intellectuelle et sentimentale dont nous avons conscience, et dont nous endossons la responsabilité probablement illusoire, tout un domaine s'étend, obscur et changeant, qui est celui de notre vie inconsciente."

C'est ce domaine mystérieux qu'explorent aujourd'hui les romanciers avec des méthodes très différentes.

Les uns, qui sont purement des *objectifs*, au lieu de mettre au jour la psychologie des personnages en des dissertations explicatives, la font simplement apparaître par leurs actes. Les dedans se trouvent ainsi dévoilés par les dehors, sans aucune argumentation psychologique.

Les autres, comme M. Paul Bourget, font pour ainsi dire la géographie morale des gens qu'ils présentent au lecteur et ils entrent jusqu'au profond de leur âme pour dévoiler les mobiles de leurs actions. On pourrait appeler ceux-ci des métaphysiciens, et ceux-là des metteurs-en-scène.

Mais il faut encore distinguer parmi les romanciers deux grandes tendances générales. L'une qui pousse les analystes à simplifier l'âme humaine observée; à faire, en quelque sorte la somme des nuances de même nature pour frapper le lecteur par un trait typique, par une note unique et caractéristique; l'autre qui les détermine au contraire à saisir et à montrer une à une les plus vagues, les plus fugitives sensations de la pensée, les plus obscures évolutions de la volonté, à ne négliger aucun détail d'aucune nature, aucune nuance d'aucune sorte.

Ces derniers auraient donc, au contraire, une propension à compliquer. On les pourrait appeler les subtils.

Dans les œuvres des premiers la vie apparaît par images comme dans la réalité. Les visions passent devant les yeux du lecteur, éveillant en lui plus ou moins d'attention, plus ou moins de réflexion; il en tire, suivant le degré de son intelligence, des conclusions plus ou moins profondes, et des déductions plus ou moins étendues. Il peut, à son gré, s'il n'est doué d'aucun esprit de pénétration, se contenter de regarder se dérouler l'aventure et agir les personnages comme il regarderait un accident et des passants dans la rue.

Les subtils, au contraire, forcent les lecteurs à un travail de pensée délicieux pour les uns et pénible pour les autres. Il faut, pour suivre toutes les finesses de leurs aperçus et les arguties de leurs remarques, demeurer toujours en éveil, toujours au guet; on accomplit à leur suite un voyage d'exploration dans le cerveau humain; il faut un effort constant d'attention et d'intelligence pour marcher derrière eux, dans ce dédale.

Parmi les écrivains classés dès aujourd'hui comme des maîtres (je ne parle que des observateurs artistes), Flaubert représente parfaitement le type du romancier essentiellement objectif, tandis que les frères de Goncourt sont des subtils.

Parmi les écrivains actuellement en plein labeur et en plein talent, deux hommes nous montrent, avec des qualités très différentes, des manières de voir et d'écrire très opposées, et une valeur tout à fait supérieure, deux types très différents de subtils.

Ce sont MM. Catulle Mendès et Paul Bourget.

Catulle Mendès

Chez lui, tout est subtil et tout est séduisant. C'est un poète charmant, un poète même en prose.

Il n'a qu'un souci médiocre de la réalité, et se contente de demeurer dans le possible, par suite, sans doute, de cette certitude que "tout arrive."

Je veux dire par là qu'au lieu de chercher à frapper l'esprit par la vraisemblance éclatante, indéniable des caractères et des faits, ce que veulent obtenir les Réalistes en négligeant les vérités exceptionnelles pour ne choisir que les vérités constantes, il aime, il préfère les personnages qui ont un grain d'anormal, et les sujets où se mêle un peu d'étrange. Sa fantaisie charmante, imprévue et bizarre se plaît hors la regle commune. Elle évoque des êtres capricieux, délicats, pervers, toujours subtils, toujours compliqués, toujours intéressants par le mystère, souvent criminel de leur âme.

Il a bien fait ressortir toutes les ressources surprenantes de son exquis talent dans cette série de singuliers portraits qu'il intitula "les Monstres parisiens."

Il vient de publier deux volumes où il montre sous deux faces nouvelles ses admirables qualités d'observateur indépendant et fantaisiste. L'un de ces deux livres est fortement osé, il s'appelle "les boudoirs de verre." L'autre, non moins délicat et rusé, mais plus honnête, a pour titre "les jeunes filles."

Dans l'un et dans l'autre apparaît cette subtilité alerte, pénétrante, si artiste, si personnelle qui est la marque de son talent, qui fait de Catulle Mendès un maître curieux ne ressemblant à personne, ne pouvant être classé dans aucune école, ni comparé à aucun écrivain.

Son style fin, agile, malin, sournois a des hardiesses secrètes, des hardiesses jésuitiques que personne ne tenterait. Sa pensée masquée et mérveilleusement servie par l'incomparable artifice de cette langue, ne recule devant rien, et si on poursuivait les écrivains, aucun magistrat ne pourrait relever un outrage à la morale dans ses contes d'une corruption sans pareille, mais d'une telle adresse de phrase qu'ils braveraient les plus adroits inquisiteurs.

Paul Bourget

Il vient de publier un très remarquable volume, *l'Irréparable*, qui donne bien la note de ce penseur, de cet observateur profond et mélancolique. Celui-là est surtout un délicat, un effarouché devant les brutalités de la vie, un vibrant et un spleenétique à la manière anglaise.

Tout préoccupé des phénomènes mystérieux de l'âme, il les suit avec une subtilité sérieuse et les exprime en une langue précise, un peu philosophique, mais qui dévoile merveilleusement toutes les obscures évolutions de la pensée et de la volonté chez l'être humain.

C'est sur les femmes que s'exerce le plus volontiers son analyse pénétrante et bienveillante, car on sent qu'il aime les femmes d'un amour infini et désintéressé. Il les connaît, les raconte, les montre avec une étonnante sûreté de vue, et la délicatesse presque exagerée de sa pensée apparaît à tout instant, soit qu'il parle des hommes qui veulent seulement *avoir* des femmes, verbe brutal qui décèle bien la secrète brutalité de ces sortes de rapports cruels entre les sexes, qu'on appelle pourtant du bon nom "d'amour," soit qu'il analyse un de ses personnages qu'il montre atteint d'une maladie étrange bien moderne, observée et exprimée par lui avec une rare perspicacité: "Il était malade d'un excès de subtilité, toujours à la recherche de la nuance rare, et, quoique supérieurement intelligent, il ne devait jamais atteindre à cette large et franche conception de l'art qui produit les œuvres géniales."

Il dit ailleurs (c'est une femme qui parle): "J'étais toute jeune alors, je n'avais pas acquis cette indulgence que donne le sentiment de l'inachevé de la vie. . . ."

Quoi de plus juste, de plus saisissant et de plus aigu que ces observations qui tombent de sa plume, au cours du récit, de page en page? Il semble qu'il porte une lampe, une petite lampe vive et mystérieuse comme celle des mineurs et qu'il éclaire, d'une rapide lumière, par une ligne, par un mot, à mesure qu'il fait agir un personnage, le fond secret de sa pensée. Et il donne en même temps, lui aussi, d'une façon discrète, et un peu triste, son avis sur les choses et les hommes. Il laisse apparaître sans cesse ces déductions, ne laissant pas au lecteur le choix et la liberté, soit de conclure dans un sens ou dans l'autre, soit de ne point conclure du tout.

Paul Bourget qui avait pris, comme poète et comme critique, une place éminente parmi les écrivains de ce temps, vient de se placer aussi au premier rang des romanciers observateurs, psychologues et artistes.

Maufrigneuse

BIBLIOGRAPHY

In the preparation of this study I have consulted innumerable books and articles dealing with Maupassant, some of which I found to be valuable and stimulating while others were wholly negligible. It would be pointless to give here a complete list of such works, since an excellent bibliography already exists in Artine Artinian's *Maupassant Criticism in France 1880-1940*, which provides as well an account of contemporary critical reaction to Maupassant's works as they appeared. The list given below, therefore, is not intended to be complete, but is offered as a record of the books and essays which I consider particularly useful for the student of Maupassant's novels, with a brief evaluation of each. A few works are included which should be used with caution, for although they pertain to the subject, they are misleading or inadequate. A list of publications dealing with Maupassant's *chroniques* is given in the notes to the Introduction.

Addamiano, A. *Guy de Maupassant, La Vita e l'Opera*, Rome, Ausonia, 1949.
> Contains a lengthy description of the novels; *Une Vie, Pierre et Jean,* and *Fort comme la mort* are considered "cose perfette."

Albalat, A. *Souvenirs de la vie littéraire*, Paris, Crès, 1924, pp. 183-201.
> Notes some borrowings from earlier material in *Une Vie;* random anecdotes on Maupassant.

Artinian, A. *Maupassant Criticism in France 1880-1940*, New York, King's Crown Press, 1941.
> Excellent account of critical reactions in France; contains most complete bibliography of books and articles on Maupassant ever published.

Barthou, L. "Maupassant inédit, Autour d'*Une Vie*," *Revue des deux mondes,* October 15, 1920.
> Comparison of early MS of *Une Vie* with the published work.

Bourget, P. *Nouvelles Pages de critique et de doctrine*, vol. I, Paris, Plon, 1922, pp. 65-74: "Un Roman inachevé de Maupassant."
> On *L'Ame étrangère*; a highly exaggerated estimate of the fragment.

Boyd, E. *Guy de Maupassant, a Biographical Study*, New York and London, Knopf, 1926.

Mainly concerned with Maupassant's madness; violent antipathy toward Maupassant and sees little merit in his works.

Brandes, G. "Portraits littéraires, M. Guy de Maupassant," *Revue bleue*, September 2, 1891, pp. 329-335.

A good general appreciation of Maupassant by the Danish critic; high praise for all the novels.

Châtel, G. "Maupassant peint par lui-même," *Revue bleue*, July 11, 1896, pp. 41-48.

Superficial account of autobiographical elements in Maupassant's works; notes on the originals of some of his characters.

Conrad, J. *Notes on Life and Letters*, New York, Doubleday, Page, 1921, pp. 25-31: "Guy de Maupassant." First appeared as Introduction to *Yvette and Other Stories*, New York, Knopf, 1904.

Admirable brief essay on Maupassant's essential traits.

Croce, B. *European Literature in the Nineteenth Century*, tr. by D. Ainslee, New York, Knopf, 1924, pp. 344-358: "Maupassant."

Maupassant as a poet of matter and the senses, ingenuous and amoral, yet "moral" in his results.

Deffoux, L. and Zavie, E. *Le Groupe de Médan*, Paris, Crès, (1925), pp. 55-76: "Guy de Maupassant romancier de soi-même."

Genealogical data and a sketch of Maupassant "homme du monde et accaparé par ses admiratrices."

Dorchain, A. "Notes de la semaine: Quelques Normands," *Annales politiques et littéraires*, June 3, 1900. Reproduced in Lumbroso (see below), pp. 57-65.

Report of Maupassant's reading part of *L'Angélus*; valuable information on the plan of the book.

Doumic, R. *Ecrivains d'aujourd'hui*, Paris, Perrin, 1894, pp. 47-96. First appeared as "L'Œuvre de Guy de Maupassant," *Revue des deux mondes*, November 1, 1893, pp. 187-209.

General estimate of Maupassant's career; discounts the novels.

Dumesnil, R. *Guy de Maupassant*, Paris, Armand Colin, 1933. Republished by Tallandier, 1947, with a few additions, pp. 228-238.

A standard account of life and works with strong emphasis on Maupassant as a Norman.

Faguet, E. *Propos littéraires*, IIIe Série, Paris, Société française d'imprimerie et de librairie, 1905, pp. 195-209. First appeared as "Guy de Maupassant," *Revue bleue*, July 15, 1893, pp. 65-68.

Maupassant as the impersonal, impassible observer, "le romancier réaliste par excellence."

Filon, A. "Courrier littéraire," *Revue bleue*, August 2, 1890, pp. 154-156.

A flippant and superficial review of *Notre Cœur*, considered as a brilliantly written but badly composed novel.

France, A. *La Vie littéraire*, vol. II, Paris, Calmann-Lévy, 1890, pp. 28-35. First appeared as "M. Guy de Maupassant critique et romancier," *Le Temps*, January 15, 1888.

Review of *Pierre et Jean*: penetrating analysis of the novel and a rejection of the ideas of the preface.

Galsworthy, J. *Castles in Spain and Other Screeds*, New York, Scribner's, 1927.

His debt to Maupassant as a novelist; see pp. 212-214.

√Gaudefroy-Demombynes, L. *La Femme dans l'œuvre de Maupassant*, Paris, Mercure de France, 1943.

Thesis classifying Maupassant's female characters.

Gelzer, H. *Guy de Maupassant*, Heidelberg, Carl Winter, 1926.

Considers Maupassant's novels unimportant: "Der Roman ist nichts anderes als die verlängerte grande nouvelle"; severe criticism of Maupassant's style.

Gelzer, H. "Maupassant und Flaubert," *Herrigs Archiv*, 1920, pp. 222-239.

On Flaubert's corrections of Maupassant's manuscripts, especially *Des Vers* and *Boule de Suif*; some material on *Une Vie*.

Green, F. C. *French Novelists from the Revolution to Proust*, New York, Appleton, 1931, pp. 290-296.

Excellent short account of the novels.

Gregh, F. "Les Œuvres posthumes de Guy de Maupassant," *Revue bleue*, April 13, 1901, pp. 465-467.

Brief mention of the posthumous works and a sketch of Maupassant's career.

Guérinot, A. "Maupassant et la composition de *Mont-Oriol*," *Mercure de France*, June 15, 1921.

Three sources of the novel: "En Auvergne," "Malades et Médecins," and "Mes vingt-cinq jours."

√Hainsworth, G. "Pattern and Symbol in the Work of Maupassant," *French Studies*, January 1951, pp. 1-17.

A very interesting article on Maupassant's use of natural objects and animals as symbols or prefigurations of the explicit theme.

Hainsworth, G. "Un Thème des romanciers naturalistes: La Matrone d'Ephèse," *Comparative Literature*, 1951, pp. 129-151.

Death of Forestier in *Bel-Ami* is linked to the Matron of Ephesus theme.

Hermant, A. *Essais de critique*, Paris, Grasset, 1912, pp. 353-404.

Excellent essay on Maupassant; penetrating discussion of literary generations, naturalism, and distinction between *nouvelle* and *roman*; sees Maupassant as more *nouvelliste* than *romancier*.

Hytier, J. *Les Arts de littérature*, Paris, Charlot, 1945.

Stimulating observations on the art of the novel; pp. 132-133 on Maupassant.

Jackson, S. *Guy de Maupassant*, London, Duckworth, 1938.

A poor biography of Maupassant as a victim of syphilis doomed to insanity; almost nothing on Maupassant as a writer.

James, H. *Partial Portraits*, London, Macmillan, 1888, pp. 243-287. First appeared as "Guy de Maupassant," *Fortnightly Review*, March 1, 1888.

Brilliant critical appraisal of Maupassant's work up to 1888.

Lemaître, J. *Les Contemporains*, Ve Série, Paris, Société française d'imprimerie et de librairie, 1898, pp. 1-12. First appeared as "Portraits littéraires: M. Guy de Maupassant," *Revue bleue*, June 29, 1889, pp. 801-804.

Penetrating observations on Maupassant's career in a review of *Fort comme la mort*, "ce merveilleux livre."

Létourneau, R. "Maupassant et sa conception de l'œuvre d'art," *Revue de l'Université d'Ottawa* iii (1933), 364-390; iv (1934), 478-490.

Very little on Maupassant's conception of the work of art; deals mainly with his materialism, pessimism, and general ideas.

Lion, F. *Der französische Roman im neunzehnten Jahrhundert*, Zurich, Oprecht, 1952.

On Stendhal, Balzac, Flaubert, Zola; appendix on Maupassant, pp. 147-149.

Lubbock, P. *The Craft of Fiction*, New York, Scribner's, 1921.

Classic discussion of the "pictorial" method in fiction as opposed to the "dramatic"; Maupassant as an example of the latter.

Lumbroso, A. *Souvenirs sur Maupassant*, Rome, Bocca frères, 1905.

An invaluable but chaotic volume of letters, anecdotes, and personal testimony about Maupassant.

Mahn, P. *Guy de Maupassant, sein Leben und seine Werke*, Berlin, Fleischel, 1908.

Analysis of the novels, *Fort comme la mort* considered as most successful; chapter on Maupassant as a journalist.

Martino, P. *Le Naturalisme français*, Paris, Colin, 1951, pp. 122-146.

Brief account of the novels, pp. 134-138.

Maupassant, *Œuvres complètes de Guy de Maupassant*, 29 vols., Paris, Louis Conard, 1908-1930.

Valuable notes on Maupassant's manuscripts and excerpts from contemporary criticism.

Maupassant, *Œuvres complètes illustrées de Guy de Maupassant*, 15 vols., Paris, Librairie de France, 1934-1938.

Useful notes by Dumesnil throughout and in vol. xv a detailed but incomplete and often inaccurate bibliography of Maupassant's works. For corrections see Sullivan and Steegmuller, "Supplément à la bibliographie de Maupassant," *Revue d'Histoire littéraire de la France*, October-December 1949, pp. 370-375.

Maynial, E. "La Composition dans les premiers romans de Maupassant," *Revue bleue*, October 31 and November 7, 1903, pp. 562-565, 604-608.

On previously published material used in *Une Vie* and *Bel-Ami*.

√ Maynial, E. *La Vie et l'Œuvre de Guy de Maupassant*, Paris, Mercure de France, 1906.

A very good biography and still most useful; Dumesnil's work supplements this but does not replace it.

Neveux, P. "Guy de Maupassant," *Boule de Suif*, Paris, Conard, 1908, pp. xv-xc.

A good essay on Maupassant as a short story writer; little enthusiasm for the novels, utter scorn for the critical writings.

O'Faolain, S. *The Short Story*, London, Collins, 1948, pp. 101-131: "Guy de Maupassant or the Relentless Realist."

A particularly keen discussion of Maupassant's realism with devastating comments on Faguet's point of view.

Pellissier, G. *Le Mouvement littéraire contemporain*, Paris, Plon-Nourrit, 1902, pp. 9-18.
Classic view of Maupassant as "unliterary."

Pritchett, V. S. *Books in General*, New York, Harcourt, Brace, 1953, pp. 94-103: "Maupassant."
A brief but perceptive study of *Une Vie*.

Rzewuski, S. *Etudes littéraires*, Paris, Librairie de la Revue Indépendante, 1888, pp. 195-285.
Enthusiastic article on *Une Vie* as a masterful "psychological" novel.

Saintsbury, G. *A History of the French Novel*, vol. II, London, Macmillan, 1919, pp. 484-515.
Considers Maupassant an important novelist and attempts to show that he improved with each novel, a thesis that is rendered meaningless since Saintsbury was utterly confused about the order of appearance of the novels.

Sartre, J.-P. *Situations II*, Paris, Gallimard, 1948.
Uses Maupassant as a whipping-boy in a very lively attack on all 19th-century literature; see especially pp. 179-185.

Sherard, R. *The Life, Work and Evil Fate of Guy de Maupassant* (*Gentilhomme de Lettres*), New York, Brentano's (1926) (London, Werner Laurie).
Confused and inaccurate biography.

✓Steegmuller, F. *Maupassant, A Lion in the Path*, New York, Random House, 1949.
The best biography of Maupassant; analysis of the novels with detailed account of circumstances of composition.

Tassart, F. *Souvenirs sur Guy de Maupassant*, Paris, Plon, 1911.
Notes of Maupassant's valet; some interesting background information about the composition of the novels.

Thibaudet, A. *Réflexions sur le roman*, Paris, Gallimard, 1938, pp. 132-138.
Perceptive essay on "Le Groupe de Médan."

Thompson, D. G. *The Philosophy of Fiction in Literature*, London, Longmans Green, 1890.
"Realism and Idealism," pp. 46-83, on Maupassant and Zola from viewpoint of a student of philosophy.

Thoraval, J. *L'Art de Maupassant d'après ses variantes*, Paris, Imprimerie Nationale, 1950.
A not very illuminating study of Maupassant's manuscript

corrections and an essay on his literary doctrine based on only a handful of the *chroniques*.

Tolstoy, L. *Zola, Dumas, Maupassant,* tr. by E. Halpérine-Kaminsky, Paris, Léon Chailly, 1896, pp. 93-168. ("Découverte d'un écrivain," *L'Age nouveau,* November 1951, pp. 29-34, described as *inédit,* is merely a new translation of part of the above.)

The novels judged from the point of view of morals: *Une Vie,* the best novel since *Les Misérables; Bel-Ami,* "très sale"; in the later novels the "conception morale de la vie" is more confused.

Van de Velde, M. *French Fiction of Today,* vol. I, London, Trischler, 1891, pp. 65-84.

Inaccurate and naïve.

Vogl, A. "Guy de Maupassants Lebensgefühl und die künstlerische Gestaltung aussermenschlicher Lebewesen," *Zeitschrift für französischer Sprache und Literatur,* 1938, pp. 83-108.

Maupassant's use of nature symbols and his feeling for animals and their suffering.

INDEX

INDEX

197

INDEX

INDEX